V

Régis Debray

Vers

Teachers, Writers, Celebrities

The Intellectuals of Modern France

Introduction by Francis Mulhern

Translated by David Macey

British Library
Cataloguing in Publication Data

Debray, Régis
  Teachers, writers, celebrities.
  1. Intellectuals – France – History
  2. France – Social conditions – 19th century
  3. France – Social conditions – 20th century
  I. Title   II. La pouvoir intellectuel en
  France. *English*
  305.5'5   HT690.F8

First published as *Le Pouvoir intellectuel en France*
Editions Ramsay, Paris 1979
© Editions Ramsay, 1979

This translation first published by
NLB and Verso Editions, London 1981
© NLB, 1981

Introduction © NLB, 1981

Filmset in Monophoto Ehrhardt by
Servis Filmsetting, Manchester

Printed in Great Britain by
Redwood Burn Ltd. Trowbridge and Esher

ISBN 86091 039 3 (Cloth)
       86091 736 3 (Paper)

Contents

Introduction

Preliminaries
and Two Contrasts

Francis Mulhern

The appearance of Regis Debray's *Le Pouvoir intellectuel en France* was a major cultural event in France.[1] Critical reaction was instant and passionate; the book was soon a talking-point and—on the scale appropriate to a book of its kind—a best-seller. But if the public evidence pointed straightforwardly to literary success, the occasion itself was nonetheless a complex one. *Le Pouvoir intellectuel* was an analysis of French culture and its intellectuals that blended familiar themes with preoccupations of a not at all familiar, even antithetical kind. Philosophical and theoretical at one end of its discursive range, at the other it immersed itself in the mundane affairs of its subject, freely naming institutions and individuals, restaurants and bars. It was also a political intervention, made after the emergence of the New Philosophers and the defeat of the Union of the Left, and intended as an explanation of the cultural mechanisms that had been at work in these linked events. The complexities of the work were deepened further by the career of the author: Debray was quite open about his own past associations with the institutions and milieux that he now attacked, and was too lucid not to anticipate the role of his personal publicity-value in stimulating response to his book.

The English translation appears in very different conditions; some of the issues that engaged French readers may recede now, and will perhaps be replaced by others. At all events, it is in the nature of the case that some spontaneous perceptual re-ordering will occur. It may be useful, then, to discuss some contexts and perspectives of reading, both 'original' and 'acquired', that seem appropriate to *Teachers, Writers, Celebrities*. These notes will attempt first to situate it in the history of French writing about intellectuals, and in relation to other relevant traditions; then to examine

[1] Paris 1979.

the historical specificity of the French intelligentsia and to suggest some pertinent comparisons and contrasts with Britain and the United States, paying particular attention to the phenomemon of 'intellectual corporatism';[2] and finally to look again at the complex cultural make-up of the book.

I

'Le clerc ne trahit jamais.' Debray's studied declaration at once evokes and challenges a whole tradition of intellectual self-reflection. The homeland of this tradition is France, and its inception, in its modern form at least, may be dated from the appearance of Julien Benda's *La Trahison des clercs* in 1927. The cultural matrix of Benda's book was liberal humanism, its politics, amidst the crisis of post-war Europe, an unworldly rejection of all national particularism or social partisanship in the name of the disinterested service of humanity as a whole. *La Trahison des clercs* is internationally significant as a classic statement of this outlook; its added significance in France is that it laid down the protocols of a distinctive cultural *occasion* that was to recur in subsequent crises and under the auspices of radically contrasting positions.

Benda's symbolic counterpart between the wars was Paul Nizan, whose *Les Chiens de garde* (1932) was one Communist intellectual's 'great-minded harangue' (Debray) against the political quietism of academic philosophy. Some fifteen years later, after the Liberation, Nizan's friend Sartre launched *Les Temps Modernes* with a declaration of intellectual commitment, and wrote *Qu'est-ce que la littérature?* to demonstrate that the writer was, *qua* writer, necessarily on the left. The anti-type, in the Cold War fifties, was Raymond Aron's *L'Opium des intellectuels*. May 1968 and its aftermath saw a great proliferation of such documents, of which Sartre's 1970 interview 'L'Ami du peuple' and the Godard-Gorin film *Tout va bien* are among the better-known instances. The confusions and disappointments, the reversals and the desertions of the later seventies have proved no less conducive to this traditional activity than the antithetical conditions of ten years ago. The 'bad objects' of the Parisian high intelligentsia may vary (approximately, from Power to the Gulag to

---

[2] 'Intellectual corporatism' arises when an ideology of collective unity and independence takes hold in a given intelligentsia or segment of it. 'Corporatism' as intended here differs from conventional Gramscian usage in that it does not imply the 'hegemonic' posture as its opposite.

the Devil—and back) but an unassimilable 'plebeian' stance is widely advocated as appropriate to the age. And here, now, in Debray's book, is another—oppositely intended—challenge.

This tradition, then, is not confined to any particular political or intellectual position; it has been a prominent and constant theme in the *national culture* of twentieth-century France. This consideration is decisive for any attempt to understand the phenomenon. For the moment, however, it is more pertinent to note a related, 'intrinsic' feature of the tradition: in spite of the wide variety of its tributaries, it has retained a marked discursive coherence. It has characteristically been an *ethics* (or, in the twin classical sense, a 'politics') of intellectual life. Benda's text was patently and proudly a work of moral prescription founded on an ontology of the intellectual as social being. Nizan's was structurally similar, even if the imperatives were now political and the ground of being was history as class struggle. The socialist politics of *Qu'est-ce que la littérature?* were premissed on the existentialist ethics of Sartre's technical philosophy, the intermediary being an aesthetic conception of the novel as a 'pact of freedoms'.[3] Rationalist, phenomenological or dialectical-materialist, liberal or socialist, these and kindred writings sustained a common discourse whose basic character was always (not only or even principally in the pejorative sense) *moralist*.

Teachers, Writers, Celebrities lies uneasily among its predecessors, for the main novelty of the book is precisely its practical challenge to moralism and the analytic options and occlusions characteristic of it. It represents, in fact, a major break in the tradition. Ethics is displaced here by politics, ontology by history and sociology. Benda invoked the changeless truth of a calling and prescribed its functions accordingly; Debray seeks to analyse the formation and re-formation of a determinate occupational bloc. Sartre's investigation of the relations between intellectuals and their audience concluded that writing was constitutionally leftist, that the vocation of writer was a political fatality; Debray's object, by contrast, is to discover the structured tendencies of intellectual behaviour in successive cultural production-systems and to show how these dictate the posture of the intelligentsia in given political situations. The 'mediological' discourse so initiated is markedly more historical, markedly more materialist than anything in its parent tradition.

[3] See Ronald Aronson, *Jean-Paul Sartre—Philosophy in the World*, London 1980, pp. 122–42.

Indeed, the novelty of the book remains clear in international comparison. When Debray complains that France is the 'political paradise' of the intelligentsia but the 'purgatory' of its analysts, he does too much justice to the implied national contrasts. More precisely, he underestimates the extent to which the selfsame or similar, essentially philosophico-literary discourse on 'the clerisy' permeates the cultures of the advanced capitalist world, not excepting the younger, scientific disciplines that claim to have superseded it. Such notions are active in the work of Parsons, for example, and just as clearly in that of Gramsci— whose nearly complete isolation, as a Marxist, in this field of theory and research tells its own tale.[4] Whether Debray himself has entirely settled accounts with this 'erstwhile philosophical consciousness' is a consideration that will be taken up. But the main emphasis should fall on the originality of his book. Precedents may be cited for its various themes and analytic strategies—its combination of theoretical argument and concrete analysis, the historical sketch of the French intelligentsia that forms the centre of the book, the insistence on the specific economics of culture and, related to this, the systematic integration of statistical with more conventional ('qualitative') kinds of evidence. What is novel here is the combination, and the purpose that it is designed to serve. No one, Marxist or other, has made so concerted an attempt to analyse what might be called, in Marx's terms, the 'social being' of 'social consciousness', the intelligentsia as a social category at work, in one of its major modern incarnations. By this alone, Debray's book sets a standard for future research.

2

That is one context in which to read *Teachers, Writers, Celebrities*. But certain others, two in particular, will probably hold greater significance for an English-language audience.

The first of these is Frankfurt Marxism. Debray's history of the French intelligentsia is conceived in the form of a study of the development of the

[4] See Parson's contribution to Philip Rieff, ed., *On Intellectuals*, New York 1969; and Gramsci's discussion of 'traditional intellectuals', which effectively adopts the self-image of intellectual corporatism ('The Formation of the Intellectuals', Quintin Hoare and Geoffrey Nowell Smith, ed., Antonio Gramsci, *Selections From the Prison Notebooks*, London 1971, pp. 5-14).

national cultural apparatuses—the schools and universities, publishing, the press, radio and television. It is an exercise in 'mediology', and much of its argumentation pertains not so much to intellectuals as to the laws of motion of the institutions in and by which they are deployed. Two processes are given analytic priority. The first, economic process is that of the absorption of cultural production into general commodity production, in an era when the capitalist economy is said itself to be undergoing an inner transformation, the relative determining powers of production and distribution being switched to the advantage of the latter. The second, technical process involves the development of the forces of cultural production and the institutional rearrangements induced by it. The analytic object so constituted is akin to what the Frankfurt tradition called 'the culture industry'; and the substance of the analysis is no less redolent of Critical Theory, above all in its historical pessimism.[5] Debray may not altogether suppress the distinction between the technical resources of the media and the social relations within which they are utilized, but he denies emphatically that it underwrites the possibility of cultural emancipation. The electronic media are bringing forth a culture in keeping with their own unalterable nature, he argues. The modern culture industry falls under one historical law and one only: the law of increasing symbolic immiseration, in obedience to which the criterion of intrinsic worth is displaced by that of 'mediatic surface', the complexity of the message is sacrificed to the volume of its reception, cultural labour is deskilled and its products quality-controlled to ensure the optimal incidence of sensation. A society whose 'high intellectuals' reserve their main energies for appearances on Friday-night television, Debray maintains, is in truth a 'mediocracy'. 'The darkest spot in modern society is a small luminous screen.'

These echoes of the Frankfurt School are notable enough in a writer of Althusserian and Leninist formation. But such arguments stir stronger, more familiar and far more improbable associations. For many of the topics and themes of his book, and even, in places, its tones and cultural accents, were anticipated fifty years ago in the early writings of F.R. and Q.D. Leavis. The former's *Mass Civilization and Minority Culture* and the latter's *Fiction and the Reading Public* showed the same preoccupation with the contemporary economic reorganization of culture that now motivates

[5] See, for example, Theodor Adorno and Max Horkheimer, *Dialectic of Enlightenment*, London 1979.

Debray (though he naturally thinks of the economy as capitalist, a specification that the Leavises thought secondary in the essentially monolithic conditions of 'industrialism').[6] 'Standardization and levelling down' was their conventional shorthand for the same tendencies that Debray now describes as inherent in 'mediocratic' culture. His acid accounts of intellectual life in the Latin Quarter and Montparnasse recall the Leavises' attacks on the 'coteries' of metropolitan London. His analysis of the circuits of influence and advantage in reviewing and promotion is parallel to theirs. For Bernard-Henri Lévy, actor-manager of the New Philosophy, read (say) Michael Roberts, the strategist of the *New Signatures* and *New Country* anthologies in the early thirties. For Pivot, the tele-journalist with the power of life and death over the season's new titles, read Arnold Bennett, the star reviewer of the London *Evening Standard*. In temper too there is a striking similarity. Cool and concentrated, but then suddenly mocking, indignant or openly angry, both the Leavises and Debray here display a tense combination of fatalism and defiance. Debray might well cite, as he has done in the past, Gramsci's famous borrowing, 'pessimism of the intelligence, optimism of the will',[7] for this motto registers the stress at the heart of his book, the same stress that was defined in the perhaps more lucid Leavisian phrase, 'desperate optimism': the stress of a cultural voluntarism armed only with its conscience and always-already-defeated, if its own strategic estimates are really to be believed.

This is not to say that Debray's mediology is 'really' a belated, stray variant of *Kulturkritik*. The theoretical constitution of the book will prompt many questions, but these are best posed in the light of prior and more widely applicable historical questions. How should we regard this improbable confluence of English cultural criticism and French Marxism, and what does it suggest about Debray's relationship with the national history that he discusses? But first, is there anything further to be said about the specificity of the French case, or by way of pertinent contrast, about the differing cases of England and the United States?

3

Debray distinguishes three 'cycles' in the past century of French intellectual history: the academic, which he dates from 1880 to 1930; that

---

[6] Cambridge 1932 and London 1932 respectively.
[7] 'Schema for a Study of Gramsci', *Prison Writings*, Harmondsworth 1975, pp. 161–66.

of publishing (1920–1960); and the mediatic, initiated in 1968 and still in its ascendant phase. These chronological periods delimit not life-spans but hegemonies. Just as the university displaced the Church in the last years of the nineteenth century, so in the inter-war years publishing and its culture displaced the university milieu, reorganizing the latter in a subaltern position. Then, in the 1960s, the press and broadcasting apparatuses restructured both, creating a pyramidal culture in which a mediatic elite became paramount over a subordinate publishing sector and an abject educational system. There was a symbolic succession from Alain to Gide to Glucksmann.

This was not, it need hardly be said, the common destiny of the West. But, to the extent that it was rather a distinctive French experience, general theses concerning the development of capitalist commerce and of communications technology cannot fully explain it: by definition blind to national variation, they are at once too much and too little. Other elements besides these were involved in shaping this distinctive historical passage.

The so-called 'second industrial revolution' came very late in France, and when it did arrive was correspondingly intensified in its rhythms and effects. The trustification and technical rationalization of industry, the introduction of scientific 'research and development', the production of machines by means of machines and the opening up of the mass market had begun in the United States at the end of the 1890s, and by the end of the First World War had already largely transformed the American urban economy—the baptism of Ford's assembly-line in 1915 symbolized the start of the new era. Over the same period, the multiple conjunctions of commercial pressure and opportunity with technological innovation were responsible for a whole complex of culturally decisive changes: the transformation in the status of advertising and the financial reorganization of the press, the growth of publishing of all kinds, the ascent of Hollywood and the consolidation of a nationwide broadcasting network. By 1930 the cultural format of 'mass', 'consumer' capitalism had been designed and patented. In Britain, it was the war itself and the ensuing depression that triggered the process already known as 'Americanization'. The results, in an economy weakened by technical senescence and over-reliant on the stored fat of Empire, were naturally unequal. Yet within twenty years the economy had been considerably remodelled (most evidently in the sphere of distribution) and the national culture had been transformed—by the promotional revolution, the huge expansion of publishing and the cinema, and the creation of the British Broadcasting Corporation. The 'American' motif was prominent among the attractions of Weimar Berlin for young English writers at that time; Paris, in contrast, was the gathering-place of American intellectuals drawn to an older Bohemian style. It was not surprising, for no comparable transformation was experienced in inter-war France. The component processes of the 'second industrial revolution' unfolded slowly and piecemeal, each in its own space and according to its own tempo, in a society that remained archaic overall. A further twenty years and a full constitutional cycle passed before *le défi américain* finally forced a quickened and coordinated pace of modernization on Gaullist France, the breakneck pace that led to the social collision of 1968.

Higher education forms a second plane of comparison. All three countries laid the foundations of their modern university systems around the same time: roughly, in the last quarter of the nineteenth century and first ten years of the twentieth. The great university reforms of the Third Republic date mainly from the 1880s. In England, where the foundation of London University had already weakened the hegemony of Oxford and Cambridge, the next decade saw the first 'redbrick' institutions of learning chartered as independent universities. Across the Atlantic, in the same years, the first public universities emerged from the old system of Land Grant Colleges. However, the French case stood apart from the British and the American in two decisive respects. The emergent systems in the latter cases were based on recent foundations—Liverpool or Sheffield, Wisconsin or California. The old institutions—Oxford and Cambridge in England, and in the United States the Ivy League colleges—were by-passed, so to speak, in an ambiguous gesture that signified both supersession and untouchability. But the French reforms concerned precisely the old foundations, the Sorbonne and the *grandes écoles* of the Latin Quarter. Beneath this contrast lay a fundamental difference. The late-nineteenth-century innovations in England and the United States belonged to waves of educational expansion that were themselves part of broader processes of economic and cultural change. The innovations of the Third Republic were in this sense socially blank, as the next half-century revealed. By 1930, the national academic corps had grown by under a quarter to 1,405, less than half that of slightly less populous Britain. At the same date, the United States, little more than three times the size of either country, possessed more *institutions* of higher education than France did academic *personnel*, and could claim a university and college student population ten times that of France's secondary schools.[8] In sum, the reforms of the 1880s had not been expansionist or even, in any sense that Britain or the United States might have echoed, modernist. The French 'multiversity' lay very far ahead still—as far ahead as the 'second industrial revolution'. The university remained the exclusive, hierarchical institution it had long been. Yet, as Debray explains, it had indeed been reformed: not so much in what it was or how it functioned as in what it represented.[9] The consequences for French culture were decisive.

The purpose of the reforms was directly, expressly political: it was to win the university to the role of a secular, democratic successor to the Church, to create in it the loyal and effective ideological custodian of the new, third Republic. The teaching community, with the Sorbonne and the Ecole Normale at its head, was to be invested as a republican clergy—in the words of the Charter of the Union for Moral Action, as 'a militant lay order based on private and public duty'. The collective initiation of the new order in the struggle over Dreyfus—the very moment when the noun *intellectuel* was added to the language—is powerfully recounted here, but its lasting significance is insufficiently stressed. 'The primal scene of politics', Debray observes elsewhere in the book, is the prince with his scribes. If that is so, then the 'screening memory', in the collective psyche of the French intelligentsia, is of Conscience in the company of the Republic.

The entente between the University and the Third Republic was the formative experience of the intellectuals, the mould of a dual posture that could seem at times the defining attribute of intellectuality as such. In its 'negative' moment, the posture was factional, one of permanent readiness in the defence of threatened allegiances; but there was also the inseparable 'positive' moment that claimed generality, in cultural terms (transcendent values) and often also politically (popular-democratic 'typicality'). *La Trahison des clercs* at once exemplified and depended upon the paradigmatic authority of this dual posture, the posture of a 'republican clergy'. When the old Dreyfusard attacked the 'organizers of political passions', he cited only opponents of the Republic, on the extreme left (Sorel) or right (Maurras). Durkheim, conceivably the most effective

---

[8] See Debray's figures (pp. 52–3 below), and for the USA see Donald R. McCoy, *Coming of Age*, Harmondsworth 1973, pp. 116–44.

[9] See Chapter Two below, especially pp. 58–63.

intellectual-politican of the pre-war era, was nowhere mentioned. The Third Republic was more than a 'political' allegiance; it was the *republique des professeurs*, the constitutional ground of Reason itself.

This was not a doctrine or a programme; it was rather an objectively constituted repertoire of postures and occasions, a part of the cultural inheritance of generation after generation of French intellectuals and of the audiences to and 'for' whom they spoke. As such it persisted into the publishing and mediatic cycles of the middle and later decades of this century, as a necessary support of the milieux and the practices that Debray describes. True enough, a phenomenon like the New Philosophy presupposed late-capitalist distribution and promotion and the electronic media; and the French apparatuses, being of relatively recent date, are advanced of their kind. It also presupposed the unique degree of centralization that makes Paris the political, academic and lay cultural capital of the country (a fusion of roles elsewhere distributed among, say, Washington, Boston and New York, or London and Oxbridge). But it was quite unimaginable in the absence of the cultural syndrome that ensured that the road to Damascus would be lined with editors and paved with contracts, outside a culture in which the Pauline style was known, expected and prized.

Underlying Debray's tricyclical history there is a continuous tradition whose forcing-house was the reconstitution of the republican state after 1871. Its epitome is the career of Jean-Paul Sartre—brilliant *normalien*, privileged stipendiary of the house of Gallimard, regular focus of controversy in the media and, in the end, petitioner at the Elysée Palace. Merleau-Ponty once charged that Sartre's dramatic style of socialist 'commitment' was dictated by his unreconstructed philosophical individualism, by a 'conception of freedom that allows only for sudden interventions into the world, for camera shots and flash-bulbs'.[10] But if Sartrean 'commitment' was a distinctively existentialist creation, the press cameras that sensationalized its public moments plainly were not. Sartre inherited not only a philosophical tradition that went back to Descartes, but the established morality, the 'spontaneous ideology' of a corporation. His great personal distinction was that he accepted the role of 'intellectual' with the utmost self-consciousness and passion, and reached its limits in the rarest and most creditable of ways—by pressing its possibilities to the point of exhaustion.

[10] Cit. Aronson, p. 226.

The legendary contrast that is the British intelligentsia was shaped by a radically different political history. No one could take the Third Republic for granted: the opposite of a historical fatality, it was a project to further or to thwart, a point of controversy in its own right. But in Britain a remarkably continuous state history had the effect of largely withholding basic constitutional questions from political debate; the great issues of nation and state remained, in local parlance, 'above party politics'. The inevitable beneficiary of this history has been the Conservative Party, since the First World War the 'natural party of government' in Britain. The real hegemonic strength of Conservatism may be judged not by its celebrated pragmatism but by the fact that it alone of the parliamentary parties in the last sixty years has a proven capacity for disruptive confrontation—from the break-up of the Lloyd George coalition in the twenties to the onslaught on social provision today. That the power of political initiative is monopolized by the oldest and most continuist of the parties is both cause and consequence of the exceptional constitutional quietism of the polity.

The culture and the intelligentsia formed in this matrix were correspondingly distinctive. The institutional sequence university-publishing-media was repeated, but within a shorter time-span and accordingly to a different principle of combination. Here, the older would characteristically *license* the newer, ceding this specialized function or permitting the extension or duplication of that, or it would encroach upon the newer, after an initial recoil perhaps, to secure its own advantage in the new territory. In neither case was there a decisive transfer of hegemony. The university expansion around the turn of the century was part of a far-reaching process of cultural change, but it scarcely dimmed the radiation of Oxford and Cambridge: if by the mid-twenties these institutions taught only one in every three university students,[11] their traditions weighed just as heavily on the other two—whose Oxbridge counterpart, now the elite of an elite, in fact enjoyed the old prestige to the second power. At the beginning of the twenties, relations between the university and the lay culture based on publishing were close only among the most archaic and reactionary circles of both, the scholar-gentleman and the bellelettrists (the Bloomsbury Group was an exceptional case). For the rest, the contemporary reciprocal hostility of specialized teachers and writers made glib by commissions and deadlines was already quasi-institutional.

[11] C.L. Mowat, *Britain Between the Wars, 1918–1940*, London 1968.

Yet within twenty-five years the old guards had been dislodged, each by new generations below them, and a new relationship was instituted in which the power of the university was manifest. The end of the forties saw the closure of England's last successful literary magazine of extra-academic provenance, *Horizon*. Throughout the fifties, the eclipse of 'creation' by 'criticism' and of the freelance writer by the academic was widely but unavailingly complained of. By the end of the decade, the major reviewing spaces in the weekly journals and supplements and the prime ideological occasions—'the new Naipaul' or whatever—were largely reserved by a corps of professor-journalists, many, perhaps a majority of them from Oxford and Cambridge. The experience of the electronic media has been in important respects similar. The BBC, as befitted a national broadcasting service, was apparently born venerable. What it lacked in years was made up in the funereal propriety that Reith prescribed as its institutional style. Yet a long time passed before radio, and far longer before television, won the assent of British intellectuals and their established institutions. The politico-cultural innovations of the wartime service, the inception of the Third Programme and, ultimately, the creation of the Open University (complete with Vice-Chancellor 'and all the trimmings', lest any misunderstand[12]) were among the crucial steps in the acceptance-colonization of broadcasting.

It would be perverse to argue that the electronic media are the least powerful of cultural institutions. But it would be equally perverse to insist that when the doyen of Oxford history appears on prime-time television to discuss, say, the Second World War, truth's last citadel has fallen to mediatic barbarism. British continuism has the effect of rejuvenating the older institutions at the expense of the newer. But the rejuvenation of the old, seen from the other side, is the legitimation and regulation of the new, and this is the real strategic value of cultural continuism. The university in effect acts as a licensing authority for other cultural institutions, recognizing and/or regulating the extent and demarcation of their various claims to knowledge and endowing them with something of its own accumulated prestige. The resulting institutional configuration is perhaps unique in its conservative adaptability.

The people whose work was in these institutions were not accustomed to think of themselves as 'intellectuals'. No form of corporate conscious-

[12] Thus Jennie Lee, the Labour minister responsible (see Raymond Williams, *Politics and Letters*, London 1979, p. 371).

ness either drew them together or defined a social role for them as individuals. If the French intelligentsia formed a 'republican clergy', their English counterparts were decidedly Anglican in temper: aware of higher things but careful not to become tedious on that account, and not really in much doubt of the basic good sense of the nation and those who governed it. It is not, of course, that they constituted a kind of collective 'happy consciousness' willingly allied with the dominant classes. But two contrasting political histories produced two distinct types of intellectual formation. 'Independence' here signified not a self-defining corporate invigilation of a transcendent general interest but the freedom to pursue one's particular (usually occupational) interest without ideological distraction or politico-juridical interference, in conditions where 'the Constitution' was not a redoubt to be defended or stormed, not even an arena of free civic activity, but a half-noticed, hardly changing country landscape.

The sectoral distribution of political allegiances also differed from one country to the other. In France, according to Debray, academics and teachers have traditionally inclined to the left, writers to the right. This was so during the Dreyfus affair, in the political crisis of the mid-thirties, and is the case again today. But in Britain, it is probably true to say, the intellectual radicalization of the thirties was more marked in the lay culture dominated by writers than in the universities. The new phase of political division that opened in the mid-seventies has taken yet another form. In keeping with the apparent international pattern of the misnamed 'crisis of Marxism',[13] the rupture has occurred within the nationally dominant politico-cultural formation of the workers movement: not, as in France, Marxism of any kind but *Fabianism*. The old centre-left consensus has been largely dispersed, leaving the intelligentsia polarized both in its academic and in its lay sectors.

Other, not directly political motifs of intra-cultural antagonism recurred here, but again in variant forms. The struggle between Paris and the provinces, between privilege and merit, between the versatile amateur and the specialized professional, was epitomized in the hostility between

---

[13] The first outbreaks of the 'crisis' occurred in the Maoist or semi-Maoist far-left currents of France and Italy, extending also to the Communist Parties, particularly in the latter case, and involving a number of independents as well. These circumstances were taken—in many cases avidly seized—as evidence of a general crisis of *Marxism*. The less sensational but better attested hypothesis of a crisis of Maoism, or of culpably lingering illusions in Stalinism, was less enthusiastically bruited, being not so flattering to the renegades or ideologically so serviceable to their new allies.

the university and the Academy, between the schools of the Latin Quarter and the salons of the Right Bank. A similar deployment of values was apparent in England between the wars, but here the lines of battle were drawn *inside* the universities, dividing the scholar-gentlemen from the young professionals whose only resource was talent. The main issue in the struggle was the cultural authority of the new discipline of English, whose cause was championed by the Leavises and the writers based on the quarterly *Scrutiny*. The campaign was in one central sense successful. By the end of the Second World War the new generation had effectively displaced the old guard on their own terrain, and within a further ten to fifteen years they had extended their influence over much of the lay literary culture outside the universities. But the profession of English, as it took shape in England, was both an occupation and a claim, the one quite inseparable from the other. The claim was, in effect, that English could and must become the organizing centre of an intellectual elite capable of interpreting the general interest to a society structurally incapable of self-direction—the centre, that is, of an intelligentsia of the 'classic', 'French' type. The fortunes of this cultural effort were complex, but to the Leavises it came to seem like an unending defeat. French intellectuals could claim to represent a general interest as if by public statute; the Leavises' attempt to win the same prerogative for their discipline was met with scorn. The underlying paradox of the French intelligentsia was that its corporate independence was seen as a positive warrant of constitutional stability; it was much the same paradox that appeared, greatly exacerbated, in Leavis's increasingly wilful, subjectivist insistence that he, more or less alone, defended the 'real' world of English culture against its actual, degraded simulacrum. Every assertion of intellectual corporatism served only to emphasis the irreducible difference between the two national cultures and their respective types.

The Leavises would occasionally couple the United States with France in favourable contrast with England. There too, in the vast American public education system, careers were open to talent. At other times, they would represent the USA as England's future. It was the historic model of all the changes that were remaking traditional patterns of consumption and recreation between the wars, yet its traditions of intellectual independence were such that it seemed also to offer the most advanced paradigms of opposition to the march of 'industrial civilization'. There was demonstrable point in both suggestions, but neither really registered the historical uniqueness of the US social formation, which fostered a distinctive intellectual stratum and a remarkable national variation on the phenomenon of intellectual corporatism.

The United States on the morrow of the armistice contrasted with France and Britain not only in the degree of its economic development (it was now the world's premier capitalist economy); it was also an exceptionally decentralized and in important respects fragmented society. Federal institutions and activity had developed rapidly in the first twenty years of the century, and would acquire unprecedented centrality in the course of the thirties, yet there was no commensurate evolution towards a genuinely 'national' system of political parties or media along familiar European lines. Regional and other particularisms (religious and/or ethnic) remained proportionately strong in US politics and culture.

However, if in this sense US national institutions appeared under-developed, in another sense their politico-juridical ground-plan, the Constitution itself, enjoyed a corresponding prominence. The genesis of the modern United States might be said to have inverted the normal historical relationships of nation-state formation, a small and compact settlement achieving a basic state-form which it then 'filled' with populations and territories many times its own size. The state created the nation, as it were, in a process that continued right into the 1920s. (As late as 1920, fully *one-third* of US citizens were first- or second-generation settlers.) But the nationalism that arose in these conditions was necessarily different equally from the separatist and the unificationist nationalisms of Europe. Lacking—by definition—that popular prehistory of kinship and custom from which to fashion an effective 'national consciousness', an inclusive US nationalism could look no further back than the Constitution, before which there was, mythically, nothing but a wilderness and a latter-day project of Creation. Thus the founding texts of the US polity and the themes that cluster around them were internalized, in a kind of para-nationalist constitutional fetishism, as one of the true *longues durées* of American culture.

The US intelligentsia, as it took shape in the early decades of this century, reproduced this para-nationalist thematic in its own dominant collective ideology. This was, in effect, the dominant ideology of its main institutional emplacement, the national educational system, and, in its most elaborated version, the intellectual achievement of one profoundly influential thinker: John Dewey. Dewey's educational thought was radically and expressly functionalist: it envisaged a school system that would produce adequate numbers of young adults trained in the skills and attitudes required to sustain the American economic and political order. It was, in this respect, a creed of active national conformism, and in conditions where the weight of pre-bourgeois educational and other cultural values was virtually nil, its hegemony over the intelligentsia was assured. Yet pragmatism as a whole was more than this, and even in its applied forms could plausibly claim to be more than a policy-maker's schema. For the underlying warrant of its conformism was not some ancient *Volksgeist* but a body of postulate and argument, a constitutional rationalism that in principle transcended particular interests. The Deweyan watchword 'education for citizenship' was not only functional-ist; it also evoked notions of an order based always and everywhere on free, reasoned participation and valuing critical independence as a cultural norm. Dewey's later career itself showed that these notions were not always and everywhere mere pieties; but only very special cultural conditions could so enhance their power that they became dominant in the ideological formation of a whole segment of the intelligentsia—as was in fact to happen in the milieu of *Partisan Review* and the 'New York intellectuals'.[14]

The nucleus of this intellectual formation was triply marginalized within its cultural environment in the thirties. First, many of its members had come out of the East European Jewish immigration, at a time when that community was only partly assimilated and discriminatory practices—most relevantly the *numerus clausus* in higher education—oppressed their children. Second, the dominant political influence in the group was Trotskyism, here as elsewhere a controversial minority current within the intellectual left. Third, their cultural orientation was defiantly internationalist and avant-garde at a time when the Popular Frontist

---

[14] Dewey was an important intellectual influence on several at least of the *Partisan Review* circle, most notably Sidney Hook and James Burnham, but also James T. Farrell. The Commission on the Moscow Trials and the Committee for Cultural Freedom brought the philosopher into direct contact with the journal. (See James Burkhart Gilbert, *Writers and Partisans*, New York 1968, pp. 201–3 and passim; and Alan Wald, *James T. Farrell: the Revolutionary Socialist Years*, New York 1978). Yet Dewey attained a *national* cultural influence that *Partisan Review* could never emulate. It was very much a New York journal throughout, and New York's relationship to the USA was not at all like that of London or Paris to their respective national settings.

literary intelligentsia had joined with an older generation of nativist ideologues in an intolerant cult of 'Americanism'. These were not auspicious circumstances for any new, independent magazine starting out in 1937. But the writers around *Partisan Review* embraced their individual and collective vulnerabilities and made them the substance of a programme, an ethos and a style. The 'New York intellectuals' were anti-academic, and even where (as increasingly) they drew their main income from university teaching, they practised a versatile, generalist mode of writing that was at odds with the prevailing 'Germanic' emphasis on specialized scholarship. Their cultural stance entailed outright opposition to the emergent 'mass culture' of the American city, but they were equally firm in their rejection of conservative nostalgia, whether populist or elitist. Their political disinterestedness was the opposite of quietist; only a minority was ever directly politically engaged, but politics was always a central reference for them, and furnished the occasions of their most vigorous polemical sorties. Bohemians in the academy, moralists in the market-place, intimates of a literature beyond factions yet veterans of the politics of culture: such were the members of what was arguably the 'alienated intelligentsia' par excellence.

Or such, rather, was what Lionel Trilling—the Arnoldian of the circle—might have called their collective 'best self'. For the historical record of the New York intellectuals was one of increasing incorporation and dependence. They may have been 'alienated' from the dominant culture but they belonged to it nonetheless. As Stalinism and the run-up to war drove their politics into crisis, the editors of *Partisan Review* came increasingly to define this alienation as the characteristic state of the displaced, propertyless intellectual. In doing so, they both mistook the real determinations of their original isolation—which had been their minoritarian politics and aesthetics—and misread the cultural affinities of the ideal of 'intellectual' in the American context. This ideal had first emerged in the writings of Van Wyck Brooks and his Westport school as part of an explicitly *nationalist* cultural programme; and the evolution of the New York intellectuals showed that the association would be a lasting one.[15]

---

[15] Brooks's programme was the deviant continuation of Randolph Bourne's, which had envisaged a balanced combination of nationalism and internationalism. *Partisan Review* criticized Brooks's nationalism before the war, citing Bourne's position as more acceptable and more radical in its affinities. But cultural cosmopolitanism alone was not a sufficient safeguard against nationalist attitudes, after the subsidence of its own radicalism.

Partisan Review entered the 1950s utterly transformed. Its political poise had been badly shaken by the war against the Axis and shattered by the Cold War that followed. The journal now supported the US State Department's global effort to contain the spread of Communism. At home, it favoured a pre-emptive ideological strike that would deal with the political menace while averting the risk of an over-vigorous right-wing assault on civil liberties—the political proclivities of America's 'liberal' intelligentsia were the target of Trilling's major post-war intervention, *The Liberal Imagination*. In the outcome, the journal's solicitude did nothing to avert the McCarthy repression or—Rahv's solitary and heavily qualified disquiet notwithstanding—to resist it when it was unleashed. By 1952, alienation was sufficiently assuaged for the *Review* to run a symposium on 'Our Country and Our Culture'.

Thus, a rhetoric of independence coexisted with a record of conformity. 'The intellectual' and the free play of 'mind' became cultic objects in a milieu that, much in keeping with the surrounding culture, was deeply conservative in the fifties, liberal and even radical in the sixties and early seventies, only to swerve rightwards again thereafter. Prominent writers were sharing drinks and ideas at the White House before the Elysée Palace was added to the social map of the high intelligentsia; and Parisian Gulag chic has its tougher-minded equivalent in the New York-Washington 'military-intellectual complex'.

The post-war history of the New York intellectuals is perhaps most starkly illuminated by the career of one of their younger representatives, Norman Podhoretz. Podhoretz studied with Trilling at Columbia (and then Leavis at Cambridge) in the immediate post-war period. Having completed his academic studies, he joined the prestigious New York magazine *Commentary*, of which he became editor in 1960. Formed in the *Partisan Review*'s 'liberal anti-Communism', he later embraced an idiosyncratic 'radicalism' based on Mailer, Goodman and Norman O. Brown. But by the later sixties this amalgam had disintegrated, and Podhoretz turned towards the neo-conservative politics whose most clamorous publicist he now is. The main purpose of his recent memoir, *Breaking Ranks*, was to recapitulate and defend these successive allegiances, but its most powerful demonstration is of a whole tradition quite radically blocked. The 'alienation', or what remains of it, is of a wayward society from the quintessential American standard represented by the 'intellectual'. And that appellation, claimed compulsively on page after page, is no longer primarily important as a reference—to a milieu, say, or a programme; it is now above all the symptom of a measureless self-regard.[16]

4

The purpose of these comparative notes is not to set the scene for general theoretical conclusions; that would presuppose more exacting historical scholarship and finer analytic tools than any utilized here. But it is difficult, as one considers these divergent yet oddly echoing histories, not to feel curious about the sources of Debray's polemical energy, not to inquire what exactly it is that underwrites his freelance oppositionism.

The main impulse in *Teachers, Writers, Celebrities* is undoubtedly political. It is political first of all in the general sense that its inquiry into the development of the French cultural apparatuses is shaped by a strong strategic preoccupation with the forms of bourgeois power and the answering forms of an adequate socialist programme. But Debray's more topical and more intimate concern here is with the political fate of a whole intellectual generation. The strength of this motivation can be measured by its very persistence. In 1967, in the first of what was to have been thirty years in a Bolivian goal, he wrote 'In Settlement of All Accounts', a vivid memoir of his students days at the Ecole Normale.[17] He was already conscious then of a certain unreality in the political attachments of his milieu, and of the rising pressure of careerism and competition inside it. Within a decade his worst fears had been borne out. His *Modeste contribution aux discours et cérémonies officielles du dixième anniversaire*, published in 1978, depicted the May explosion as a functional crisis of development for consumer capitalism in France, and attacked its

---

[16] *Breaking Ranks: a Political Memoir*, New York 1979. Podhoretz's latest production is *The Present Danger* (New York 1980), a bugle-call summoning America to the reconquest of its rightful place in the world. The early history of *Partisan Review* has been replicated institutionally by the *New York Review*. On the left in the sixties and early seventies, when it was an influential platform for anti-war sentiment, the journal has moved rightwards in recent years, while retaining its broad cultural interests. A further parallel is the reliance of both journals on English contributors—a policy more marked in the case of the *New York Review*, which has actually launched a sister-publication in London. Among the *Review*'s most prominent regular writers is Susan Sontag, who might be seen as complementary to Podhoretz, conserving the modernist commitments, the range, vigour and essayistic flair that distinguished the best writing of the New York intellectuals.

[17] *Prison Writings*, pp. 169–207. This essay has never been published in France.

intellectual notables for their regression to irrationalism and political reaction.[18] The present work is a more ambitious attempt to lay bare the specifically cultural structural mechanisms that led to the all but total collapse of the Parisian left intelligentsia in the later seventies, by one of its very few honourable survivors.

However, Debray's politically intransigent Marxism is not his only resource. His mediology produces a 'Frankfurtian' analysis that explicitly denies the presence of politically sufficient contradictions within the cultural order. How, then, is his own position sustained? This is the function of a second level of his text. From time to time Debray will pause to meditate on the trans-generational continuities of the old *lycées*, or to demand 'total support' for the few surviving literary reviews of the old kind, or to brood on the possibility of a world without *Le Monde*. These passages are intermittent and brief, but they are more than rhetoric. They are outcrops of a discourse that underlies the expanse of *Teachers, Writers, Celebrities*: the classic discourse of the French intellectual tradition. The undeclared activity of this discourse is responsible for certain anomalous features of the text, very notably the systematic recourse to anatomical and zoological metaphor, as if in compensation for a forbidden ontology. 'External' circumstances also suggest the ambiguities of the association. The fact that a Marxist reflecting on the involution of the French intellectual tradition can spontaneously reproduce the themes of its minoritarian English counterpart of fifty years ago is a sign that strong cultural currents are running in channels that remain to be opened for investigation. One can know only what one refuses, says Debray, paraphrasing Goethe. Mediology, with its emphatic commitment to the primacy of explanation, suggests the necessary correction. The maxim is a half-truth whose necessary complement is its inverse: one can refuse only what one *knows*.

[18] An extract from this work has been translated in *New Left Review* 115 ('A Modest Contribution to the Rites and Ceremonies of the Tenth Anniversary', May–June 1979, pp. 45–65) together with a reply by Henri Weber (pp. 66–71).

Translator's Note

The neologisms generated by Debray's mediology (*médiologie*), or science of the media, have been transposed directly into English, *médiocratie* being rendered as mediocracy, *médiatique* as mediatic, and so on.

The translation of educational terminology poses specific problems, since French frequently distinguishes only between the *instituteur* (primary teacher) and the *professeur*, a title applied to teachers in secondary schools, university lecturers and professors—that is, faculty or departmental heads—alike. Where the ambiguity of *professeur* is essential to the argument, the French term has been retained. Elsewhere, the closest English equivalent has been used.

Translator's notes are distinguished from the author's by the use of an asterisk rather than arabic numerals.

I am grateful to Margaret Atack for her comments and criticisms.

David Macey

Foreword

This text was originally the concluding part of a broader theoretical work entitled *Traité de médiologie*, which is about to be published. The first volume will delineate the symbolic function in Western societies, retracing the history of its vectors and clarifying its organic relation with State power; the second will attempt to analyse both the notion of the *medium* and the new political and cultural technology introduced by the modern *mass media*. The concrete analysis presented here results from the application of the conceptual field so isolated to a concrete situation, that of the modern French intelligentsia. It has been decided to publish it separately because it forms a whole, as does its object. The method of observation and the *ultimate* stakes will become apparent only when the notions of intellectual, medium and State have been systematically located. I must therefore ask the reader, if indeed there is a reader, to grant me a limited stay of credit until the *Traité* appears.

As for the immediate stakes, which have a certain topical interest: the strategic role played by the high intelligentsia (*haute intelligentsia*) of France in both national and international political class relations cannot much longer remain concealed by its apparent marginality and lack of numerical importance. The alliance that the intelligentsia has forged with the *new mediocracy* (from *media*, 'means of mass communication', or 'means of production of opinion on a mass basis' and *kratein*, 'to govern'), with which indeed it is beginning to merge, ensures it a monopoly in the production and circulation of events and values, of symbolic facts and norms, over an increasingly wide area; initially in France, from top to bottom and from east to west, and then on the periphery of the Western world, where nations and cultures are normalized, planed down and homogenized from the commanding heights of the centre. The price of this integration into the main means of diffusion, whereby the high intelligentsia has bought its social supremacy, has been a considerable degradation of the intellectual function. The struggle for culture has rarely been so closely bound up with the struggle for emancipation; just as its capacity for historical innovation depends upon the maintenance of its cultural traditions, so the fate and independence of a people cannot be separated from the fate and independence of its intellectual 'elites'. Seldom have the management of minds and the conduct of business affairs converged so. 'Governing means convincing people', said Machiavelli. In France today, those who monopolize the government of opinion sit, sometimes unwittingly, in the government of the Republic, which is kept in power only by the 'opinion' of its citizens. It is therefore impossible to overthrow the coalition of interests that exploits and rules the majority of men and women, in France and all over the world, without deposing or overthrowing the social power that allows this state of disorder to establish itself inside our heads day by day as though it were a state based on law and liberty. There is more than one way to occupy a country and undermine the sovereignty of a people: the least blatant is not necessarily the least effective. The mediocracy is the main pillar of bourgeois domination in France. The now ritual division between civil society and the State (a methodological distinction metamorphosed into a real dissociation in the object) no longer stems solely from a massive theoretical misunderstanding as to the nature of political power: it has become a practical alibi that allows a number of 'intellectuals' cynically to pass themselves off as heroes of civil society when they are in fact the most efficient statesmen available to our system of bourgeois domination. In this age of dupes, the elite of our 'intellectual party' has kept for itself the best role in this comedy of a hundred different masks: one with all the advantages of authority with none of the disadvantages of power.

Our purpose here is not to display ill-temper, indignation or resentment, but to analyse. Although a polemical situation may be the moving force behind thought, the pamphlet is to our eyes a degrading genre at odds with any ethics of knowledge. A rational discipline like mediology (which aims to be rigorous and must show itself to be so) can help fashion tools to make reality intelligible and weapons to transform it; inasmuch as it acknowledges the real, it can also serve those who find advantage there. The names we will use as landmarks are to be taken simply as supports for generic relations whose internal logic, in its necessity, is our sole concern.

Let no one be surprised, then, not to find any obviously self-critical allusion to a personal lived experience. Is it not more urgent to explore an objective logic than to beat one's breast for the *n*th time? It is clear that the author of these lines has in the past used and abused the intellectual power objectivized here. Like everyone else, he has pranced about the stage in a minor role. Without ever having sat on the Administrative Board for National Intelligence, he has on occasion pinched directors' fees from those entitled to them by going through pockets and loitering in corridors. He has experienced the intoxication of journalistic fame, contrived polemics and the bravura of advertising. Once, in 1975, he even went on television to prate with his peers on *Apostrophes*. To object that he was not yet aware that television is an ideology or that he had not yet added up all the abdications, usurpations and confiscations that an intellectual worker effects when he agrees to fill the small screen with his fame is simply to admit that it was not in his interests to be aware of it, or that he put his interests as an author in search of a personality before his conscience—damning compromises for a would-be paragon of virtue. Our sole ambition now, in the field of *moeurs*, is to transform unawareness into experience; and to elicit from the risk that the doors of intellectual legitimacy will be closed against us, a desire to dismantle the mechanisms that dictate to whom and to what these doors open; and to see the conditions on which they do so. 'One only really grasps what one repudiates', said Goethe. To know is to refuse, but how can one refuse something one has yet to penetrate? What could someone who has never belonged to the 'society of thought' described here know of the laws that make it function? A first-person account of that 'journey across Paris' might well be amusing, even if it did last only four or five years (1973–8). To objectify a personal trajectory is one thing; a string of anecdotes and revelations is quite another. There is a time and a place for everything. In a time and a country drunk on 'autos', where the shop windows are packed with autobiographies, the TV with auto-portraits, tribunals with *autogestion*, the papers with *auto da fés* and the streets with automobiles, it seemed to me that yet another 'auto', even if it were an autocritique, could wait.

One last comment: the demarcation or intersection, in one person or social group, of the artist, intellectual and scientist raised too many questions (not difficulties, but a coherent set of facts and definitions tackled elsewhere) to figure in this volume. That problematic, which would lead to a refinement of the reading grid, would allow us to take into account and fully appreciate, in each period, the fascinating phenomenon of the renegades from the high intelligentsia, which excludes all those who exclude themselves from it. It also excludes them from what the lofty personages in question think of not as (intellectual) value, but as (social) position. For a creator, belonging to a class is a matter of resignation, not fate, and it is always possible for an individual to stand up to his fate. Remember Genet, Michaux, Char, Leiris, Beckett, Chris Marker, Rezvani and all the others who resisted, and whose names will crop up here and there in these pages (even if their faces are not seen on TV). They all exemplify a certain remove from the mood of the times—'black holes' in the fluorescent superfluities of the great spectacle of the West, from which, tomorrow, the inventors of the present will spring.

I would like to express my sincere thanks to those who were good enough to benefit this manuscript by their comments: Claude Durand, Clara Malraux, Christian Baudelot, Daniel Lindenberg and Bernard Cassen, Gérard-Humbert Goury and Erik Orsenna, as well as to Michel Serres and Pierre Bourdieu, who spared the time to calm my scientific doubts. On economic questions, Michel Gutelman's suggestions have been most valuable. I would also like to thank those who agreed to answer the questions of an investigator eager for details—M. Michel Peyney for information on the work and criteria of AGESSA (Association pour la gestion de la sécurité sociale des auteurs); Alain Desrosières, Laurent Thévenot and Christian Baudelot again for statistical data from INSEE and for help in deciphering it; Bernard Pingaud for information on the history of the Union des écrivains; Marie Cardinal for information of the aims of the Syndicat des écrivains de langue française—and Colette Ledannois for her unfailing help.

Balzac,
or Zoology Today

Animals have no history: what is the point of a history of the intellectuals?
The temptations of zoology make one dizzy. And how can we avoid
shrinking back before the mocking shades of those three great animal
painters of the nineteenth century who lie in wait for us here? The most
discouraging thing is not that we owe the most accurate X-rays of what was
yet to be called the intellectual to Hegel, Balzac and Nietzsche, but that
they are so obscenely up to date. The analysis of the creature was a good
century ahead of its evolution. At the start of a short essay in social history,
it is not inappropriate to recall that nature sheds more light on the secrets
of the men of culture than history does, and that the naturalists of the
human mind saw through them sooner than the historians of society. As
early as 1807, long before Nietzsche and his 'ruminants of higher
education' and 'camels of culture', the coherent figure of the intellectual as
'an individuality which takes itself to be real in and for itself' emerged in
the *Phenomenology*'s 'community of animals'[1]—and not just anywhere,
but at the most crucial moment in the development of the Spirit: mid-way
between the world of Reason and that of Spirit, in the transition between
abstract theoretical forms and the concrete history in which the Spirit will
be made incarnate. This figure of consciousness, a temporary but necessary
station on the Spirit's 'way of the cross', is known as the 'intellectual
animal'. Balzac may not have read Hegel, but he does introduce us to a
very special animal—or a very peculiar *social species*—duly classified
under the label 'Ordre: *gendelettre*', with a classificatory table of its genera,
sub-genera and varieties. This study in zoology, taken from *L'Histoire
naturelle du Bimane en société*, is entitled *Monographie de la presse parisienne*

---

[1] Hegel. *The Phenomenology of Mind*, New York 1967, p. 414 f. See also Roger Establet, *Le
Conflit des consciences et l'oeuvre commune* (Diplôme d'études supérieures, 1964).

and dates from 1843.[2] As can be seen from the synoptic table, the taxonomy used here is closer to Linnaeus than to Cuvier (with the order as an intermediary category between the class and the family); Balzac did not use the same terminology in all his works. On the other hand, the debt to Buffon, from whom he takes the classical idea of the 'unity of the plan of nature', remains constant, and Balzac remains faithful to the theses ('unity of composition') of Geoffroy de Saint Hilaire—theses which already look like ecology and come from the man who in 1854 was to coin the term 'ethology' for the study of animal behaviour. These classificatory criteria no longer have the weight of authority, but what has made publishers ignore Balzac's micrography until now is probably not its anachronism so much as its truly embarrassing modernity. A modern reader could put a face to every species and variety described here without the slightest difficulty (the tenor, the blonde critic, the Jack of all trades, the prophet, the guerrilla). The morphology of the mammal seems not to have varied any more than its physiology. Looking at these daguerreotypes is like flipping through your own family album. Must we fall back on the dogma of the fixed nature of living species?

The discovery of writing has transformed the immobility of a natural species into a human history, and it may seem unacceptable to stuff scribes for dispatch to the Natural History Museum. It is right to rebel. The naturalist hypothesis lays us open to two symmetrical errors: a doctrine of innate qualities, or of curiosities. In the former, the infinite play among individuals dissolves into the genetically programmed continuity of the species and all the richness of social history is absorbed into phylogenesis. In the latter, a jumble of secondary qualities conceals the essential unity of the class and a biographical rhapsody of ontogenesis juxtaposes more or less eccentric 'phenomena' which are inconsequential since there is no principle behind them. The result is pathological proliferation in which any central norm disappears behind the glitter of appearances and any functional necessity behind an endless procession of Rameau's Nephews from everywhere and anywhere. Biology concludes that 'there is nothing new under the sun', teratology that 'everything is picturesque'; and the two finally come together in a comforting 'it has always been that way'.

[2] Published in Volume 2 of *La grande ville, nouveau tableau de Paris, comique, critique et philosophique* by MM. Paul de Kock, Balzac, Dumas . . . with illustrations by Gavarni, Daumier, Henri Monnier, etc. (Balzac, *Oeuvres diverses*, Tome I, Librairie Ollendorf, 1907, p. 227.)

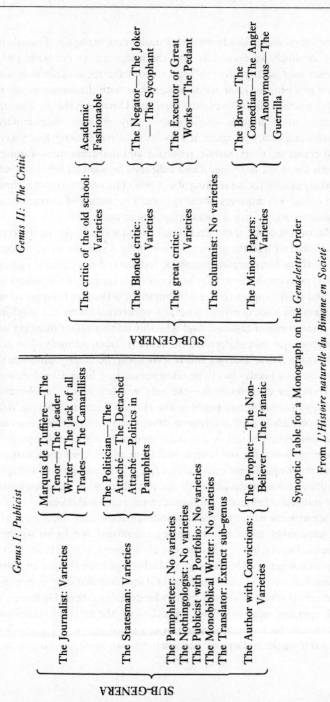

Order: Gendelettre

Genus I: Publicist

The Journalist: Varieties { Marquis de Tuffière—The Tenor—The Leader Writer—The Jack of all Trades—The Camarillists

The Statesman: Varieties { The Politician—The Attaché—The Detached Attaché—Politics in Pamphlets

SUB-GENERA

The Pamphleteer: No varieties
The Nothingologist: No varieties
The Publicist with Portfolio: No varieties
The Monobiblical Writer: No varieties
The Translator: Extinct sub-genus

The Author with Convictions: Varieties { The Prophet—The Non-Believer—The Fanatic

Genus II: The Critic

The critic of the old school: Varieties } Academic Fashionable

The Blonde critic: Varieties } The Negator—The Joker — The Sycophant

The great critic: Varieties } The Executor of Great Works—The Pedant

The columnist: No varieties

The Minor Papers: Varieties } The Bravo—The Comedian—The Angler —Anonymous—The Guerrilla

SUB-GENERA

Synoptic Table for a Monograph on the *Gendelettre* Order

From *L'Histoire naturelle du Bimane en Société*

Balzac, *La Grande ville* (1843)

Ecclesiastes shakes hands with M. Prudhomme yet again. This is a blind alley in which we eventually find the image we set out with, just like tourists on a package tour to 'exotic' countries: the *gendelettre* as a stock figure in a timeless fashionable play, always with the same plot, manners and characters. Rivarol replaces Hegel, and Offenbach Balzac. The eternal frivolity of 'bourgeois intellectuals'—why go into their cowardice, venality and vanity yet again? It's always the same old song. Every day that God grants us, every author, professor and journalist sings it under his breath about the dear friend and colleague he has just left—and who is thinking exactly the same thing about him. The banal satire of manners is part of the very manners of the species. The botany of character cannot replace sociology; it is a sociological object itself.

But the sociology of the intellectual milieu will only give up its secrets if it is treated with all the gravity of philosophy. From the outset we have to reject all the banal arguments about fashion and the sarcastic comments about 'ready-made thought'; they themselves are part of the fashion of the day and serve simply to conceal the meaning of the play from the actors by avoiding the basic question: what *can* intellectual life be if it is subject to the phenomena of fashion? And why this fashion rather than any other? The grotesque side of Parisian life has to be taken seriously. The gravity with which Balzac analyses and reflects upon the literary and journalistic buffoonery of his day has to be taken seriously. Lucien Chardon, soon to be known as de Rubempré—the very emblem of the intellectual—is perhaps the most tragic figure in the Human Comedy; his long *Bildung* ends in suicide in the Conciergerie. It may be a comedy, but it ends badly. The intellectual world is a cellular one over which unhappiness and loneliness hover: the self is separated from others, from the Cause or the Ideal, from what Hegel calls the real fact (*die Sache selbst*), in a chapter of the *Phenomenology* dealing with the lost illusions of self-consciousness. The intellectual animal—a figure of absolute individualism—comes face to face with the failure of 'the most individual solution'. He wants to make his personality his work, attributing essentiality not to his (literary or scientific) works, but to his subjective ability to create and thus to his talent or personal genius. He claims to make his 'operations' serve an objective Cause, but really he cares nothing for it and systematically fails it. So the intellectual deceives himself, just as he deceives others. He has no work and 'operates' in a void. After this false exit, the unhappy consciousness has to turn back on itself. Again, it is a failed odyssey. The intellectual animal struggles and strives to return to his own being, but his true being is nowhere. For Hegel and Balzac the intellectual is an individual non-entity who begins by thinking he is someone and finally discovers that he is nothing.

By rooting his fictional descriptions in a law of variations taken from Geoffroy de Saint-Hilaire, Balzac completely escaped the triviality of naturalism. He took the rules of method laid down in the *Foreword to the Human Comedy* quite literally, and red-handed; 'the animal is a principle which takes its outer form or, to be more accurate, its difference in form, from the environment in which it is called upon to develop. Zoological species derive from such differences.' This principle must explain why we still feel contemporary with that splendid creature called Rubempré and with the horde described in what Balzac himself called the 'most important work' of his cycle, *Lost Illusions, or A Great Man from the Provinces in Paris*—or how an obscure failed poet from Angoulême went to Paris, the great arena, and dragged himself to the heights of success by becoming a fashionable journalist. Apparently the first act of a period melodrama, this was in reality, the first handbook on how to dismantle the material cogs of hegemony. Balzac's contemporaries placed him in the same 'sub-genre' as Eugène Sue. As it happens, the genre of the *Mysteries of Paris* reveals the thorny mysteries of thought as political behaviour a hundred years before Brecht's notes, and of politics as the destiny of thought a hundred years before Gramsci's. If power, like love, has no history, the intellectual as 'animal of power' is as close to us as the great political animals of antiquity. The 'old way of the world' which depressed Chateaubriand so much shows no signs of getting any older. How many thousands of Rubemprés have there been since the original? They no longer come from Angoulême; the fashionable editor is no longer called Dauriat; the editor-in-chief to be won over is no longer on the *Journal des Débats*; the big name who will get you the front page (as they say on *Le Monde*) or the 'cultural page' (as they say on *Le Nouvel Observateur*)* is no longer called Janim; the militant's path—still disappointing and tedious, and from which one has to stray to escape anonymity as soon as possible—no longer leads to a Saint-Simonian cenacle; the Rocher de Cancale is no longer the 'amusing bar' where one can rub shoulders with ministers and stars. But the mechanisms used by the class in power to corrupt-promote the noble in spirit have not changed substantially. In terms of its inner functional logic, the *milieu* is still the same, which is why

* Each week, *Le Nouvel Observateur* invites a 'celebrity' to write on his/her choice of films, broadcasts, concerts, etc., during the coming week.

we feel so much at home in the labyrinth of Balzac's plots and portrait galleries. It is all there, right down to the latest recipes for mediatic success, the tricks of the press attachés and the harassment of our friends, their protegés: the need to stir up a polemic 'around' the book, the 'great intellectual debate' as absolute commercial imperative, the race against the clock to get 'a reaction from the press in time' (because of the faster stock rotation in the bookshops), the need to court the three or four journalists who 'count' just before publication, the exorbitant cost of promotion, tempered by the hope of free advertising in leaders which, as we all know, is so much better. If we go beyond those details—symptoms of a serious and contagious illness—we find that there is already a new deal, a new game and new stakes: the growing supremacy of the press over literature, of journalists over authors. There is a crossroads, already quite clearly outlined, which every young and unknown talent reaches sooner or later: to the left, the long career of the intellectual-militant or the academic-researcher; to the right, the very short career offered him via journalism and social climbing by the class that controls the objective means for self-realization and keeps the keys to glory and wealth. The ledgers of the intellectual's trade (ease balanced against difficulty) may use new indices and scales, but the picture painted in 1839 still applies to the Paris of 1979. There is no history without a given nature, but that nature itself has a history. Balzac was present at the beginning of an era in French cultural history and we are present at its end, even if we are still struggling with it. That is why it all looks so familiar.

There were men of letters before then, but no *gendelettre*. As a historian, Balzac witnessed the birth of a new species which has reached maturity in our day and which is unlikely to die out in the near future. Despite appearances, its conditions of existence are connected with the industrial revolution, which gave the order both its letters patent, its full political function and its social base. Other scientific and technical revolutions were to follow, and each determined an internal restructuring of the politico-literary intelligentsia (and not simply of the scientific intelligentsia, as common sense might suggest) and gave it more power. But it was the beginning of the industrial age in the West that signalled the start both of mass literary consumption and of monopolistic concentration in its production. The popularization of the written word (through the expansion of primary and then secondary education), the extension of the reading public and the subordination of writers to the ruling bourgeoisie, go hand in hand and have a cumulative effect. By destroying the material basis of peddling, the railways did away with chap-books and erected barriers that suddenly separated popular from élite culture, 'novels for chamber maids' from 'novels for the salon'—the almost official opposition of which Stendhal complained and which he wanted to overcome with *Le Rouge et le Noir*.[3] The railways meant that Parisian newspapers could achieve a nation-wide circulation. Advertising became the 'foster-mother of the press'. In 1836, Emile de Girardin (the founder of a line which, a century later, would produce the Prouvosts, the Lazareffs and the Hersants) made advertising part of the recipe for running a newspaper for the first time, and launched *La Presse* with capital subscribed thanks to it, guaranteeing a lower cover price and an amazing success. *Le Constitutionnel* and the *Journal des Débats*, the great newspapers of the Restoration, had circulations of 16,000 and 13,000 respectively. *La Presse* immediately found 40,000 subscribers, thus marking the start of an upward curve that reached the one million mark in 1885 with *Le Petit Journal*, launched in 1863 and costing one sou. By hitching itself to the locomotive of journalism through the serialized novel (and Balzac was the first author to be serialized by Girardin), and thanks to literary criticism, which had become a professional activity, literature itself suddenly took off in the same way; over the same period, print runs rose from one or two thousand in 1830—which was then considered excellent—to one hundred thousand with Zola's *Nana* in 1880.[4]

What makes our own period so similar to the July Monarchy (and, in the same way, to the Second Empire) is this twofold movement of accelerated economic change combined with an obvious symbolic depression. Just as the latter caused the intelligentsia to return to the political scene in force (because of the in-draught), finance capital burst directly into intellectual production via the press and publishing. Under the Orleanist financial bourgeoisie, the press was transformed into the main regulator of the intellectual market: the very basis of distribution, and therefore of intellectual production, was turned upside down. Then as now, the power of high finance could do without moral values, but because of its own logic

[3] See *Projet d'article sur Le Rouge et le Noir*, sent by Stendhal to Count Salvagnoli and dated October, 18, 1832. (Pléiade edition, I, p. 700.)

[4] In England, where the industrial revolution was fifty years ahead of France, the hundred thousand mark was reached by Byron and Walter Scott fifty years earlier. See Robert Escarpit, *Sociologie de la littérature*, and his thesis on *Lord Byron, un tempérament littéraire*, Paris 1955.

it could not therefore stop itself indexing the circulation of symbolic values to its scale of economic values. Papers like *La Presse* and *Le Siècle* gave novelists (in particular) the chance not only to make new and considerable gains, but also to achieve unprecedentedly wide moral and ideological influence (Eugène Sue is a case in point). Previously, writers sold their books or failed to sell them. From now on it was the newspapers that sold books, because they themselves had higher sales. In other words, writers sold in so far as and on condition that they got the newspapers to buy them. But who owned the papers and why did anyone start one? As early as 1836, Balzac was tracing, *in nuce* but *in vivo*, the dotted lines of a syllogism which time would fill out in black and white: literature was becoming dependent on the press; the press itself was dependent on the big holders of capital; therefore the writer would more or less become a servant of capital, whether openly or not. Middle term and go-between: medium.

Balzac was an artist and the role of an artist is to ask questions, not to supply answers. The surprising thing is that the questions were so well put, just at the right time, namely before their time and against the current. This was presumably because Balzac did not take himself for what he was, but for a notary or a zoographer. The aesthetes, who at this time were training their voices and flaunting their blazon, could produce nothing more than ideology and received ideas such as the mystification of 'the artist' as a consumptive, misunderstood pariah: Vigny's *Chatterton*, and then Murger's heroes. Then there was the traditional satire of artistic cliques and the picturesque side of the literary Bohemian—more reassuring images: Théophile Gautier (Preface to *Mlle de Maupin*, 1835) and Scribe (*La Camaraderie ou La Courte Echelle*, 1837). Balzac spat out the rind and bit into the hard centre: 'the horribly comic manners of the press, the only eccentrics of our day'. It is no accident that his work alone has not become dated—in the press, as in capitalism, everything has changed except the inner logic. This admirable journalist was the first lucid enemy of the 'popular press'. Rousseau's disdainful fulminations against newspapers belong to the past, being based on a misunderstanding.[5] The clear-sighted analysis of Balzac, the legitimist and the reactionary, anticipated our future, which he certainly did not enter backwards. One only understands the things one rejects. Expecting

[5] 'What is a periodical book? An ephemeral work with neither merit nor nobility, casual reading matter which is despised by literate men and which serves only to give women and fools vanity without learning'—Rousseau, 1775.

nothing from the journalists of his day and having even less to thank them for, but having had the good fortune of personal dealings with those who never stopped running him down, Balzac was able to stand back from his times, reconstitute the order of its organs and correlate its essential forms, like Cuvier bending over the fragments of a fossil. He could thus lay bare what was to become the spinal column of the mammal known as *gendelettre*—a species with a national vocation, but still in its formative stages. 'A great sore of the age, a cancer that may devour the country'— this was his prognosis for the ridiculous benign tumour that was journalism in 1839. The fact is that, one hundred and fifty years later, it has not only devoured the country by domesticating its people; it has allowed the country's ruling class to cook and devour its intelligentsia.

This preliminary but by no means 'literary' tribute was necessary, for it brings us to the heart of the subject: the medium as intermediary link between money and power. The cards are now dealt differently, but the rules of the game are the same. The twenty-five-year battle over the *Encyclopedia* allowed Diderot to explore a basic triangle of mediology in practice before it had even taken on its true social dimension. It is no accident that the three-sided genius of Diderot—that portrait of Balzac as democrat, his left-wing alter ego—reached its greatest heights in what might be termed, to use a coherent anachronism, putting political power in its rightful place (*Essai sur les règnes de Claude et de Néron*), putting the 'intellectual' on stage (*Le Neveu de Rameau*) and updating the question of the media (*Lettre sur le Commerce de la Librairie*).[6] But the fact remains that the novelist was the first observer of the modern world to focus on all three sides of our problem, namely 1. the material conditions of existence of thought (stationery, foundry, typography, printing); 2. the product of intellectual labour as a commodity subject to market constraints; 3. the organic relation between the intellectual producer and the field of politics—and this last aspect made him a veritable military expert on cultural life (hence his constant metaphors: the army of the press, the literary war, the arena of Paris). *Lost Illusions*, or how a book is made, how it is sold, how it fights; three links in the cultural chain, three successive novels in one, three stages in Lucien's initiation into the void. Taken

---

[6] Echoed, perhaps without the author's being aware of it, by Balzac's *L'Etat actuel de la Librairie* (3–10 March 1830) and *Lettre aux écrivains français* (1834). A Société des gens de lettres was formed to support Diderot in his publishing efforts. The present Société des gens de lettres was born of Balzac's legal and professional efforts.

together, they recompose the cultural sphere into a pyramid of power with a social base which finds its concrete expression in the system of hierarchical relations that make up the internal unity of the ruling intelligentsia and in the individual ascent through the hierarchy as the road to state power. The analyst makes a synchronic section, the novelist takes a diachronic route. The 'most important work' in the cycle merged the two.

It was a prophetic focalization. Balzac observed all the things that Marx did not see. One can see why Marx dreamed of devoting the rest of his life to studying his novels. There is no contradiction between a zoology of intellectual power and an analysis of the capitalist mode of production. A zoology completes it (or transcends it and assumes it into itself). If Denis Diderot was the great-uncle of mediology, Honoré de Balzac was definitely its founding father. The gateway to mediology has as its pillars the *tutti* of the evening at Florine's and Lousteau's monologue in the Luxembourg.

Let none enter except Balzacians.

One

Surveying

Paradoxes

First, a disappointment: 'there is no such thing as the intelligentsia'. As he sets out on his long march through the intellectual milieu, the investigator inevitably comes up against this profession of faith offered as a statement of fact. The higher placed his interlocutor, the stronger the denial. In the intelligentsia, this leitmotiv is both a password and a member's badge. It is as though 'we do not belong to the same family' were the motto of all its members. After a few weeks, the investigator will be inclined to class rejection of the definition among the most reliable criteria for the delineation of the category.

Second, a surprise: the term most frequently heard in this milieu is 'power'. The French intelligentsia applies the term to the most varied collection of professional bodies, institutions and nouns, often pertinently, but never to itself. It never stops talking about the mechanisms, network and diagrams of the past and other places, but seems to maintain a stubborn silence as to its own mechanism of selection-censorship and promotion-exclusion *hic et nunc* in the university, publishing and the media. Could it be that intellectual power does not exist in the eyes of the intellectuals? Very few people notice how odd this is. Power is always, it would seem, the power of others and never the power exercised by me.

What good has the investigator's pilgrim's staff done, apart from discouraging him? Appearances and tendencies are no substitute for analysis. The paradoxes he meets on his way are symptoms. But of what? Of the fact that one cannot 'be' and at the same time see oneself 'being', or that no one can be himself without simultaneously mistaking himself for someone else. The same vicious circle confines both individuals and social groups. The fact that the ideologues' self-consciousness is ideological merely attests to the spontaneity and universality of the curse. But that the sociology of sociologists should remain so underdeveloped is a case apart. The intellectuals' silence about the intelligentsia requires investigation. Just as the silence of writers—whose professional work is talking about themselves—about writers as a social body is of primary interest to the sociologist of literature, so the fact that those who wield symbolic authority show so little interest in the causes, nature and extent of their authority is something that should attract the attention of the theorists of power—if, that is, 'truth is recognizable by its attempts to conceal itself'. Let us ignore facile objections, and not simply because the sign of a gentleman is his discretion about the basis of the agreement: our manners will not be so elegant. They say that in the mafia you can do anything but call it the mafia. The law of silence certainly ensures that honourable men stick together, but the silence with which the intellectual machine protects its cogs should not suggest *omertà*, for it would be a serious error—of taste rather than judgement—to compare the high intelligentsia to a mafia, even if they do have some things in common. The intellectual milieu has its code of reciprocal good manners, but one of the technical conditions for plying the *trade* is a certain lack of self-awareness: it is easier to spread the 'light' if you yourself stay in the shadow. In that sense, the intelligentsia can best exercise its specifically political function by effacing itself as a rigorously structured social subject.

As a sociological aporia the 'intelligentsia' appears at first sight to derive from a purely ideological or even polemical categorization without any real content or identity. The fact is that, when an intellectual decides to take the intelligentsia as an object of reflection, it is usually as a subject for a confession, curses or a sermon and not as an object of study. The normative passion inhibits any concern for description from the outset, and the discourse of value—be it valorization or devaluation, the effect is the same—shields its author from the elementary demands of observation and logic. It is as difficult for a citizen to speak of the intellectuals in the city as it is for a historian to talk about the Jews in history without being caught between zionism and anti-semitism. No one describes the intellectual: you defend him or attack him, as one did the Jesuits and Freemasons of the past. It is a classic problem: Barth and Péguy speak for the prosecution, Herr and Zola for the defence, and there is no one in between. Benda denounces *La trahison des clercs* in order to pay tribute to the clerisy; Nizan

denounces its dishonour without having any interest in how it functions.[1]
Raymond Aron writes *L'Opium des intellectuels* and Sartre a *Plaidoyer pour
les intellectuels*. Even if we restrict ourselves to listing works by French
writers on the French intellectuals during the latest 'B period'[2] in which
most of them are concentrated, the documentary inconsistency is amazing.
Raymond Aron, for instance—a positive thinker, if he is to be believed—
achieves the remarkable feat of writing four hundred pages on the subject
without giving a single *definition* of the word, any *number* count, *history* of
the category or *indication* of its means of subsistence. The only rigorous
work on the subject (in its time) has been deleted from the catalogues and
is out of print: it was not by a 'big name'.[3] France, which rightly has the
reputation of being a political paradise for the intellectuals, appears to be a
purgatory for their sociologists. The two things go together. The Germans
had Mannheim, Weber, Schumpeter and Michels; the Americans, Lipset
and Wright Mills; the Italians, Gramsci and his followers. France had the
Dreyfus Affair and has been resting on its laurels ever since. If on top of
that old handicap—which means that a French *savant* can elaborate a
learned theory on the role of white coffee in the cultural practices of the
West without mentioning the part played by hot water—we think of all
the obsessive fears deriving from the current ideological conjuncture, we
might graciously excuse the corporation's pompous silence. 'Crude
positivism', 'naive empiricism' and 'vulgar sociology' are unforgivable
crimes. Many people know that and keep quiet. Others exorcise the danger
by accusing their rivals and disqualifying them before the race has even
begun. The majority ward off sarcasm by contrasting these mortifying
deviations with their own work, using punctuation as a foil. In the suction

---

[1] Edouard Berth, *Les méfaits des intellectuels*, Paris, Riviere, 1914 (Preface by Georges
Sorel). Péguy, *Notre Jeunesse* (1916) and passim. Lucien Herr, *Choix d'écrits*, Paris, Rieder
(1932) and D. Lindenberg and P.-A. Mayer, *Herr, le socialisme et son destin*, Calmann-Levy
(1977) Emile Zola, *La Vérité en marche* (1901, a collection of articles, including the celebrated
letter to the President of the Republic, dated 13 January 1898. This collection is at the origin
of the *Manifeste* and the noun.), and *Nouvelle Campagne* (1897), a collection of articles
including 'La Vertu de la République', 'L'Elite et la Politique' and 'Lettre à la jeunesse'.
Julien Benda, *La trahison des clercs*, Paris 1927, *La jeunesse d'un clerc*, Paris 1937, and *Un
régulier dans le siècle*, Paris 1938. Nizan, *Les Chiens de garde*, Paris 1932.

[2] 'B Periods' are periods when there is a divorce between coercive power and symbolic
power within the apparatus of authority. The Fourth Republic is one example. A complete
bibliography will be given in Volume 1 of the *Traité*.

[3] Louis Bodin, *Les Intellectuels*.

pump of the intellectual club of France, which one can join only by excluding someone else, these conjurors' formulae are used both as mutual deterrents and for personal enhancement. The high intelligentsia has in recent times had the wit to endow itself with a *savoir dire* that makes the labour of thought much lighter, so that crudity of thought can be gauged by precision of language, and subtlety of discourse by inaccuracy. Concealment of the real behind the symbolic—the optical focus of national ideas for the last twenty years (Lacanian psychoanalysis, structural anthropologies, learned Marxisms, semiology and linguistics)—has the advantage of combining lofty thoughts with lazy-mindedness in those who have to make a living in the wake of the research of the masters. The common virtue of theoretical 'problematics' and 'conceptual apparatuses' on the one hand and 'the site from which I speak and the statute whereby my discourse is ordained' on the other is that what I say will be heard all the better if no-one knows *what* or *whom*, and a fortiori *how many* individuals or which historical period or country I am talking about. With the exception of some of the pupils of Foucault and Bourdieu, it is left to the proletarians of the lower intelligentsia—'second-rate' historians, sociologists and researchers who are quite logically the dupes of quaint ideologies of doing things properly—to provide the empirical verifications, the bookish compilations which are the mark of the rank-and-file intelligentsia. And so the hierarchical demarcation between high and lower intelligentsia is extended from top to bottom, from school desks to the masters' dais.

So let us not be afraid of being academic: old debates raise new questions. A certain Marxist scholasticism has been trying for decades to find the right pigeon hole for the intellectuals. What is the right word: class, group, caste, or category? Empirical sociology may well be a blind alley when it comes to studying the intelligentsia. But in order to find out, we have to plunge fearlessly into it. And since we have nothing to lose except time, here are some doubts, dates and figures.

Definitions

Position

Although it is inserted into the capitalist mode of production and dependent upon it, the intelligentsia cannot be defined by its position in the material process of production, or be referred to a simple economic category (ground rent, wages or capital) for its means of existence. It is not a *class*. Although it consists of a set of men and women connected by reciprocal communications, relations between them are sustained by an armature of institutions and behaviour: it is more than an informal *group*. Membership of the intelligentsia is not hereditary; one can leave it and enter it. It is not a *caste*. It does not have any governing council, internal regulations or, *sensu strictu*, a monopoly over its own reproduction: it is not a *corporation*. It would therefore seem prudent to fall back on *social category*, which has the advantage of not committing us to anything. It is in fact, and as we shall see, at once more and less than that: less because the personal status of its members is as varied as their class background; more because it functions on the institutional model, but without the juridical impedimenta of the great guilds.

First Definition

Its very function as a mediator or intermediary indicates that the intelligentsia is a frontier-category straddling several areas: liberal professions on the one hand and senior administrative personnel on the other; or self-employed artisans and wage-earners in the state sector. If one of the criteria for the homogeneity of a socio-professional group is that its members do indeed consider themselves as belonging to it, then the intelligentsia is a decidedly heterogeneous stratum. By statute, so to speak;

for if only the homogeneous can be collected together, there can be no intellectual collectivity: each member is irreducible to his neighbour and it is precisely that difference that makes him an intellectual. The intellectuals are not short of excuses for denying their existence as a group and for claiming to be merely an - aggregate of complex individualities. As representatives of the qualitative, they are naturally confused when it comes to dealing with discrete quantities, being accustomed by their function to a system based on property qualifications, in which individuals are weighed, not counted. Presumably that is why one of the category's peculiarities is that it is more easily seen from outside than inside, from below than from above. The authorities require a homogeneous system of weights and measures to decide on the allocation of resources, just as the courts require a definition of the laws to sanction their infringement. For the state's 'great enemy' receives aid from the selfsame state, which has therefore had to find out to whom the aid should be sent and according to what criteria.

With admirable succinctness, the jurists here defined what is meant by *author*, *writer*, *work*, *reproduction*, and so on, in order to protect and guarantee the right to property—in the law of 11 March 1957, which, although partly out of date, is still used. 'Any person whose printed works are distributed through the channels of the book trade is considered to be a writer.' Technological change has broadened this narrow frame of reference, and the category of 'Lettres' has grown now to include writers of film or television scripts, radio sketches and so on. Hence the new definitions of the *author* proposed by the 'Lettres' group on the Commission for the Plan in 1970: 'Anyone who gives life to something through the agency of an original text' and/or 'Anyone who produces an original text either in the classic form of the written word or by any other means independent of the support of paper'. As for the 1975 law establishing a social security system for 'artists, authors of literary, dramatic, musical, choreographical, audio-visual, cinematographic, graphic or plastic works', this required a whole series of decrees and ministerial orders to define its various fields of application.

The notion of *production* or *creation*, with its connotations of novelty and originality, allows an immediate, initial line of demarcation to be drawn between the *intellectual professions* (doctors, lawyers, engineers, magistrates, senior army officers, the clergy, and so on) and the *professionals of the intellect*. There is in France a Confédération des

Travailleurs Intellectuels (CTI) with about a hundred organisations affiliated to it and classified under four main headings: arts, letters and sciences; liberal professions; salaried intellectual workers; students. The definition adopted by the CTI in 1952 refers to a sphere that is much broader and less precise than that of intellectuals 'in the strict sense': 'An intellectual worker is one whose normal activities require mental rather than physical effort, with all that this implies in initiative and personality'. In plain language, the Germanic-Russian term 'intelligentsia' usually refers to the aristocracy of intellectual workers, those who *create* as opposed to those who administer, distribute or organize, those who invent as opposed to those who repeat (secondary teachers are to primary teachers what skilled workers are to the unskilled, who carry out repetitive tasks). How many of these 'direct producers in the sphere of ideology and culture' (Michael Löwy) are there in the population of France today and how are we to identify them? The two statistical questions really come down to the same thing: breaking down and counting up are functions of one another. But throughout modern history, the sequence of figures has depended upon the choice of labels. We must therefore begin with taxonomy.

The History of a Category

What do we find if we go through the various grids that have been applied to the population of France, from that used to assess direct taxation under the Ancien Régime to the present codes used by the Institut National de la Statistique et des Etudes Economiques? A professional group known as the 'intellectuals' appears surreptitiously and is then swallowed up and disappears.[4] In the 1695 Capitation, which divided the population of the kingdom into twenty-two classes, ranging from 'the dauphin and princes of the blood' (1) to 'soldiers, labourers and journeymen' (22), 'professors of law, headmasters and college principals' appeared in class 16, along with 'officers responsible for bailiwicks, elections, the salt tax, waters and forests, constablewicks, admiralties and trade, advocates in council, bailiffs, corn merchants, wine merchants, wood merchants, tradesmen, some farmers and husbandmen'.[5] But there is no numerical data to go with the classification. An outline socio-professional code for the eighteenth

[4] The following information is taken from Alain Desrosières, *Eléments pour l'histoire des nomenclatures socioprofessionnelles* (INSEE, roneotyped, 1976)—essential reading.

[5] Adeline Daumard, *Revue d'histoire moderne et contemporaine*, juillet–septembre 1963.

[6] Marion, *Les Impots indirects sous l'Ancien Regime*, Paris 1910.

century, drawn up after the fact by a historian for heuristic purposes 'and using the same scale as INSEE (from 0, farmers, to 9, miscellaneous) does not isolate a special category for an intellectual stratum—which is quite logical, as it had scarcely begun to exist—but it could well come under class 7: *Professions connected with the liberal arts* (notaries, lawyers, bailiffs), which comes between *King's Service* (6) and *Secular Clergy* (7). Transposed into the nineteenth century, the same classification placed 'private tutors' in the lower category of *liberal professions*, between *public service* (6) and *miscellaneous* (7). The information became more explicit with the first census in 1872, which broke the liberal professions into three categories which correspond with or are tangential to the idea of an intelligentsia: profession 50/51, 'secondary and primary school teachers', 48,362 men and 14,491 women; 52, 'scientists and men of letters', 3,676 men and 150 women; 53, 'artistes', 18,177 men and 4,338 women. Neither the nomenclature nor the proportions changed in 1876 or 1896. In the 1911 census, state and private education appeared as a separate category, distinct from the clergy and the liberal professions. The word '*intellectuals*' appeared for the first time in the 1946 nomenclature, in the 'Administrative work and intellectual professions' (89–96). In 1951, when the first *Code of Socio-Professional Categories* was drawn up, code number 30 isolated a group of 'intellectual professions', as distinct from 'liberal professions and clergy'. There were two categories in this group: *intellectuals in executive positions* (estimate: 100,000) and *subaltern intellectuals* (estimate: 410,000). Immediately after the war, the 'intellectuals with executive responsibilities' were numerically as strong as or stronger than the clergy (80,000) and the engineers (80,000). In 1954, then, the intellectuals lost their statistical identity—perhaps because their numbers had swollen—and were given their definitive code number: 32, *literary and scientific professions*, a category within the broader classification *liberal professions and senior management*, which is now the fourth of the nine categories into which INSEE divides the active population. The artistes returned to their present position along with the clergy, the army and the police in the ninth and last category—a crude amalgam, but one with a certain finesse. Finally, in a last and significant adumbration of sociological taxonomy, the nomenclature used for the Sixth Plan merged 'literary professions and professions dealing with *information*' and put them in the same category as *senior management in the tertiary sector* (1976).

3

Numbers

The Intelligentsia: First Count

We will now look at categories 32 and 80 in the last four censuses.

32 (teachers, literary and scientific professions) includes the typical case of 'teacher in higher or secondary education, astronomer, writer, but also: art critic, geologist, *censeur*** in a *lycée*, hospital doctor (salaried), chemist, veterinary surgeon, art teacher'. It includes, then, civil servants and 'self employed persons'.

80 ('artistes') includes the following professions: 'painter, singer, musician, radio or television announcer, actor, chorus girl, circus performer, fakir, astrologer, professional sportsman, mountain guide, fencing master, cover girl, model'.[7] The number of 'artistes' has remained

	1954	1962	1968	1975
32	80,380	125,126	213,420	377,215
80	45,089	42,184	50,196	59,075

* Senior administrative member of staff in a school, with no teaching responsibilities.

[7] It will be noted that ceramists are classified under the socio-professional category of *artisans* (CSP No. 2) and that music teachers and primary teachers are classified under *middle management* (No. 4). 'Artistes' still come at the bottom of the list, along with cops. Writers (32), liberal professions (31), engineers (33) and senior administrative personnel (34) make up CSP No. 3

stable (since 1872 when France had a population of 36,102,921, of whom 47,995 individuals made a living directly or indirectly from artistic activities). The numbers in the 'literary or scientific professions' have risen by leaps and bounds, thanks to the huge increase of those working in education. As a result, the teachers move into literary activities in force—it should be remembered that the number of teachers in state secondary schools rose from 66,387 in 1958 to 223,792 in 1974.

The Intelligentsia: Second Count.

The table again uses INSEE information and the 1975 census, but this time the numbers have been calculated on the basis of the *Code des métiers* and information from the subjects concerned, who categorized themselves by declaring that the profession in question was their main source of income.

Here we have the self-declared ideological producers, less the 7,080 men and women scientists who cannot be classed as ideologues on the basis of their profession (although they may well also pursue ideological activities in relation to their discipline or any other subject). Teachers, doctors and lawyers have not been included, as their main activity (education, medicine, the bar) is their main source of income—not that that stops a number of them from publishing or writing books, articles, commentaries, petitions, manifestoes, and thus figuring in the forefront of the high intelligentsia.

For reference purposes, here follow the figures for those whose income derives from an artistic profession:

The Intelligentsia: an Estimate.

All the figures supplied by INSEE call for some correction and most should be adjusted downwards. For example, the 1,500 publishers in the census include publishers of brochures and postcards, and a large number of publishers with a low turnover. The number of publishers listed (somewhat arbitrarily) by the Syndicat National des Editeurs in 1976 was 386.

Conversely, our inquiry demands that some figures be adjusted upwards, such as those mentioned in several official documents that put the number of 'professional writers' living by their pen at between four

	Men	Women	Total
Publishers (and booksellers-publishers)	1,100	500	1,600
Men of letters (musical controller, literary, art or music critic, screen-writer, calligrapher, art dealer, littérateur, philosopher, poet, novelist, script-writer)	2,760	800	3,560
Intellectual Professions (archeologist, research assistant or supervisor, economist, ethonographer, market research officer, geographer, historian, linguist, marketing manager, palaeontologist, psychologist)	7,040	4,840	11,880
Scientists	5,320	1,760	7,080
Advertising specialists (media studies officer, advertising sales, station controller, advertising executive, advertising manager)	8,160	4,800	12,960
Journalists, reporters (press attaché, public relations officer, special correspondent, journalist, reader, editor, editor-in-chief, sub editor, reporter, editorial secretary . . .)	15,820	6,600	22,420

and five hundred. In late 1978, the Association pour la Gestion de la Sécurité Sociale des Auteurs (AGESSA) listed almost 4,000 writers living by their pen—the term 'writer' here including *all* who write (thrillers, pornography, technical manuals, or whatever). If other branches of the profession are taken into account, almost 80,000 people are in receipt of royalties of varying amounts, on a regular or an irregular basis. 90% of these people have some other form of social insurance, usually through the state (teachers and academics). AGESSA predicts that within the next few years—once the surveys and affiliations are completed—some 7,000 or 8,000 people will be paying insurance contributions through it; this defines the number of people whose main source of income is their

	Men	Women	Total
Artists, sculptors (+animator, restorer of antiques, picture restorer, artist in glass)	9,020	3,180	12,200
Musicians, composers, lyricists	9,260	2,040	11,300
Entertainment (theatre, dance, cinema, radio, TV) (actor, radio or TV compere, choreographer, comedian, commentator, dancer, extra, conjurer, maître de ballet, quiz master, presenter, announcer)	3,840	4,020	7,860
Circus, music hall and variety artistes	1,400	800	2,200
Directors, producers (cinema, radio and TV)	3,660	1,240	4,900
Stage managers	760	100	860
Editors (film and TV)	940	940	1,880

royalties. The Maison des Artistes (painters, sculptors, engravers) has 4,500 affiliates, out of an approximate 40,000 plastic artists. SACEM has over 15,000 members. There are 15,000 card-carrying journalists (Commission de la carte). The number of actors can be put at between 8,000 and 10,000, of whom about 5% actually make their living from their profession. To sum up: if we agree to include only teachers in higher education (50,000) and to leave out the majority of secondary teachers (those teaching *classes terminales* should be classified under higher education, given the specialist nature of their teaching and the level of qualifications), what we refer to as the *French intelligentsia* includes between 120,000 and 140,000 people (1978). According to the 1975 census, France has an active population of 21,775,000. To judge by the figures, then, the professionals' lack of interest seems perfectly justified: the intellectuals are not worth tuppence.

Alarm Bells.

It really would be disastrous if two alarms, widely separated in time and space, failed to wake the dogmatists. Two comparisons may perhaps set the indifferent on the road to reason. The first is with the socialist countries, the second with the Ancien Régime.

The Socialist Regimes

It is common knowledge that there is no simple correspondence between the place and the function of an element in a social structure. Observation of (dominantly) capitalist systems adds a particular proviso to that general theoretical remark, since one of their peculiar features is that the formal indices of the existence of an element are often in inverse proportion to its true gravitational force. Hence the paradox that it is in (dominantly) socialist systems that the intelligentsia appears under its own name in the nomenclatures and is listed and classified as a specific socio-professional stratum and, accordingly, has its own political representation; but it is also there that its existence as a subject of historical action is most tenuous. In contrast, the intelligentsia does not appear as such on the social scene in capitalist countries, except perhaps as an informal confederation of personal positions; but it is there that it plays a decisive role. Weak characterization, high functionality, and vice versa: the sociology of the socialist regimes integrates the intelligentsia into its official framework in order to neutralize it as a political force; the sociology of real capitalism ignores (or marginalizes) it in order to conceal it as an active political force and to perpetuate the illusion that it does not exist.

Every socialist country has its Writers' Union and its Journalists' Union, complete with statutes, governing body, congress and organs. But the statistical tables and the socio-economic analyses class journalists and writers together along with artists, scientists and, to some extent, students as 'intellectuals', a rubric within the broader sphere of the intelligentsia.[8] The amalgam is functional, for the two criteria for membership of the intelligentsia in a socialist country are a university education and access to the means of mass communication. In Poland, for example, more than half

---

[8] *La Presse, les intellectuels et le pouvoir en URSS*, Documentation française, avril 1970. What the Soviet Union refers to as the *intelligentsia* in the broad sense—as distinct from the *creative intelligentsia*—is what we call the 'intellectual professions'. Hence the definition in the *Dictionary of Philosophy* (Moscow): 'The intellectuals are an intermediary social stratum composed of men devoted to intellectual labour. That stratum includes engineers, technicians, lawyers, artists and scientific workers.' Estimated at 2,725,000 in 1926, the Soviet intelligentsia included 15,460,000 people in 1956 (according to the Central Statistical Office) and more than 30 million in 1970.

the members of the Writers' Union work in the press, radio, television, publishing or the cinema. In the USSR, the 'creative' intelligentsia is an individualized social group which is regularly represented in the Supreme Soviet where, in proportional terms, it is stronger than on the Central Committee of the Party. That, together with its well-known integration into the official mechanisms of the State, is the final index of its subordinate position amongst the various political pressure groups. According to the official figures, in 1970 the Soviet republics had between them 100,000 writers and journalists, all duly classified. Their political representation in the various soviets is probably greater than their numerical strength; but if this includes a certain honorary surplus value, it does not give them the benefit of any added *political* value. The absence of anything officially recognized as public opinion by the authorities in socialist countries (a result of the systematic impossibility of distinguishing between civil society and state) and the reduction of the press to a mere 'conveyor belt' preclude any possibility that the writer or journalist, or a fortiori the artist or scientist, might appear on the social scene as an interlocutor of any importance. There can be no interlocutor if, for want of an autonomous logos, there is no interpellation—except in the canonical and programmed forms of the 'open letter', public interventions in professional meetings or collective petitions, none of which have any effect since they are very rarely reproduced in the central press and (in the case of Soviet society) are deadened by the compactness of the popular consensus. The idea that 'socialism favours intellectuals, just as capitalism favours property owners' (Jacques Julliard, Paris, 1977) is a nineteenth-century ideologism that is refuted by the evidence of 'real socialism' in the twentieth. It might almost be said that in the system of real socialism, the intellectuals are useless, being reduced to their functional logic: they therefore have the consistency of an institution. Conversely, liberal capitalism cannot reproduce itself as a system without the intellectuals: they are therefore invisible, dissolved into society in an almost colloidal solution. Although they crystallize here and there around certain nodal points of communication, their distribution seems random—radio, TV, universities, research centres, publishing houses, theatres, cultural centres, and so on—and therefore insignificant.

The Clergy.

It is not always necessary to establish a *frontier* in order to mark out a *field* (and the field in question would not basically be altered if we decided to include secondary education in it), and it is not always necessary to isolate *organs* in order to identify a *function*. In that sense, sociological information is precious (and expensive), but the investigation of the size and contours of the professions should come after rather than before the identification of their function. Ernest Labrousse has pointed out that, of the three factors brought into play by social hierarchies, the Ancien Régime emphasized birth, the bourgeoisie of the nineteenth century wealth, and the state apparatuses of the twentieth, function. It has been demonstrated more than once that function now cuts across both birth and wealth—especially in the educational and administrative apparatuses. But the monarchic regime did not exclude functional criteria from its institutional divisions, and the solution does not therefore lie in a continuity between the modern bourgeois intelligentsia and the clergy under the Ancien Régime. That they are much the same size is an index, not an argument. In so far as it as a group is collectively responsible for hegemony—leadership, supervision, execution—the intelligentsia fulfils the same social function. In so far as it is an intermediary between rulers and ruled, it occupies an analogous place, at once autonomous and ambivalent. In so far as it is an eminently hierarchical body, horizontally compartmentalized and vertically stratified, it has all the hierarchical complexity of the clergy. The smallest of the orders of the Ancien Régime—130,000 members before the Revolution—was also the most important of the three in terms of prerogatives and pre-eminence. The French intelligentsia obviously does not have the juridical status of the old orders: tolerance, connivance and privilege have replaced prescriptions and rules. But the same division runs through both.[9] What does a parish priest on a low income and sharing the life of his peasant parishioners have in common with a bishop at court who, in terms of income and lineage, is closer to the great nobles? What does a *professeur* in a Collège d'Enseignement Technique have in common with a *professeur* at the Collège de France? Their institutional positions produce solidarity (even if it is hierarchical); their social situations create antagonism (expressed politically). When the States General met at Versailles, the nobility stood aloof and formed a bloc, as did the third estate. The clergy was the *only* order that was divided. The intellectual hierarchy is traversed by multiple

---

[9] There is no longer a state religion, but there is state education. There was a first and a second order within the clergy, just as there is primary and secondary education, junior lecturers and first and second class prefects. Is grading inherent in the organic? Or hierarchy inherent in the state?

hierarchies which both interfere with and reinforce one another. The least visible of the dividing lines now appears to be the most important. The frontier that allows a distinction to be drawn between the high and the lower intelligentsia is *each member's ability or inability to gain access to the means of mass communication.* That ability is not individual: it is socially determined. It is not aleatory: it presupposes the observance of strict rules. It is not a complementary or side issue: it involves the intellectual activity itself, the realization or non-realization of its concept as the action of man on man through symbolic communication, as a project of influence. That is why the question of the media runs right through the intelligentsia, cutting across categories, disciplines, political backgrounds and affiliations like a watershed, a definition that none escapes, whether they know it or not, be they researcher, painter, writer or teacher; Communist, monarchist, anarchist or nothing at all.

That group socially authorized to express individual opinions on public affairs independently of the normal civic procedures to which ordinary citizens are subject will be referred to as the *high intelligentsia,* to distinguish it from the mere *professionals of the intellect.* Those authorized to speak usually belong to the intellectual and liberal professions (which require higher education), but their membership of the high intelligentsia is not a function of their professions: a scientist or teacher may or may not belong to it whilst still remaining within the horizons of his profession, whereas a lawyer, a doctor, an actor or an explorer belongs to it in so far as he has acquired an authoritative public individuality outside his professional activity, but thanks to it. Individual authors of legitimate opinions—whatever the content of those opinions—are obviously recruited from within the ruling classes, but neither their class origins nor their professional activities are decisive criteria. It should be remembered that the high clergy of the Ancien Régime (abbots, bishops, canons in cathedrals) numbered less than 4,000. The lesser clergy numbered 125,000, more or less evenly divided between the regular and the secular. The lower intelligentsia is numerically larger, but the proportions are much the same, and a figure of 4,000 does not seem an unreasonable ceiling for the high intelligentsia.

The historians of the Ancien Régime seem to have paid relatively little attention to the clerical order, if one thinks of the number of studies devoted to the nobility and the third estate. By some curious parallel, the sociologists of modern France seem to take as little interest in the contemporary French intelligentsia. There are monographs on top management and the top civil servants. But what is there on the top intellectuals and the modern high intelligentsia? Perhaps people have been discouraged from studying the senior hegemonic personnel by two impressions, an under-estimation and—who knows?—a difficulty.

(a) The impression of heterogeneity. What do the following have in common: a Nobel prize winner in physics, an actor, an auctioneer, a *professeur* at the Collège de France, a priest, a doctor, a former far-left militant, a free-market ideologue and a theatre director? Obviously not their socio-professional background.

(b) The impression that it is not organic or closed. There is a diplomatic corps and a medical profession. There was once a teaching corps and the great organs of the state are visible to the naked eye: they are made up of the senior personnel of the political apparatus or the central administration. But is there an intellectual corps and if so what is its bond-structure? How are we to identify its limits, and what terms can we use to identify it? The upper spheres of the private and public sectors are practically all listed in the Bottin Mondain; they meet in clubs and well-defined circles (the Jockey Club, the Automobile Club, the Rotary, the Saint Cloud golf club and so on). Where do the upper intellectual and moral circles of the country congregate? There is still no *Who's Who* of the intelligentsia.

(c) The under-estimation. In his remarkable *Essai sur l'élite du pouvoir en France* and *La classe dirigeante en France*, Pierre Birnbaum ignores the top intellectuals on the grounds that they are not part of the French ruling class or the state apparatus, being, so to speak, the former's perks and the latter's incidental expenses. This omission, which is based on a hypothesis, is never made explicit as such; the author simply takes it for granted and begs the question. 'If we accept', he writes, 'that the socio-professional categories that make up the ruling class can be divided into ruling fractions (civil and military state bureaucracy, industry and finance) and non-ruling fractions (intellectuals, the liberal professions), *with the latter wielding a purely symbolic power* that is very important in terms of the socialization of individuals and the formation of a common culture that legitimates the power of the ruling fractions . . .'. The concession does not rectify the omission. In matters of state, serious things are solid and can be measured: senior civil servants, big banks, industry, something the student can get hold of. Symbolic power is unstable and can be left to one side: it only has side-effects. After an excursion through Weber or Parsons, modern sociology seems to be getting back to the principle behind Marxism's disdain for the question of the intellectuals: serious applicants only. 'The bourgeois intelligentsia is the cream on the cake, let's get to the filling'. But cream is no longer a mere ornament in the new cuisine. It is the cream that makes the cake edible. Leaving gastronomy to one side, if the symbolic is not the oil that lubricates the cogs and reduces friction, but the very petrol on which the state runs in an 'advanced' country, should not the diminutive be replaced by a substantive? Can the sociology of power accept the traditional division of the political field at face value: the symbolic on one side and the political and administrative on the other?

We are all agreed.[10] Empirical sociology is obviously less well equipped than historical research (not to mention mediological method) to discover what all these scattered individualities might have in common and what the infrastructure that ensures their organization might be. The individuals have at least one thing in common: they are all personalities, authorities who collectively sign weekly manifestoes, appeals, petitions and hold press conferences that have 'repercussions'. The notion of 'personality' derives from *social history*, that of 'repercussion' from a certain *mediatic technology*. And that of 'authority' from a science of the concrete conditions of hegemony.

(d) There may, finally, be a difficulty: what if those who wielded the conceptual and material instruments for this study were themselves part of the high intelligentsia or had aspirations in that direction? The result would be the traditional lack of self-awareness that typifies social agents in general, together with the denials of being part of it that typify the high intelligentsia in particular. This is no more than a hypothesis, which will be ignored for decency's sake.

To my knowledge the one, remarkable exception to the intellectuals' lack of interest in the intelligentsia, which deserves a study in itself, is the work of the Collège de Sociologie Européenne and particularly the work of its director, Pierre Bourdieu. It is quite true that this kind of reflection is scarcely welcomed by a profession whose attitude seems to be summed up

---

[10] Pierre Birnbaum would be the first to agree; he, of all people, should be spared such unfounded criticisms.

by Cocteau's comment that mirrors should think twice before reflecting. But if researchers in the social sciences, whose job it is to reflect others, do not look at themselves in the mirror, and if writers whose vocation is looking at themselves in mirrors refuse to undergo a collective X-ray, what right have they to criticize those who try to do it for them?

Two

The Three Ages

Two

The Three Ages

On the situation forced upon the
intellectual party by the accidents
of temporal glory.
Charles Péguy

A history, like a society, is a *continuum* that historians and sociologists compulsively violate and tear up into *periods* and *categories*. If it were not broken up, the continuum would in effect be unintelligible. In order to understand the contemporary French intelligentsia, it seems necessary to distinguish three ages or cycles in its recent history. Despite the risk of arbitrariness, the distinction seems all the more necessary in that the cycles overlap and intersect *quite naturally*. We have already said that to opt for nature means ultimately to transform history into nature and practice into mysticism. It is therefore preferable to produce an approximate history of the intellectual corps than the thousandth version of the immobile mythology of the 'clerical' soul.

It is a vocation proper to the 'spirit that denies' to assert itself by denying the events that produce it. The intellectual corps of a nation may be said to be the soul of its civilization, provided we add that the soul grows, ages and dies along with the physical organs of that civilization. In France, as in Italy and England, the university developed before the book, the book before the newspaper and the newspaper before the audio-visual media. Each body has its soul. These avatars are spread across seven centuries and the whole of the Western world. If we put them together in one century and one country, we, statesmen and members of the French 'intellectual party', have our history. Although it is apparently continuous and homogeneous, there is nothing sleek or smooth about it. It is a coherent series of accidents, a sequence of innovations, dismissals and metamorphoses.

'The situation forced upon the intellectual party by the accidents of temporal glory' has, then, varied as much as those who distribute glory and distil power. In 1906, Charles Péguy called the university of his day 'the great apparatus of discernment', an apparatus dreaded and venerated by a Republic that made it redoubtable and venerable: 'It is fortunate for the stability of the Republic that men like Andler and Lanson* are staunch republicans'. The university grading machine has been replaced, but the new mechanisms of selection reproduce its effects. Péguy continued: 'The men in France who accept or reject French-born candidates for the *baccalauréat*, degrees, the *agrégation*, the Ecole Normale, grants and even travel grants, the men licensed to create doctors and normaliens will always have unlimited power in France. And there will always be many who are dependent upon them'.[1] Only one word was out of place: 'always'. For the power of the men who are still licensed to create doctors and *normaliens* is rapidly approaching its lowest ebb. The power of 'the party' has been displaced. For a while, just after Péguy's death, it lay with the men who were licensed to create *authors*. It now lies with those who are licensed to produce *journalists*. And at each stage the 'stability of the regime' has been fortunate in the party leaders hand-picked for it by the most conformist of filters. It is as though the 'apparatus of discernment' were made for the state, or vice versa, or as though they were made for each other. The chronological sequence of filters—the university, publishing, the media—corresponds quite well to the sequence of the last three Republics, each with its chosen bourgeoisie, its industrial revolution, its favourite sciences, its jargon and its means of transport. The way in which 'those who want partisans' and those who want 'the glory of ruling others' (Péguy) recruit their followers has had many avatars, but the 'intellectual party' is still with us, like some eternally recycled phoenix. It alone is our concern, with its glory and its ashes.

---

* Charles Andler (1866–1933): early member of the SFIO, an associate of Lucien Herr and author of a thesis on 'The Philosophical Origins of German Socialism'. Gustave Lanson (1857–1934): philosopher and teacher, sometime head of the Ecole Normale Supérieure.

[1] Péguy, *Oeuvres complètes*, Slatkine Reprints, Geneva, 1974, III–IV.

The University Cycle
(1880–1930)

Anticlerical clergy, lay priesthood, state congregation: for a long time, the intellectual corps attracted these nicknames because of its genealogy in the University. That was, in substance, the history of the French University as it adapted to the gradual secularization of the State during the nineteenth century. Whilst we are not qualified to retrace it in all its details (Antoine Prost's excellent synthesis describes the main stages), let us recall the circumstances of the birth which was to shape the adult body,[2] beginning with its baptism as a corps in the image of the great corps of the State that appeared for the first time in an Imperial law of 1806.[3] When the First Empire replaced the teaching congregations decimated by the Revolution with a teaching corps whose spiritual unity was to rival that of the religious institutions, it demonstrated yet again that one only destroys things that one can replace and that one can only replace what one can reproduce. The University may have been an imitation, but it was no masquerade. 'I am making you the head of an order,' Napoleon told Fontanes when he made him a Grand Master. 'Choose your men; that is your concern.' They may not have appeared in the habits of soldier-monks, but total commitment ('the obligations') was still demanded of the members of the University who were required to be celibate and to lead a communal life, and were subject to the power of the Grand Master in exchange for autonomy in their internal administration (the University Council, the rectorates of the Academies). Although it was again put under ecclesiastical control by the Restoration (the Ministry for Ecclesiastical Affairs and Public Education, set up in 1824), the University Corporation

---

[2] Antoine Prost, *Histoire de l'enseignement en France 1800–1967*.

[3] The law of 10 May 1806 which established 'a corps known as the Imperial University, with sole responsibility for teaching and public education throughout the Empire'.

maintained its monopoly over conferring degrees and reached its first apogee under the July Monarchy (which extended its monopoly to include awards in secondary education). After 1848, the counter-revolutionary backlash brought the Falloux law (1850), which re-established freedom in private education (or, to be more accurate, sanctioned its expansion). Having handed the management of minds back to the Church, the Second Empire logically enough began to weaken the power of the University and to restrict its autonomy. The least equivocal criterion for gauging the degree of virulence of a period of reaction is the attitude of the authorities towards the University and the teaching profession as a whole. For over a century, the criterion of criteria has been the position of philosophy teaching in the schools and that of the *concours* in philosophy. After the Second Empire, only Vichy, and then the current regime, have evinced the same degree of hostility towards the *agrégation* in philosophy (for although market philosophers are being cultivated in high places, the teachers of non-market philosophies are again being decimated; the two things go together). Introduced in 1828, when it was separated from the *agrégation* in French, the *agrégation* in philosophy was abolished in 1853, along with that in history—a somewhat less subtle process than the Haby reform.* Ten years later, it was reintroduced: the cure had proved worse than the disease, being said to have exposed a disoriented younger generation to the dangers of materialism.[4] It is to be hoped that our present ministers will learn from that mistake.

The real birth of the French University presupposed the defeat of Bonapartism and the Church. It was between 1871 and 1885 that the Third Republic (returning, paradoxically enough, to the traditions of the Jacobin First Empire) laid the institutional foundations and outlined the contours of a *university milieu*.

The Liberal Empire did of course found the Ecole Pratique des Hautes Etudes in 1868. And the Ecole Normale (like the Ecole Polytechnique and the Conservatoire des Arts et des Métiers, a creation of the Thermidorean Convention) did survive the Second Empire, taking one year with the next, because it was independent of the University (and remained so until 1903) and was under the strict control of the Ministry for Public

---

* A major reform of secondary education introduced in 1975.

[4] Victor Duroy: 'The true cause of the spread of negative doctrines amongst certain young people is the decline in philosophy teaching in our *Lycées*. The study of philosophy is the only cure for materialism.' (Cited by Jacques Derrida in 'La philosophie et ses classes', *Qui a peur de la philosophie*, Paris p. 447.)

Education. But it was in the 1880s that higher education took on its present features—now becoming blurred before our very eyes. Here are a few dates in the struggle to 'tear the soul of French youth away from the Jesuits'. 1887: grants to study for degrees; the birth of the 'lecturer'. 1880: dissolution of the Society of Jesus and establishment of a state monopoly over conferring degrees (enjoyed until then by the Free Universities); introduction of grants to study for the *agrégation*. 1882: introduction of 'closed' lectures at the Sorbonne (until then open lectures had been the rule); the 'arts *student*' appeared (the term had previously applied only in medicine and law).[5] 1885: *agrégations* in literary subjects were granted definitive status; the diploma in higher education was introduced. 1889: the Sorbonne building in Paris was completed. In a word, the institutional organization of the corporation (the introduction of degrees, diplomas and rituals, and so on) was not ideologically neutral. The state makes its civil servants in its own image. Yet this scarcely represented state annexation of the intellectual. The alternatives facing the intellectual then were not freedom or constraint, but Church or State, state service or the Congregations—or, more succinctly, bourgeoisie or aristocracy, republic or monarchy, positivism or spiritualism, Littré or Ollé-Laprune. In the long run, the university milieu made its choice, perhaps because its very existence depended upon it.

It was a restricted, withdrawn milieu, somewhat turned in on itself. What weight did the 650 teachers in the French universities in 1890 carry, compared with 6,500 magistrates; or the 9,751 civil servants in state secondary education in 1887, compared with 31,000 officers and 80,000 inspectors in the Ministry of Finance? More than their numbers might suggest: for, like the clergy, the vast majority of officers and magistrates refused to have anything to do with the Republic—when, that is, they were not plotting against it. The *professeurs* were its generals and its bishops; the *instituteurs* its hussars and its country priests. The diffusion of knowledge and the political crusade were one and the same thing. The savant was also a militant *because* he was a savant. In France, the intellectuals were born 'progressive' because they were the offspring of a regular union between state and Enlightenment—or, to be more accurate, between the bourgeois Republic and liberal rationalism. A middle-class marriage, certainly, but it caused a scandal at the time. For a state

[5] It will be recalled that the word 'University' originally referred to the union or corporation of three faculties: law, medicine and theology.

surrounded by a Catholic population, it meant nothing less than filing a divorce suit against the Church of France, Rome and official obscurantism. The couple may have aged, but those who refused to recognize the marriage in the first place have lost none of their energy.

One hundred years later, has the Republic won? Scarcely, for in the meantime a second dilemma has appeared: state or market? State service or a private foundation? Competence or popularity? The third term, which no one could foresee, has caught the actors unawares. In history, it is always the unexpected person who clears the board. The state has not won the game; capitalism has beaten the state by subordinating it to its economic logic. Higher education has been industrialized and made to submit to the inexorable laws of productivity and profitability, just as a state-owned firm submits to the norms and procedures of private capital before coming directly under its control. The diploma market has fallen in line with the labour market. We will not describe the death throes of the French university here—modesty forbids, not to mention competence—even though the end of a historical cycle is conducive to overviews. What concerns us here is less the decline itself than the redistribution of forces it produced within the intellectual order and, more generally, the modification of the basis of hegemony in France.

The decline obviously did not start in 1930. 1930 was only a pause, not the end—at most, the first break in a long period of almost regal power and calm happiness. From the 1880s to the 1930s, staff-student ratios remained stable in both the universities and the secondary schools. It would take fifty years for university lecturers to double in number: 503 in 1880, 650 in 1890, 1,048 in 1909 and 1,145 in 1930 (a further fifty years, and there would be 43,000 of them, including assistant lecturers). Nor was there any great rise in student numbers before 1930, for in fifty years the number of teachers in higher education and the number of pupils in state secondary schools (73,000 in 1881 and 110,000 in 1930) merely doubled. Demographic stagnation, class segregation, the selection of 'scholarship students', the Malthusianism of the 'inheritors': it was the narrow basis of recruitment into the university that made it the main sorting office within the intelligentsia and ensured the club its hegemony over public life and over the intellectual corps itself. When it suddenly expanded, the University lost its hegemonic strength. The power of an élite is in inverse proportion to its numerical strength. No longer the privileged site of selection, either from above (increased numbers of teaching posts) or from below (soaring student numbers), the University can no longer ensure its own renewal within the ruling class—although it may still be able to reproduce class inequality in society as a whole—nor, a fortiori, within the intellectual aristocracy of that class. Since 1880, the population of France has risen by only a quarter, but the number of arts students has risen from 1,000 in 1882, 7,000 in 1914, to 191,600 in 1976! Such numbers lead to devaluation. There has been a similar population explosion in the teaching profession which, ipso facto, has been proletarianized.[6] Assistant lecturers, the skilled workers of higher education, are already working on an assembly line; they will soon be on piece-rate and working in shifts. No more research. And so the teaching élite merges with the white collar workers, deafened by the background noise of repetitive work (practicals) and plunged into the anonymity of a service industry. With the prospect of unemployment pure and simple for graduates in Arts subjects, Law and the Human Sciences; that sector of the market has been flooded too. The one attribute which has not been taken away from the university—its corporate monopoly over its own reproduction—thus becomes the very thing that is hastening its destruction.

Like any social class threatened with expropriation, the scientific and literary intelligentsia has, of course, found ways to parry its industrialization. The more access the lower strata are given to higher education, the more the elite looks for emergency exits. It flees to the Centre National de la Recherche Scientifique, to the Collège de France, the Ecole Pratique or to private foundations (which ultimately means the USA). Malthus lives: he may be condemned in theory, but in practice he is still very useful. The way university staff are creamed off compensates for the institutional spread of the universities, which downgrades the symbolic weight of names (Sorbonne) until they are mere numbers (Paris I) and diminishes the weight of positions and titles by multiplying them. It is in these rarefied places that the elite of the elite reproduces itself by cooption and after long probationary periods. The selection of the many by the few on the floor above recreates the asymmetry and denotes the gap inherent in any relation of domination. It is a general law, basic to the economy of institutions (national or international), that as those from below reach a certain level of equality, the old inequality is displaced on to a higher level, which thereby becomes the new decision-making centre. The imbalance restores the initial balance, namely the old imbalance. There is a law of

[6] See the table on p. 103.

hydrostatics in human inequality: a century ago it applied to the granting of universal suffrage in the politics of the West; we can now see it at work in the international arena—in the UN for example.[7] It is, of course, because the next floor has already (but discreetly) been furnished that the door downstairs can be opened to the vulgus. Being hierarchically structured, the French intelligentsia does not escape this law.

The break-up of the university corps obviously relates to the organic decadence of French society: it is both symptom and factor, cause and effect. In immediate terms, it is equivalent to a transfer of power. The ideological field is magnetic: as one force of attraction weakens, the other grows stronger. But the iron filings still form a pattern; and as the intellectuals must cluster around something, they will go wherever the organicity, and therefore the potential for organization and promotion, is greatest: the more ambitious into the media and private capital, the more scrupulous into the state administration. The disorganization of the university means the historical disorganization of the intelligentsia, or in other words its reorganization under the aegis of rival hegemonic interests. Public rumour and private gossip all point to the appearance, within the university field itself, of 'unusual' criteria for allocating credits to one or another laboratory or institute and for making teaching appointments in centres of higher education: the greater or lesser social visibility—or mediatic surface—of a researcher; the effect of a particular line of research on public opinion; a candidate's personal position in the apparatus of mass diffusion. We are seeing something more serious that the mere displacement of one institutional hierarchy (in the university: assistant lecturer, lecturer, senior lecturer, full professor) by another external to it (in the media: freelancer, columnist, sub-editor, leader writer, editor-in-chief). We are seeing the university corps and, at a more general level the intellectual corps, voluntarily relinquish *its own logic of organization, selection and reproduction* and adopt the market logic inherent in the workings of the media (already present in the old publishing market,

[7] Important (practicable) decisions stopped being taken in the General Assembly when— all sovereign states being equal—decolonization put the West in a minority; these are now taken in specialist organizations where the voting is weighted, where, that is, a property qualification is involved (IMF, FAO, the World Bank). The rich countries and their information agencies therefore speak scornfully of 'automatic majorities' in the UN (where the Third World and socialist countries have a de facto majority). In 1950, the majority was equally automatic, but it was in favour of the West. It was then known as 'a consensus of the community of free nations'. Automatism is for the poor—having no soul, 'barbarians' are machines.

though not to any critical degree). It is a logic whose strict incompatibility or, to be more accurate, contradiction can be demonstrated. Its reconciliation—such modesty—with 'civil society', in other words with the laws of the market (supply and demand), will probably take the form of normalization through advertising, which already applies to the supports and content of mass information (press, radio, TV) and which could equally well apply to the institutional supports of the intelligentsia (in so far as there is still a difference between the two). Dependence on the state was never the ideal of the clerisy; dependence on the opinion market and therefore on a commercial plebiscite for moral and intellectual validation may well become a nightmare for it. In terms of the cost-benefit ratio, domestication by capital may be more restrictive and humiliating than domestication by a generic and ultimately not very fussy power, given the historical origins of the state and the effect on it of a hundred years of working-class and petty-bourgeois struggles. The status of civil servant does not seem to have prevented Althusser from teaching Spinoza, Machiavelli and Marx to his apprentice civil servants at the Ecole Normale Supérieure, or Derrida from teaching Malebranche or Nietzsche, but French civil society being what it is (one of the least democratic in the world) who can be certain that they might not be well advised to change their subject, or even their profession, if one day they somehow came to be dependent on Bleustein-Blanchet,* Jacqueline Baudrier or the Peugeot Foundation? Philosophy (particularly materialist philosophy) not only lowers the announcer's audience-ratings, print runs and budgets because it is intrinsically unattractive; it also provokes spontaneous protests from the vast *majority* of listeners/readers/clients, because everyone knows that philosophy turns little despots into big ones. (It's *true* because *everyone* says so on the radio, on TV and at dinner parties). 'Surely you don't want our readers to cancel their subscriptions, our listeners to switch off and our announcers to break their contracts, do you?' What would become of our 'Foundation for the Freedom of Thought' if it had no money in the bank?

New ideological productive forces have come into being below the old, but also, paradoxically enough, above them. The big bourgeoisie of France will at last be able to rid itself of the hard core of the classic intelligentsia, that irritating stone that formed in the arts subjects (including philosophy, sociology and history) over the years. The Second Empire opted to expel it brutally, through a direct surgical intervention.

* Bleustein-Blanchet, advertising specialist and chairman of the Compagnie d'Agences de Publicité. Jacqueline Baudrier: President of Radio-France, former news producer.

48

Since '68, the Fifth Republic has preferred to see the foreign body passed
as sand in urine, with the help of the reorganization of knowledge and the
necessary decline of the humanities. It will move towards other,
predictable and safer fields of gravitation. And so, through a process of
homogenization and dissolution, the last pocket of independence in the
heart of the superstructures, which owed much of its undeniable capacity
for moral and intellectual resistance (or counter-offensives) to its organic
and administrative cohesion, will disappear. In comparison, and despite
adaptations and *aggiornamenti*, the army, the clergy and the top state
bureaucracy are showing an unexpected capacity for resistance and
personal survival because they have preserved their institutional exclusivity and autonomy. Here, then, is a useful counterweight for the ruling
class, which is only too happy to see these unhoped for, if somewhat dated,
reinforcements looming up in the distance. If and in so far as the death of
the university is indeed a murder, there can rarely have been such a
willing, almost ecstatic, victim. The tragedy of periods of decadence is that
the social actors collaborate with the very thing that will destroy them, like
the heroes in Greek tragedy. But in the case of France, it is to be feared that
a note of spinelessness is being added to the traditional motif—for
originality's sake.

As the core of the university crumbles, it may take with it a particular
moral philosophy; deontology, which is the gateway to all possible moral
philosophies. In so far as it subjects its users to the universality of
discourse and is no respecter of persons, the pedagogical canon postulates
a formal equality between master and pupil. It is one thing to criticize the
element of mystification in that equality, but it is quite another to criticize
the equality itself by mocking the rationalism of teachers who know
nothing of genetics. Those who jeer at schoolmasters and at studies
prefects—a common pastime of men of letters—knowingly confuse the
rules of critical discourse with a *dogma* of reason so as to avoid the
elementary obligations of truth under the pretext of escaping the mediocre
prejudices of schoolboys. 'All praise to the old Masters of the University;
they were honourable and upright; they were men of heart and men of
integrity.' The young Péguy's refrain still rings in our ears—he at least
paid tribute to his youth before rallying to Joan of Arc, the glebe and the
soul. 'With their every example, with all their heart and all their soul they
perpetually produced the virtue of *credo colendam esse virtutem*, which is
the sole strength of republics.' The same 'nonsense' is also, and for the
same reasons, the sole strength of socialism, and although the old Masters

have changed their names since 1914, until very recently education and abnegation were still synonymous. Integrity, obscurity, selflessness; the words raise a smile, but the archaism of the vocabulary derives from the downgrading of the practices of the schools, not vice versa.

Those who had the good fortune to learn to think on the benches of the Sorbonne in the 1950s may well have known the last Socrates. At least they will be able to play the Ghost Sonata for their grandchildren and tell them what was meant by the morality of intelligence in an age when philosophers still knew some philosophy and did not pose for *Paris-Match*. In their turn, they will murmur, 'All praise to Bachelard, Canguilhem or Hyppolyte! All praise to Jean Wahl, Merleau-Ponty and Althusser!', and inwardly marvel at the unconscious chain of generations that reduced the entropy of time and fought against it. Nothing is more easily forgotten than the unforgettable and 'immortal principles' are always the first to die. Because of the stability of its institutions, education was able to be an exception to the rule and to preserve at least a pocket of memory, a tribal reservation for the ethics of truth. The natives reproduced well and aged less rapidly than the colonists. The master was rejuvenated by the disciple and the disciple by the master. The line of descent through the philosophy classes, the *khâgnes* and the *thurnes** meant that thanks to a teacher at Louis-le-Grand (Maurice Savin), who had been a pupil of a teacher at Henri IV (Emile Chartier, better known as Alain),* who was himself the old pupil of a teacher at Michelet (Jules Lagneau), a schoolboy in the 60s could still see before him the shade of a lay saint who was born just after 1848 and was 'capable of living what he taught until it killed him'. The odds are that the laureates of the *concours général* (competitive examinations) are no longer presented with copies of the 'Célèbres Leçons et Fragments' of the founder of the Union pour l'Action Morale, whose charter (*Revue Bleue*, 1892) stipulated: 'We will refuse *to seek popularity* and we will reject all ambitions *to be someone.*' Or again: 'The new society will stand by its principle alone: we are trying to create unanimity; we do not claim to be starting out from it. That will not prevent us from actively sympathizing with anything done in any church or party which is in accordance with that spirit, without any *concern for competition*. Whether the best works through us or through others is unimportant: that which *deserves* to exist will exist.' *Action Morale* saw

---

* *Khâgne* is one of the preparatory classes for entry to the *grandes écoles*; in student slang, a *Thurne* is a room at Ecole Normale Supérieure.

* Alain (1868–1951): the principal philosophical spokesman for Radicalism.

itself as 'a militant lay order based upon private and public duty'. Let us not be too quick to smile at the teachers' appeal to 'all men to subordinate their immediate interests to the accomplishment of what they believe to be just, right and true'. For, five years later, this became the charter of the Dreyfusards. Such idealism is religious. It therefore produced fighters. This tiny but tenacious minority was the first to rise up against the eternal trilogy that Thibaudet identified in 1927 in his *République des professeurs*: 'vested interest, the press, Paris'. For years they were the only ones to do so. One has to be something of a priest, a little soldier, to refuse to obey those powers, which have been in league since the Dreyfus Affair and which are now more powerful than ever before. A priest or, to be more accurate, a pastor: for the university clergy, of which, according to Thibaudet again, the philosophy teachers were the elite, resembled the Reformed Church rather than the Roman.[8] Protestants presided over the founding of the teaching orders under the Third Republic (Buisson, Rabier, Steeg, Pécaut); and were the first to launch the campaign for a revision of the verdict in the Dreyfus case (Scheurer-Kestner, Pressensé, Gabriel Monod).

The decline of the *teacher* is the rise of the *author*, both in education and in the city. Inner values are weighed in the old scales: as the pan of lectures goes down, the pan of publications rises. The public counterpoint to the twilight of the University is the return of the Academy: the Dreyfus Affair in reverse. Today's Dreyfuses—who are collective rather than individual—will stay on Devil's Island. That is a statement of fact, not a prognosis. Let me explain . . .

The rivalry between the Sorbonne and the Quai Conti follows the line of a secular fault. It will be recalled that the French intellectuals climbed on to the plinth of the university despite and in the face of the Academicians, So there are two material bases, two spiritual families and two political camps. Many people still say that the Dreyfus Affair marked the triumph of the 'intellectuals' without realizing that the condition of their triumph was the defeat of the 'writers'. The Ligue des Droits de l'Homme versus the Ligue de la Patrie Française meant the provinces versus Paris, the schools versus the salons, the scholarship men against the

---

[8] 'There is, in the vocation of the philosopher, something analagous to the vocation of the priest. Even if he becomes a corrupt politician or a dishonest banker, anyone who has prepared for the *agrégation* in philosophy has, at some point, been touched by the idea that the greatest of all human achievements is a life devoted to the service of the spirit, and that the University *concours* provide places which make it possible to take up that service' (Albert Thibaudet).

inheritors (to use Thibaudet's terminology). It meant the 'German' university against 'French literature'; 'the rue d'Ulm versus the rue Saint-Guillaume, the *Revue historique* versus the *Revue des deux mondes*' (René Rémond); the left bank versus the right bank (of the salons); the university corporation with its learned journals, its seminars and *L'Aurore*, the black sheep of the popular press (which was won over, logically enough, by 'opinion' and therefore anti-Dreyfusard), versus the entire Academy, practically all the Parisian newspapers, and all the literary salons (factories for turning out Academicians, to use Daudet's phrase). Such was the underlying drama acted out by actors called Barrès, Bourget, Lemaître and Coppée on one side and Monod, Herr, Andler and Péguy on the other. It is the posthumous legend of Zola, rather than his spectacular rallying to the cause, that blurs the boundary line in the eyes of posterity (and it still runs through our midst, like a dotted line that every national crisis carefully inks in). By 1898, Zola had already been refused entry to the Académie Française ten times, always in the most humiliating fashion. According to the 'Prince of Youth', this popular novelist 'whose great output tires the attention and whose superficial thought never becomes interesting' (Barrès) was simply 'one of the commercial strengths of French publishing'. All that Zola had going for him (or against him, on the floor above) were his print runs and his reputation abroad. But in France and in the eyes of everyone 'who counted' in the French literary world, 'Homais on Sinai'* was out of date and vulgar. As the leader of a dated naturalist school that was being overtaken by the rise of the psychological novel (Loti, Brunetière, Bourget), Zola was not welcome in any salon worthy of the name. 'The great pig' was not socially acceptable.[9]

* Homais is the apothecary in Flaubert's *Madame Bovary*—a symbol of mediocrity.

[9] C. Charle's fascinating research on 'Les Ecrivains et l'Affaire Dreyfus' (*Annales*, March–April 1977) leads me to extend these comments, without, however, altering the basic content. Charle shows that the division between Dreyfusards and anti-Dreyfusards in the literary field distinguished a dominated pole (symbolists and naturalists) and a dominant pole (the Académie Française, the Parnassians, the psychological novelists). The ambiguity comes from the split in the intermediate sector (Anatole France, Hervieu, Sardou). The ruling pole sided with the ruling class and the aesthetically subordinate avant-gardes with politically subordinate positions. Zola, an author with a mass audience, but ideologically a non-conformist, initially straddled both camps. But the real surprise was Anatole France, a member of the Académie Française (elected in 1896), a psychological novelist and a literary critic on *Le Temps*. This fashionable figure of authority chose the losing side in the wake of Zola, returning his Légion d'Honneur when Zola was stripped of that decoration. After Zola's *J'Accuse*, it was the young writers of the *Revue Blanche* (Marcel Proust, Halévy, Gregh) who had been won over to the avant-garde who took the initiative by petitioning the recognized masters.

In so far as it was an intellectual battle, the Dreyfus Affair marked the victory of the lower intelligentsia over the high intelligentsia. A Saint-Simonian would say it was a victory of the meritocracy over the aristocracy of the mind. A Proustian would make it quite clear that it was the victory of the Verdurin over the Guermantes clan, even though the *patronne* took a long time to make her mind up. As a sociologist, Marcel Proust could easily find excuses for her prevarication: 'The majority of fashionable people were so anti-revisionist that a Dreyfusard salon seemed as impossible as a Communard salon did in the past.'[10] Apart from Vallès and Rochefort, the writers were all against the Commune. If they had the last word—and what language!—on that occasion, it was largely because the university clergy no longer really existed (or did not yet exist) in 1871, having been treated very badly by the Second Empire.[11] The writers were against Dreyfus too and, had it not been for the university, they would again have had the last word. But the authors and the inheritors found themselves up against the teachers and scholarship men, those despicable but conscientious parvenus. The inheritors were born with good taste, but the scholarship men had to win their grants in competitive examinations: and grants, *concours* and examinations all came into being between 1871 and 1898. Barrès had already scented the danger in *Les Déracinés*, where he caricatured his old philosophy teacher, Jules Lagneau, a modest scholarship man of peasant origins from Metz, in the ignoble features of Boutellier. And it was indeed the Boutelliers of the lycées and the provincial universities who defeated the big Parisian names by succeeding in having the case revised. 'In Paris,' noted the author of *La République des professeurs*, 'the great corporations are the Académie, the Institute, literature, journalism and the Bar. The University comes a long way

[10] *Sodome et Gomorrhe, Oeuvres complètes*, tome II, p. 744. The subordinate position of the university academics compared with the great writers is illustrated by Brichot, or Chochotte as he is known, a *professeur* at the Sorbonne and a pillar of the Verdurin salon. Like the second-rate writers brought in by the *patronne*, who were 'of no social use to her because they were Dreyfusards', he contributed to the 'great set-back inflicted on the salon by the social mistake of the Dreyfus affair' (*Le Prisonnière*, Pléiade III, p. 236). In contrast, the writer Bergotte frequents the salon of Mme Swann, the future Mme. de Torchville, who has nationalist and anti-semitic leanings, and who has difficulty in tolerating her husband's unexpected Dreyfusism.

[11] Flaubert to George Sand: 'I am in favour of sending the whole Commune to the galleys and of forcing these bloody imbeciles to clear the ruins of Paris with chains around their necks, like convicts' (November 1871). Théophile Gautier: 'The Commune makes me sick'. Nohant's good lady; 'A crisis of vomit'. See Paul Lidsky's *Les écrivains et la Commune*, and for the finer points, Francine Mallet's *George Sand*.

behind and is of secondary importance; the *instituteur*, of course, does not count. In the provinces, the *professeur* comes first, and once the *curé* has gone from the village, there is only the *instituteur* left.' The side of the people is rarely popular—at first. Fortunately the democratic messianism of the scholars was not electioneering, as otherwise the *professeurs* would never have become Dreyfusards. As one socialist put it, 'Dreyfus was never a popular cause in France'. The street was the realm of the nationalists—until after the trial at Rennes. The university mystique enshrined by Lagneau introduced a certain mystique of unpopularity, just as the death of Socrates was the outcome of a democratic vote: truth and justice are not majority values. The ideology of French common sense orchestrated by Jules Lemaître and Barrès was openly plebiscitary, resting upon a consensus of the little men of France. Intellectuals who support elections always belong to the High Intelligentsia. In that sense, the premonitory modernity of the Dreyfus Affair—that bloodless civil war— is not to be sought in the ancestral alliance of pen, sabre and holy water. The July Monarchy, the first *monarchie des professeurs* (with Guizot, Villemain and Cousin), had already clashed with that Holy Alliance: Orleanists versus Legitimists. The men of the pen are by their very nature creatures of the salon and, then as now, 'society' brings together fashionable ladies, the Quai d'Orsay and the Quai Conti. The modernity of the Dreyfus Affair lies rather in the alliance between society propaganda and mass propaganda, between the salon, the elite and the popular press, an alliance which was signed on a local basis and very late in the day. In modern terms: between the high intelligentsia and the mass media.

It can never be said too often that, if the Affair was a battle between newspapers, then the Dreyfusards faced odds of a hundred to one, because truth was fighting opinion. There were no opinion polls at the time, fortunately, but the circulation figures of the dailies served the same purpose. On one side, *Le Petit Journal* (circulation 1,500,000), *La Libre Parole* (500,000 readers), *L'Intransigeant*, *Le Gaulois*, *Le Petit Parisien*, *L'Echo de Paris*, plus, from start to finish, the Assumptionist and Catholic press (130 million copies per year); on the other side; *L'Aurore* (circulation 100,000—200,000 when *J'Accuse* was published), later joined by some second- and third-rank papers (*Le Siècle*, *Le Radical*, Jaurès *La Petite République*). The high intelligentsia ('Paris') rallied the press and therefore 'the interests' for, in the opinion market, it is the *market* that rules and those who control opinion are governed by its laws. The top intellectuals and the popular press thus acted in concert. In 1897, *Le Figaro*, which had published Esterhazy's letters, found itself unable to stand up to a campaign of subscription cancellations and chose to bow before reason of State because 'public opinion was against it' (hence Zola's departure for *L'Aurore*, owned by the radical politician Clemenceau). A university lecturer has no customers to please: he can therefore allow himself the luxury of a conscience. That is why most of the *professeurs* stood firm during the storm, whilst most writers bent before the wind. The former moved towards unanimity, the latter—with a few exceptions—moved in the opposite direction. It was as though the High Intelligentsia had already found its modern place and function: taking the part of the newspapers against the party press. The lower intelligentsia had yet to find collective institutions to lean on in the face of opinion; the faculties and lycées served as its parties and trades unions.[12]

When, three years after the Cartel des Gauches,* Thibaudet noted that *L'Action Française* was still 'the headquarters of the literateurs' of his day, he suggested that 'the writer's trade inevitably leads those who practice it to the right'—just like that of the economist or the financier. The wall of money is still standing; so is that of 'letters'. And the left regularly breaks against both. In France, the stock exchange index has its counterpart in the world of letters, but this is really a political barometer and provides more information than the former. The parties of the left lost the battle in 1978 because they lost the intellectual battle as early as 1976 (without even having fought, but that, historically, is a banal paradox). The unspeakable inadequacy of the parties on this ground does not mean they have no solid excuses. The underhand dismissal of the *professeur* seems to be one of them. Ten years after '68, the political left once again found itself caught between the pincers of the Academicians and the media, but this time without any fortifications to shelter behind in the University, as the old citadel was by then on the plain and was being pounded from above by the heavy artillery. No last minute paratrooper could prevent this mediological Dien Bien Phu.

Our purpose here is not to sketch a political history of the intelligentsia;

---

[12] A further indication of their relative strength: whereas the Ligue des Droits de l'Homme (founded in February 1898) had 8,000 members at its height, the Ligue de la Patrie Française (founded in December of the same year) immediately gathered 100,000 signatures.

* The electoral alliance of left-wing parties that came to power under Edouard Herriot in 1924.

we are only interested in the mediological premisses. Since the Affair, it has been customary to situate the Académie 'mainly on the right' and the University 'mainly on the left'.[13] Despite appearances, the prelude to the Popular Front confirmed the rule. In 1934, it fell to three important academics to launch and chair the 'Comité de vigilance des intellectuels antifascistes': Alain, Langevin and Rivet. The 'authors' followed: Barbusse, Gide, Romain Rolland, and hundreds of other authors of stature. But during the intellectual battle for and against Ethiopia in 1935, the lists were again opened by the flower of the Académie and the cream of the University. When the history of the manifestoes of the post-Dreyfus intelligentsia in France is written, along with that of the three watershed appeals which unconsciously (and sometimes literally) echo one another— *Le Manifeste de Parti Intellectuel (le Figaro*, January 1919), *Le Manifeste pour la Défense de l'Occident et la Paix en Europe (Le Temps*, October 1935) and *Le Manifeste de Comite des intellectuels pour l'Europe des libertés* (CIEL, *Le Monde* January 1978)—it will be seen that in this wordy and stubborn battle between Mind and Matter, the West and Barbarism, Europe and the Third World, the names, style and terminology of the 'authors' displace and relegate those of the *professeurs*. The same demarcation appeared—in an even more acute form—under the German occupation and in the face of collaboration. Compared with the 'dear Masters' who bent without breaking, the Mandarins on the whole stood firm, and often more than firm. It was no coincidence that the intellectual martyrs should come from the corporation (Halbwachs, Cavaillès, Politzer). Indochina, Algeria: the bastion of anti-colonialism is still the home of the 'dear *professeurs*', whereas the Académie is wrapped up in its dictionary.

To schematize the distinction (and annoy right-minded people by forcing it somewhat): until well after the war, a left-wing intellectual was a *professeur* who wrote books, and a right-wing intellectual a writer who played the *professeur*. Individualization of a generality may produce a stereotype . . . and it might be added that the late sixties somewhat confused the issue of left and right, mandarins and writers. On the one hand, the tenured professors' reaction to the corporation's loss of status

[13] René Rémond, 'Les intellectuels et la politique', *Revue française de science politique*, December 1959. Paul Valéry, a confused anti-Dreyfusard who paid his mite to the Henry fund ('Three francs, and not without reflection') was to become a member of the Académie. Gide and Proust, both somewhat retiring Dreyfusards, were very careful not to end up in the Académie Française when they became famous twenty years later.

was a spontaneously oligarchic and reactionary reflex, at a moment when many writers were taking to the streets and forming a union. The Hôtel de Massa is certainly not the Palais d'Hiver, whereas the Nanterre-la-Folie of '68 may well be the Sorbonne of '98. The Académie went back to the Champs-Elysée. In a word, the game goes on. The antithesis lies deep in the historical unconscious of the intellectual corps—a rhetorical device for inferiorization and a signal to other writers to keep their distance. Nowadays, when Jean Dutourd, a journalist on *France-Soir* who recently became a member of the Académie, wants to hammer Robbe-Grillet on *Apostrophes* (December 1978), the last literary salon of our time (and the biggest of all time), the snub is based on three hundred years of scorn— 'the *professeurs* are on your side; you've got the Sorbonne on your side'. Reflexes have long memories. In 1658, Princess Rhetoric was fighting the good fight in Furetière's 'Kingdom of Eloquence' against Captain Twaddle, 'an obscure man from the dregs of society'. The two armies met on the Plateau of Letters. Twaddle commanded a Babel-like and seditious Sorbonne where Renaissance humanism mingled with Aristotelian pedagogy. Fortunately, however, Princess Rhetoric called her forty barons to her capital, Academy, and routed him.[14] A hundred years earlier, Rabelais was fulminating against the Sorbonagres and Sorbonicoles, who were then the incarnation of power. Absolutism and Richelieu reversed the fronts. According to the latest bulletins, the Princess is doing well.

The right, as usual, is not involved in politics—nor is the Académie Française. The left has not always been content with being *involved*; the Sorbonne has on occasion *gone into* politics by fully identifying itself with the state. The *République des professeurs* is more than fifty years old: the book appeared in 1927, the phenomenon in 1924. Just as Gambetta, Waldeck-Rousseau and Poincaré gave the Republic of the lawyers its complexion, the triumvirate of Herriot, Painlevé and Blum symbolized the apogee of the power of the University. Mid-way between the Affair and the Disaster, the aristocracy of the teaching staff coincided with that of the political staff. The Ecole Normale d'Administration was part of the Ecole Normale Supérieure, which served the function of combining intellectual magistrature and state power. 'At that time, it was as though, in addition to its obvious function (training the *agrégés* who would form the elite of

[14] 'La Nouvelle Allégorique ou Histoire des derniers troubles arrivés au Royaume d'Eloquence' (Furetière, 1658). See Alain Rey's *Antoine Furetière, imagier de la culture classique*.

education and research), the institution had a latent function (training cadres for the political scene)' writes Daniel Lindenberg.[15] It was impossible to attack the Radical government without also attacking the ENS. The bourgeois Republic had two faces, so that it could be slapped on both cheeks. The Maurrasian Bourgin slated it for being a Republic; in his *L'Ecole Normale et la politique*, he denounced the professors of revolution, the rectors of decadence, the philosophers of anarchy and the sociologists of constraint. In *Aden-Arabie* and especially in *Les Chiens de garde*, the Communist Nizan slated it for being bourgeois and attacked the 'failed priests' who were betraying the proletariat and resigning in the face of human suffering. An eternal centrist, the schoolmaster is used to all this. He has been turning the left cheek to Vallès and the right to Barrès for a long time now.

Les Chiens de garde, a great-minded harangue in which everything rings true, is one of the big mediological gaffs of our day. It is a complete historical nonsense. This was not Nizan's fault, but that of the intellectual period following the one in which he wrote and which, fortunately for him, he could not foresee. The nonsense was history itself. Nizan was a revolutionary who expected a revolution and worked for its coming until it was the death of him. But television came instead, suddenly shifted all the correlations to the right, and turned his left into our right. If Nizan were alive today, the odds are that he would be defending the watchdogs. Nizan used Brunschvicg, Boutroux and Xavier Léon as means to attack Kant in the name of Lenin, and deliberately took up *L'Humanité*'s position on *La Revue de la métaphysique et de la morale*. But from the point of view of *Playboy* and the ads, Kant and Lenin are all one. Xavier Léon and Paul Nizan are saying the same thing. They watch the public quarrels between the supporters of the Académie and the sons of the lycée as might the Visigoths at the gates of Rome. From a distance, these quarrels between two philosophies reveal an identity of culture rather than an opposition between cultures. Whether one can move from Kant to Marx may be a debatable question; but if Kant disappears, there is no question of getting to Marx. The destruction of bourgeois philosophy implies the destruction of the one possible means of arriving at a philosophy that can transcend it, just as burning a Platonic codex makes a recently discovered text by Aristotle meaningless. When Nazism is on the border, the Communist outrider who thinks the freemasons are the main enemy is not showing

[15] Preface to Bourgin's *De Jaurès à Léon Blum: L'Ecole Normale et la politique*.

much political perspicacity, he is displaying the suicidal sectarianism of the Comintern's 'Third Period'. In 1932, Nizan presumably had every chance to turn Jules Lagneau's moral philosophy upside down under the nose of his students, who were then in power. It is quite true that the rule of Reason is the idealized rule of the bourgeoise and that, then as now, the 'idylls of the philosophy of the Rights of Man' mean that the cries of those without rights—since they do not have the privilege of being White Europeans—go unheard. Aside from that, the pedagogic virtues, which in themselves are no more proletarian than Ferdinand Buisson's Ligue de l'Enseignement, the Ligue des Droits de l'Homme (Francis de Pressensé) or Victor Basch, were definitely beginning to go stale for want of institutional, demographic and social ventilation. Nizan had only one programme to oppose to the old maids' embroidery: to open up the Sorbonne to the East wind which then seemed (to Gide too) to be fresher and healthier than the West wind. Basically, he took up the perennial discourse of those who love the earth as opposed to the clouds, the lived concrete experience rather than the abstraction of concepts—which does not seem to have much in common with Marx's intentions. Not that the absence of a programme or the vagueness of the theory matter greatly: the important point is that the mandarins of the bourgeoisie gave way to the clowns of the Spectacle not to proletarian scientists—which means that the shivering mandarins of yesterday have a very different place in history. Nizan criticized the *République des professeurs* in the name of a future Republic of Soviets, but it was not what he thought it would be and the People's Commissars let him down. Ultimately, the bourgeois university saved the honour of French intellectuals during the Dreyfus Affair—and again during the Occupation—and at the time of the colonial wars. When there is nothing left but the Académie Française and satellite TV, and they are hand in glove,[16] how can there be anything but dishonour?

For lack of a historical base of operations, a left-wing critique of the Radical-Socialist university therefore began to operate on the right, and the cry from the heart began to wreck a little more of the ecosystem of

---

[16] *Hand in glove*: contrary to popular belief, academic and TV fame are perfectly congruent. They are superimposed and complement one another. Not surprisingly; if TV is an ideology, the Académie Française is the same ideology. Look at the list of those who win the 'essay' section of the Académie's prizes: you will find the most 'modern' and the least 'archaic' of the ideological stars of the small screen. The institution of the Académie has nothing to fear from the audio-visual institution; it reflects its glow.

socialism, a fragile social idea that perishes along with pedagogic constraints and society's knowledge of its own archives. The concomitant decline of the bourgeois university and of working-class autonomy in French society may not prove the point, but equally they do not disprove it. The tragicomedy of time finally played a dirty trick on Nizan the materialist. He complained that the doors of the university were closed to Marxism. Marxism finally forced them. But unfortunately they closed behind it, trapping it into a learned theoreticism and a formalism from which it will have difficulty in recovering. Strictly non-operational Marxist theoretical activities have thus crystallized around the university pole, leaving the workers' movement outside complete freedom to indulge in practical activities that are distinctly un-Marxist. It is a vicious old circle, with each arc reproducing the next. But there was a Parthian shot. The decline in the social power of the teachers meant a diminution of Marxism's ideological power. The collapse of mandarin metaphysics that Nizan and also Politzer prayed for has come about, but the materialist dialectic has not risen to take its place. On the contrary: the inversion of ideological dominance between the different supports of the intelligentsia proved the support for an inversion of ideological domination, and put Nizan and Brunschvicg in the same place: at the bottom. There is nothing immoral in the story. French Marxism is simply being punished for its academic sins—academically.

2

The Publishing Cycle
(1920–1960)

Re-creation is the life blood of culture, and anything that permits continuity makes possible a radical break. It must be said from the start: there is no 'solution of continuity' between the first and second ages. The cycle of 'publishing' was a by-product of the reign of the university and shook off its guardianship precisely because it was originally closely linked with it. Why separate the two? Because at the beginning of the century, an autonomous literary milieu appeared, independent of the traditional academic milieu and very much on the fringes of the university, free of the constraints of the latter and the prejudices of the former. As to the history of this microcosm—we can provisionally call it the milieu of the *Nouvelle revue française*—Maria Van Rysselberghe's *Les Cahiers de la petite dame* has recently provided us with its book of hours, and Malraux's preface, written in the depths of 'a society in which literary milieux no longer exist', is its will. These '*Notes pour l'histoire authentique d'André Gide*', which cover a period of thirty years (1918–1948), can be seen as a field study of the *gens* 'author' in which the Gide family, the 'Vaneau'* as centre and subject of the study, serves as an ethnographic witness to its allied and collateral clans. What separates us from that world is now inseparable from what it was in itself. Despite its disappearance, its existence forces itself on each and every one of us. If all that exists deserves to perish, the world of French literature has not been without its merits.

When did the Sorbonne lose its authority to the NRF? 1920? 1930? There is no doubt about the shift itself, merely about its dating and the areas of authority involved. There is no legislation to direct the government of minds and no official demarcation between territories. Intellectual and moral magistratures are more subtle and diffuse than their political counterparts. But when the 'aura' of the *maître-à-vivre*—the

* A nickname for Gide, derived from his address in rue Vaneau.

French culmination of the intellectual master—passed from Renan to Gide, after having settled on Barrès and brushed against Bergson, it was not simply a change of style, epoch or idiom. One regime of symbolic production was displacing another, and its centre of gravity was the publisher.

Unlike the Other, the human spirit blows where it *can*. In a high wind it just blows away; but it becomes stale when closed in. In short, it needs air but hates draughts. It is difficult to strike a balance between open and closed and every intellectual worker has to strike it for himself by alternating between the two. Shutting himself up in order to produce and opening up in order to transmit and receive. Spiritual calm requires a closed space: it is in the nature of those who serve the intellect to live together—in a circle. The intellectual function requires an opening to the outside: if the circles shut themselves up with no outlet on to the outside world, the intellectual can no longer fulfil his social function of communicating and the *clerc* becomes a monk again. There is no perfect solution to this squaring of the circle in any political or social regime. But at the half-way stage (on the median line of capitalist development), the French intelligentsia seems to have found the least evil of all possible indices of closure in the *publishing house*, which gave the spiritual family a roof over its head, walls and, more important, windows. The publishing houses already existed as simple business concerns, and none of them was short on personality or even combativity for instance, Hetzel (1838), the Republican who published Jules Verne. Hachette was founded in 1826 (Zola was to work there as a clerk and then as head of advertising), Plon in 1854, and Lemerre won fame (and fortune) by publishing the Parnassian poets. But the publisher as tutelary seal, compere and source of legitimacy appeared shortly before the First World War. Bernard Grasset established his firm in 1907 and the NRF writers set up Gallimard in 1910.[17] In the latter case, it was the journal that produced the publisher and not the reverse. Gide, Schlumberger, Drouin, Copeau and Rivière had already financed thirty or so issues of the NRF with their own money (the first issue was dated 15 November 1908) before starting to look for a managing editor-cum-Maecenas and finding Gaston Gallimard, son of the owner of the Théâtre des Variétés. The story of that cooption is adequate proof that

[17] See Gabriel Boillat, *La Librairie Grasset at les lettres françaises, les chemins de l'édition (1907–1914)*, Paris 1974; and of course Auguste Anglès admirable thesis, *André Gide et le premiere groupe de la NRF (1890–1910)*, Paris 1978.

in publishing, management took second place at that time. The hegemony of the publisher, symbolized by the Gallimard imprint, lasted until the 1960s, when the publishing world began to lose the economic and intellectual initiative. As it ceased to polarize the magnetic field of the literary intelligentsia, it began itself to be polarized by a very different system of gravitation.

To publish (*publicare simulacrum*: to erect a statue in a public place) means to sell to the highest bidder. To edit (from *edere*: to give birth) means to bring something into the world. Books are published and authors are edited. The distinction is not meaningless, but it cannot mask the fact that there is no publishing without editing, and no publication without prostitution (*publicare corpus*: to prostitute oneself). It is, however, enough to give the publisher a flattering ambiguity in the eyes of the author, the public man. He is both his pimp and his true love. The pimp finds clients for his protegé and defends him from his neighbours and competitors in exchange for a percentage on the tricks he turns. The lover listens to his secrets and lets him pour out his hopes and fears. The author contracts to rent the publisher his mind, not his body; the publisher pays the printer to give the productions of that mind a typographical body, and the bookseller sells the product. Historically, the publisher was the last of the four to appear and the author came just before him. Three pieces of information are juxtaposed on the cover of a modern book: the title, the author's name and the publisher's name. Only the first is essential. Books have managed without the others in the past. Books appeared without 'publishers' from the sixteenth century to the nineteenth. During the same period, many books appeared without authors: almanachs, missals, fabliaux, lives of saints and heroes, and so on. Michel Foucault has put forward some stimulating propositions on the appearance and disappearance on the author-function in past western discourses, and the spaces of truth and type of circulation they inaugurate, depending upon the period and the category of the utterances.[18] Modern discourse still does without authors at the two extremes of scientific production and popular speech. It is as though the most dense of all the records of the intelligence craved the honour of anonymity: funny stories and graffiti no more have authors than the proverbs, tales and epics of the past. When the walls speak (*les murs ont*

[18] 'Qu'est-ce qu'un auteur', *Bulletin de la Société française de philosophie*, 22 February 1969. English translation, 'What is an Author' in Michel Foucault, *Language, Counter-Memory, Practice*, Oxford 1977.

la parole), they are like laboratories: it is their right to be apocryphal and their duty to omit all mention of the author's name. 'Attributed to' would be restrictive for one and disenchanting for the other. Scientific truth is like the poetry of tomorrow: for everyone and by no-one. In the meantime, the absence of copyright may be to the advantage of publishers of funny stories or Bourbaki, but personalized books are more profitable. In matters literary, anonymity has become an expensive nonsense, unless it works as a riddle and pushes up the sales. At the two extremes of textual authority, then, the author disappears, but in between there is an immense range of 'average books' that demand an author and await a publisher.

Before Gutenberg, all they needed was a copyist. After Gutenberg, they needed printers, who either sold the product themselves or distributed it through booksellers. These were booksellers, printer-booksellers and bookseller-printers, all assembled in one corporation on the rue Saint-Jacques and strictly controlled, first by the Church and then by the state. Technical advances in printing, together with the extension of the reading public and the possibility of larger print runs, increased both the potential profits and the complexity of the labour process. Hence the need for centralized coordination to unify the technical and the commercial tasks. The publisher as *industrial firm*, as intermediary between the *printer* (technical) and the *bookseller* (commercial), appeared in the second half of the eighteenth century. The bourgeois revolution emancipated both publishers, by abolishing the corporation of booksellers, and authors, by recognizing literary property under the law of 1793, which was to govern relations between authors and publishers for almost two hundred years. The publisher was officially established as a *juridical institution* by a Napoleonic law requiring every publication to have an *éditeur responsable*. Even today, it is the publisher and not the author who is taken to court, fined and punished in cases of libel or when a book is banned by the authorities. The publisher gradually won his autonomy, marginalizing both printers and booksellers, and in 1892 the Cercle de la librairie split into the Chambre syndicale des libraires and the Syndicat national des éditeurs.[19] The publisher was no longer one stage among others, but the very pivot of the process of literary promotion. The foundations of publishing as a *focus of cultural attraction* were laid at the end of the century.

After the explosion of the 1880s, which were marked by impressive sales

[19] See, Syndicat national de l'édition, *L'Editeur, pourquoi?* Cercle de la librairie, 1977.

by Zola, Maupassant and Renan (*La Vie de Jésus* sold 60,000 copies in six months), publishing lapsed into apathy. The ebb began in 1890 and lasted until about 1910: a novel did well to sell 2,000 copies (as in the years between 1820 and 1835). Maupassant complained of poor sales,[20] Péguy struggled to pay his bills on *Les Cahiers de la quinzaine*,[21] and Claudel complained to Gide, perhaps from the depths of China, that 'the book trade seems to me to be in a barbaric and inorganic state'. No author who was not a guaranteed success could find a home without paying for it. Publication at the author's expense became inevitable: such was Gide's fate before *L'Immoraliste*; Segalen's throughout his life, and Proust's until the war. Bernard Grasset was to cause something of a minor revolution in 'advanced' circles by offering to bear the cost of review and presentation copies (as he first did for Proust). In 1890, Verlaine sold 350 copies of his poems, and the next year 325 people bought Mallarmé's *Pages*. Gide had yet to reach the five hundred mark, and the first three pre-war editions of *Du côte de chez swann* sold 2,200 copies in all; Proust was far from unhappy with his half-success.

Initially, the NRF group welcomed the narrowness of the literary audience, but it later went on to explode it. The popular press, on the other hand, was more than flourishing (there were 2,000 periodicals in Paris in 1890) and forced pure literature into touch by normalizing and popularizing the academic production of the sub-D'Annunzio's, the Edmond Rostands and the Octave Mirbeaus. Gide and his followers rebelled against 'the suffocating flood of abject rubbish poured into the country by journalism'. The second issue of the NRF (1909) proclaimed its intentions of 'combating journalism, Americanism, commercialism and the self-complacency of the period'—a programme that would not be out of place in the year 1979. 'Literary France in 1909: academicism, Parisianism, opportunism. . . .' Saint-John Perse's posthumous tribute to Gide's action—'the forgers denounced as embezzlers, the rhetoricians unmasked, the mages confounded, the parasites thrown out, intellectual poverty discouraged'—recalls the very real *secession* made by the tiny

[20] 'Bookselling is in crisis. People are no longer buying books. I believe that cheap reprints and the countless 40 sou collections available to the public are killing the novel' (Letter to his mother, 1890).

[21] 'You will not find a single publisher in Paris who is prepared to launch a young, unknown man. A man without a name. No man today will do what old Michel Lévy did for the young Ernest Renan: invent, launch a man, start a firm, launch someone completely unknown, take risks, bet on him without any guarantees: no man will do that today'.

group that was, in Mauriac's phrase, to become the 'compass-card of twentieth-century French literature'. Initially, this literary religion could not avoid a certain secretarian jealousy, which was the source of Gaston Gallimard's strength. The source of the more individualistic Bernard Grasset's strength was his cult of talent and his company retained some of the eclecticism of the café Vachette of 1900. Grasset was a café-salon, Gallimard a salon-chapel. One wanted to use advertising to widen an audience that the other was creaming off with sobriety. Early in his career, Grasset distinguished himself by setting up a promotional system which he pioneered in the literary market: word-of-mouth advertising in fashionable society, paid advertisements in the press, door-to-door selling, bill-posting. Until then an author's success had depended upon his books alone, and Alfred Vallette, the editor of the Mercure de France calmly formulated the general belief as a dilemma: 'I never advertise the books I publish. Either they are bad and it is quite pointless to do anything to save them, or they are good and will eventually sell themselves.' For the love of art, Grasset introduced the technique of bluffing—'Advertising means having the audacity to say you already have something when you are merely expecting it'—high pressure selling, free gifts, canvassing for business, and so on. Not that this prevented him from discovering and retaining Giraudoux, Mauriac, Radiguet, Morand, Cocteau, Giono, Cendrars, Rilke and Ramuz. For a long time after the First World War, Daniel Halévy's *Cahiers verts* were an effective counterbalance to the 'white cover' of the NRF. The NRF finally gained the upper hand because it represented a group of conspirators and was able to found a school. The NRF imprimateur meant adoption into a family, or even incorporation into an order. That is why Proust finally went over to it (despite the earlier rebuffs), as did Martin de Gard, who went to see Gide when Grasset turned down his *Jean Barois*: 'The ranks of the NRF offered me much more; a welcoming spiritual family whose aspirations and research were similar to my own and in which I could settle without losing any of my independence of mind'.[22] Grasset's desire for popular success led him to turn down the avant-garde and fighting works that the more likeminded NRF attracted, seeming to be more interested in the future of ideas and forms than in their present state.

The apogee of the publisher's authority, which subsumed and prolonged that of the university without a break, marked the golden age of

[22] Cited in Gabriel Boillat, *Deux erreurs de Grasset*, p. 123.

French thought. All the harmony of a peaceful summer was there: full bloom, balance, maturity. The golden age—'when gold did not rule'—was open primarily to those with money: because it was more difficult then than now to make a fortune in the milieu, entrance was easier if one had an inheritance, if one was a landowner like Gide, Claudel or Mauriac, a bourgeois like Schlumberger, Rivière, Larbaud, or from a good family, like Martin du Gard and others. The *aurea mediocritas* of bourgeois happiness, mid-way between the asceticism of the priests and the vulgarization of the market-place, between the aridity of erudite long marches and the barren spasms of topicality; an age of classical proportions (of quality and audience), cultivation and nuance; 'all in exquisite taste, naturally': those last words written by the dying Gide at the end of the manuscript of *Ainsi soit-il* could in retrospect stand as its motto. It was a serenely, almost proudly bourgeois world; but although conservative and liberal, the Republic of letters was not above going in for leftist audacities and was quite capable, in time of danger, of accepting its civic responsibilities without fuss, with a certain lucidity (think of Gide and the USSR). This humanism was all the more praiseworthy for being practical rather than theoretical: it had as much to do with manners as ideas, as befits an age wherein prevailed the 'good manners' subsequently destroyed by TV and the media (in the sense of 'mass media', a later coinage), those schools of bad manners and factories of exhibitionism— and as befits a group (the NRF) whose unity was not ideological, but *tonal* (its tone obviously related to a certain conception of man and society). The family circle was more a clan than a clique and, if the distinction means anything, it would have to be termed, to use an older canon, an intellectual aristocracy (exercising power in the general interest) as opposed to today's high intelligentsia, which exercises power in its own interests and should really be termed an *oligarchy*. In the final analysis, the Gidean patriciate, open to novices and explorers alike, did not abuse its quasi-monopoly position solely to its own advantage. The milieu did of course strive to preserve an exclusivity that was partly thrust upon it (by a popular press which, by devoting very little space to literature and culture, had the side effect of producing a whole crop of specialist but widely-read reviews) and partly chosen (as a means of keeping its moral distance from contemporary events and as a precondition for aesthetic work). Rather than recount its history or describe it, which would mean recopying it (this world spent its days telling its own story and describing itself, but without drums and trumpets, metaphor or metonymy), let us try to uncover its foundations. The great world of letters—whose religion is literature—cannot be too great, for religion is synonymous with family, fasces and pact, and therefore with demarcation. The demarcation did not lead to segregation, thanks to the bridges built by the big literary weeklies (*Les Nouvelles Littéraires* was founded by Larousse in 1922, with Roger Martin de Gard's brother as its editor), the diversity of positions and temperaments, the constant call of current events, filtered but never ignored (the 1935 Writers' Congress, for example). At a deeper level, the cohesion of this dense, multiple world, allegorized by Gide for a quarter of a century, may derive from a fusion, a fragile, momentary, but productive alliance between three branches or functions that are usually rivals. If worlds are formed by miracles—a chance encounter between necessary causal sequences—this world was produced by a fusion. The distance between producer (writer), filter (the critic on the review or newspaper) and entrepreneur (publisher) had never been smaller. To break the spell, it might be said that these literary artisans verified in advance the law of industrial economics according to which productivity in a given branch rises as the level at which decisions are made approaches that where they are implemented, as management and effective labour converge. The NRF represented a merger between the three instances of production, distribution and legitimation, which are now split up. To put it another way, the merger then operated at the level of the producers and according to their norms, whereas it now operates at the level of the distributors and according to theirs. The most effective place for pre-publication or serialization is now the weekly, but then it was the review. The NRF of 1930 played the same role as *Le Nouvel Observateur* in 1970. *Le Temps perdu* and *La Condition humaine* were published in instalments in the NRF before they appeared in book form and were acclaimed by the public. The house of Gallimard allowed a mind to take on its own industrial and typographical body and to choose how it was to become flesh—and that will be its great merit in the eyes of history. From the early twenties to the early sixties, from Andre Gidé to Queneau and Marcel Arland—and not forgetting Malraux (a staff member), Drieu (who died on the job) and Sartre (who drew a stipend from the house)—those who animated and produced a culture met in the same offices and the same pages. The specialists were their own popularizers; French literature had the ability to produce its own media and to choose its own supports. It is tempting to forget how cosy and easy it all was, to temper one's rejection of castes by praising the virtuosos. When the productive circuit comes to resemble a family circle, something unhealthy begins to pollute the air; perhaps the windows should be broken. Even so there is something comic rather than melodramatic about the old annual spectacle of that elegant vaudeville show of a Gallimard jury awarding the Prix Goncourt to a Gallimard author already enthroned by Gallimard's review. Both on and off stage, the professionals were always amongst friends. The 'mutual admiration societies' have subsequently been expanded on to the national scale by the mass-information media.

A critic has an audience, an author his work. What does a publisher have? Authors. He is the author of his authors; the company is his collected works. The proof of this is that the company is normally named after him; when he 'defends his authors' he is 'defending his name', as Robert Laffont puts it.[23] Mediately, the publisher's name works as an author's name: the author squared. And he needs to have authors to the power of three at his side and above him, those Socratic midwives of the text who prefer to deliver a generation of famous men than to become famous themselves, and who were once to a publishing house what leader writers are to today's newspapers. In the days when publishing did not mean printing, but imprinting a line and sticking to it, those masters in the shadows were as vital to the life of letters as a Lucien Herr* to the leaders of French socialism in the days when socialism meant an idea and not an election. If some are to perfect what was then called a 'work', there must be others at hand to watch carefully over them, others who have no 'work' either because they choose not to or because they do not care to display it. Such mentors are not simply critics, for they have no grudge against the author and have a passion for giving as well as the ability to criticize. Desjardins, Rivière, Groethuysen: these hidden men had the souls of missionaries prepared to die for their purpose, a failing that earned them disciples for life. Through their friends, they left their mark on their times without ever having to show their claws. Someone like Jean Paulhan is definitely a member of this strange family (with Berl and Queneau as emancipated cousins), which some historian of the intellect will have to examine one day. In any case, that clandestine consistory of the spirit of the times could only pass judgment, produce or even have the influence it

---

[23] See *Robert Laffont, éditeur*, Paris 1974.

* Lucien Herr (1964–1926): A Dreyfusard and subsequently a member of the SFIO, close associate of Léon Blum. For many years librarian at the Ecole Normale Supérieure.

did so long as it was not subject to the industrial imperative of profitability. If those leader writers of the *Zeitgeist* (who signed their articles with their initials, not their full names) had not been able to challenge, both in principle and in fact, the criterion of distribution, namely immediate profitability, the logic of moral, aesthetic and intellectual research would immediately have been supplanted by the mass-mediatic logic of the search for the *greatest possible audience* and the invention of the numerators of the future would consequently have given way to the lowest common denominator of the moment. The directors would have been directed; instead of informing their time, they would have been 'informed' by it, like most of their present-day counterparts. In a word, they would have spent their lives pushing a guard's van labelled 'avant-garde'.

In 1945, the academics returned in force to the literary intelligentsia and the Sartre family seemed brutally to displace the Gide family and its allied branches. But, despite a definite difference in *tone*, both stemmed from the same trunk and clung to the same origin: Pontigny stands as an emblem of the whole period, a vault that could shelter both Jules Lagneau and Jean-Paul Sartre, the spiritualist so mocked by Nizan and Nizan's existentialist comrade. Paul Desjardins[24] was its hidden cornerstone. This philosophy teacher, cleric at heart, Dreyfusard by vocation, and stiff-necked nuisance out of necessity (according to those who knew him), a friend of Bergson and Jaurès in the rue d'Ulm (in the famous class of 1878) died in 1940. Together with Lagneau, he founded the Union pour l'Action Morale and rechristened it the Union pour la Vérité in 1905. Shortly afterwards he bought a deconsecrated Cistercian abbey, with himself as verger, and made it a meeting place where anyone who was anyone amongst the intellectuals of Europe could gather under the trees each summer. From 1910 onwards, Desjardins, a one-man link between the university and the world of letters, brought the general staff of the NRF here, where it regularly held its sittings until the very end. Who did not come to say his piece and listen to the others? Not a face is missing from the photo album: Martin du Gard, Gide, Schlumberger, Maurois, Rivière, Charles de Bos, Mauriac, Malraux, Sartre (then a student), Edmond Jaloux, Focillion, Bachelard, Jankelevitch, Fabre-Luce, Martin-Chauffier, and the rest. A society of White European Men (an official rule proposed by Gide to Desjardins: 'We will accept couples, that is, women who are accompanied by their husbands. No single women to be invited'), all adults, bourgeois,

[24] See *Paul Desjardins et les Décades de Pontigny*, Paris 1964.

leisured and 'normal' (or keeping quiet about their 'deviations'); a society whose limits and constraints have been admirably described by Clara Malraux, who went there in 1928 'accompanied by her husband' and, even so, not without difficulty:

'According to André, this place where the spirit blew should, like Mount Athos, be a male preserve. . . . The place was then reached by train. As the station was a few kilometres from the Abbey where the intellectual festivities took place, M. Desjardins came on foot to meet his guests at the station. . . . He had the face of a somewhat demonic saint, and it looked even longer because of his slightly old-fashioned grey goatee. . . . To one side of us walked a good part of the intelligentsia of France, all in stiff collars, ties and boots. . . . Not one of these men had ever committed an illegal act. Their entire lives were a non-challenge to the values handed down by their predecessors. Their debates had been with higher powers than those we were confronting. After all, Pontigny was born of the Union pour la Vérité, and the Union pour la Vérité was born of the Dreyfus Affair. Ever since, those who gathered in the rue Visconti and at the Abbey had posed their ethical questions from a Christian point of view, sometimes delicately tinged with Guesdist socialism and enlightened by humanism. The war, the Russian Revolution, and colonialism caused them little anxiety. For most of them the Allied cause was virginally pure, Communism an intrusion of barbarism into an ordered world, and the presence of Whites in Asia and Africa a requirement of civilization. At what point does one realize that the house is about to fall down? The cracks were scarcely visible. The thinkers of France knew that all civilizations are mortal, but the same Valéry who noted the fact approved of opening fire on the strikers at Fourmies. . . . Very few of those who stayed at the Abbey with us in 1928 had set foot outside Europe—were they even part of it? Of all that Asia had produced, only the mysticism interested them. Whether they realized it or not, their real debate was with the spiritual. Desjardins's ambition was to "roll under the Holy Table", and he achieved it during the Second World War. The prototype he sought to embody was purely monastic, suggested perhaps by the cathedral that overlooked the house and was connected with it by the ruins of the monastery, the great romanesque hall of the monks' refectory where we took our meals, on the floor above the library where we meditated amongst the books. . . . ,'[25]

[25] *Voici que vient l'été.*

Does not that halt at Pontigny in 1925 have some claim to be preserved in all our memories, like a popular print of a half-way stage between the cloisters of the Ecole Normale Superiéure in 1880 and the recording studios of 1970, a half-way stage on the road that, within the space of a century, took the bourgeois intelligentsia from the priesthood to the hit parade, assuming, of course, that the species can still preserve a few scraps of memories from topicality? The tone of the period was first set in this ill-disguised cloister. The most striking thing about this tone of the period is that it was such a good one, mid-way between the ecclesiastical solemnity that went before it and the shrillness of the advertising that came after. It is as though that high intelligentsia owed respect for itself and for others to a slightly ridiculous bourgeois respectability. More than a salon and less than a forum, this salon-forum in Burgundy appears to have provided excellent acoustics for courteous and subtle exchanges in which no-one was out to sell himself or make a profit, except in the sense of sharpening his wits against those of others. Internal emulation was sufficient; the speakers were scarcely concerned about being heard outside these walls. It was the tone of the nineteenth century (from which the circle inherited its custom of reading manuscripts to one another)—a talk was not yet a colloquium nor a gathering a seminar. The values quoted within the group were not indexed to the stock exchange of opinion. The floor was reserved for the privileged few, but what they were required to bring with them was not so much personal social capital (background, fame, contacts) as cultural capital (which obviously derives from the former, but cannot be reduced to it).

The Pontigny circuit has probably not been broken—or not completely. After the war, Desjardins's daughter, Anne Heurgon-Desjardins (who has since died), relaunched the summer conversations at Cérisy-la-Salle. Now, there was a freer, less starchy atmosphere, with no summonses or rules, but a very different discursive diet: that of the intervention prepared in advance and taped for transcriptions—with the eminently praiseworthy aim that nothing be lost and that the discourse of the masters may live on in a paperback. There was something amateurish about the old Masters with their gratuitous effort, their pleasure and their nonchalance. The true *professional* communicators came later, with tape-recorders and the human sciences.

Given that any serious spirituality takes the temporal in charge, the intent to publish in the classical age found a spontaneous outlet in the review, an amenity common to chapels, churches and parties, the first and last seal on the long chain of fervour. The review is as old as literature itself, and punctuated all its inflections from the romantic Restoration to the rise of symbolism, from the *Muse Française* to *La Revue blanche*. But it was after the turn of the century that the review-forum became the intellectual army's main mode of territorial organization and a support for the strategies known as schools. Intellectual warfare is subject to the same organizational laws as social warfare. No political party, no paper; but if there is no paper, there is no revolutionary party. No publisher, no review; but if there is no review there is no school. Just as a party starts with a paper, a school starts with a review. The great epoch of 'isms' was therefore also that of the periodicals. With Barbusse and its International Editorial Board, *Clarté* rooted Communism in the French intelligentsia (and, as a side effect, the Italian) a year before the Congress of Tours rooted it in the workers' movement. The same year, surrealism crystallized around *Littérature* (1919–1923), which was subsequently replaced by *La Révolution surréaliste* (1924–1929), and then by *Le Surréalisme au service de la révolution* (1930–1933), until the school broke up and dissolved into a generalized movement for want of a central journal. This is not to mention *Bifur* (1929–1931) and other fertile dissident movements. There would have been no personalism without *L'Esprit* (1932), no existentialism without *Les Temps modernes* (1945), no new French historical school without the *Annales* (founded by Lucien Febvre and Marc Bloch in 1929), no new criticism without *Critique* (founded by Bataille in 1946) and no new wave without *Les Cahiers du cinéma* (André Bazin, 1951). Segalen would not have been rediscovered and Camus would not have made his breakthrough without *Les Cahiers du sud*, which unfortunately perished with its founder in 1966 (Jean Ballard in Marseilles).

So we see that the review is isomorphic with the separate fields of the aesthetic avant-garde, academic research and political action, and welds them together. It both materializes and symbolizes the possibility of a translation, if not an equivalence, and therefore communication between them. After the Second World War, *Europe*, *La Nouvelle Critique* and *La Pensée* served to sustain a Stalinist Marxism in 'scientific and intellectual circles', in the same way that *Socialisme et Barbarie*, followed by *Arguments* in 1956, sustained a critical Marxism in the fifties. *Partisans* served the same function for third-worldism and the anti-imperialist struggle in the sixties. In literary terms, did the period opened by the NRF in 1909 come to an end in the late 60s with *Tel Quel*—right at the edge of the mediological fault, but still on this side of it?

The necessary life-span of a review is a generation, between twenty and twenty-five years, after which it either changes or outlives its purpose. Can one ideological and aesthetic generation still take over from another by using the review-form? Some are admirable, like *Change*, with its exemplary rigour and integrity. But have Jean-Pierre Faye and his friends forged an instrument of the quality they could have attained with the same tools *before* the break? There will be dozens, if not hundreds of other literary reviews, good, bad and indifferent. But in the recent ups and downs of intellectual public authority, the review seems to have gone from being a motive for action to being a stage prop that may be decorative but has no influence on the workings of the plot. Reviews are, of course, still vital in scientific domains as a site for research and elaboration, but there the esoteric aspect is not masterful but functional. In the profane world, weekly news magazines have taken over from the glorious monthlies, rejecting the canonic model to the status of a luxury figurehead and becoming more like pastimes for schoolkids.[26] As for the theoretical journals of those parties that used to have a theory, their difficulties are well-known and their decline still more so.

There has been a break, and with good reason. In its specific form, the review does not belong to the universe of the mass media: it is marketed, but it is not a market commodity. Even if by some miracle it did make a profit (it is of the essence of the review to make a loss, but accidents to happen), even if it were full of clip-off coupons, surprise gifts and four-colour pictures, it would still be the complete antithesis of a *magazine* (*Lire, Le Magazine littéraire* or *Le Figaro magazine*). The review seeks influence, not an audience, coherence and not eclecticism, truth (*its* truth) and not affability. It works with quality, not volume, and takes orders only from the values it has chosen, not from the facts that besiege it. The difference lies not in its periodicity, but in its substance.[27] A review

---

[26] There is one exception: *Les Actes de la recherche en sciences sociales* (edited by Pierre Bourdieu). Its originality consists in applying the canon of scientific research to the profane field of topicality. The telescoping effect is always enlightening and sometimes even spicy.

[27] *Les Nouvelles littéraires* (Jean-Marie Borzeix) and *La Quinzaine Littéraire* (Maurice Nadeau), one weekly, the other fortnightly, are closer to the review element than to the magazine element. That is their glory and their agony. Both deserve more than respect: total support.

prospects; a magazine exploits: which means that management may come second with the former, but must come first with the latter—that a review is the concern of an individual or a community, but a magazine is a concern, full-stop. A review needs dedication and volunteers; a magazine is a business that needs files and, above all, a mailing list. A review is pre-recorded and therefore forward-looking; a magazine goes out live and is therefore backward-looking. To say that one is a matter of duration and that the other reacts to the event of the moment is equivalent to saying that one is bound to authenticity (which stands up to both verification and the test of time) while the other is bound to ideology (the presence of the illusion stemming from the illusion of the present). Having annexed cultural life, the news factory has to produce something *new* every month, but the product that comes off the line is second-hand. A good review is always twenty years ahead of its time, a good magazine is never a week late. The magazine brings death in full colour, the review invents life in black and white. What seems to be 'advanced' is often concealed nostalgia. What now passes for a cultural review is objectively obliged to announce the liquidation of culture by advertising. A culture lives by its contradictions and therefore by debates and polemics. No serious debate about ideas is possible in five or six double-spaced sheets of typescript—the maximum length of a magazine 'article'. The great quarrels of the 30s and 50s (between Sartre and Camus over *The Rebel*, for example) would be *materially* impossible today—primarily for lack of space.

The withering away of the review-form and the flourishing of the magazine mean much more than the suffocation of news stories beneath pages of advertising;[28] they announce a glorious revival of intellectual comfort and social inertia. In this field, any awakening must come from moral will-power, not from economic logic; from a project, not a mechanism; in a word, from a publisher or a party. The publisher in the classic sense was to intellectual society what the party, in the organic sense, is to society as a whole: an apparatus that transforms an event into consciousness and consciousness into activity, which is capable, not of opposing the flow of events, but of superimposing a counter-current of

[28] To take a recent example. According to an official count made by *Le Monde* (note by Viansson-Ponté, 17 December 1978), *Jours de France* (No. 1252, 9–15 December) has 284 pages, including 185 pages of paid advertisements. In comparison, *L'Express* (No. 1431, 9–15 December) has 244 pages, including 94 pages of news stories and 150 pages of ads; *Le Nouvel Observateur* (No. 735, 11–17 December): 54 pages of news stories and 78 pages of ads; *Le Point* (No. 325, 11–17 December: 65 pages of news stories and 127 pages of ads; *Paris-Match* (No. 1542, 15 December): 92 pages of news stories and 96 pages of ads.

will and thought upon it. When the reverse happens and force of circumstance imposes itself on the will of men, the publisher becomes to the market for printed matter what the party becomes to the flow of events: a cork caught in the undertow and only too happy to bob up and down there—not an actor but an agent, not a force for initiative but a form of operation. It is not, or not only, that will-power collapses but that, where the publisher is concerned, economic constraints become harsher and that the parties are increasingly hemmed in by the so-called apolitical 'information' media. These joint declines converge towards the simultaneous eclipse of the review-form and of the serious (or militant) newspaper.

The authority of the publisher expressed the supremacy of literature within the symbolic field at the level of institutions: it is becoming dated in that sense too. But the sovereignty of literature in no way completely isolated the *gendelettre* from the rest of the city. Classical culture and belles lettres hegemonized the political field simultaneously, supplying it with its troops (parliamentary and party leadership), its emblems (myths and rhetoric) and weapons (papers and weeklies). A review was therefore not simply a publisher's anteroom, a test-bed for criticism or a pool of new talent. It looked out on to history in the raw and, after the crash of 1929 and the rise of fascism, moved quite easily between the street and the editorial office. In 1932, the NRF's Emmanuel Berl became the editor of *Marianne*. In 1935, Gide became a regular contributor to *Vendredi*, the Popular Front's polemical organ, founded by Chamson, Guéhenno and Andrée Viollis. In 1937, Aragon left *Commune*, which he and Vaillant-Couturier had set up in 1933, to become editor of *Ce Soir* (which reached a circulation of 300,000 in 1939) along with Jean-Richard Bloch from *Europe*. Louis Guilloux worked on all three at once. These are a few of the hundreds of individual itineraries that illustrate the capital, and largely forgotten, paradox that there is no more a contradiction (it is a breastwork) between the closure of the avant-garde and the openness of the militant than there was between the political and the cultural avant-gardes of that time. But that is a vast subject and mediology, which fears commonplaces (in time it will produce its own), will content itself with tracing its informational contours. But it has to be stated that in the bygone days of the European revolutions(?), social discourse had the material (economic and political) opportunity to move both ways (intellectual discourse into the discourse of the workers and vice versa) without (too many) intercalated institutions or (too much) capitulation to the weight of competition. As André Chamson proclaimed in the editorial in the first issue of *Vendredi* (November 1935): 'We have based our action on the twofold wager that there is in France a group of free writers and a huge audience of free men who want nothing better than to *communicate directly* with one another.' In the storm, and partly thanks to it, the wager succeeded. The period did see the birth of organs for both writers and the general public and even 'mass intellectual' journals, which indicates that popular, but not demagogic, communication and open and complex information are not always or in principle mutually exclusive. It also suggests that this was a period when the organization of publishing and distribution did not preclude a certain supremacy of content over form,[29] in that it did not automatically index the message to its reception or the value of the one to the volume of the other. In a word, it was a period when culture commanded the market (and was at the same time integrated into it), which is why men of culture could in the past (in the two periods we have distinguished) go to the media, whereas now they have to surrender to them. The miracle of working without getting your hands dirty: this was the privilege of a period in which the most demanding intellectual workers could control the distribution machine, either as individuals or as a group. The best proof is that most of them could make the round trip. With the exception of those who took a one-way ticket, like Brasillach and Drieu, whose very 'dishonour' bears witness to the field of honour of the printed word, where they killed and where they died without cheating, with dignity.

For throughout this half century (1918–1968), with its mixture of political baroque and mediatic classicism, there were as many stairways to the right as to the left. Communication ran backwards and forwards, up and down. *Archaïsant* historians like Bainville and Gaxotte could move from the Bibliothèque Nationale to the editoral board of a national weekly dealing with current events (*Candide*) without resistance. André Bellessort, André Rousseaux and Georges Suarez—the totem and taboo of the critical mandarinate—joined Daudet and Béraud on *Gringoire*, and even on *L'Action française*.[30] The most surprising thing about the

[29] If only graphically: the length of articles, the dominance of the text over the photos, the simplicity of the lay-out, the sobriety of the typography.

[30] This, it will be recalled, first appeared in review form in 1899. Maurras wanted to *counter* Herr's work on the *Revue de Paris*, the machine of war constructed by Calmann-Levy in 1889 to unite Literature and University under the aegis of the advanced, lay and republican bourgeoisie.

firebrands who helped make and break pre-war intellectual opinion was the rhetoric of violence and the academic tone of the insults they hurled about, conferring on partisan dishonesty an integrity of a kind. This mixture of ferocity and urbanity—if taken far enough, extremes meet— would go a long way towards making these pamphleteers look prehistoric, were it not recalled that the Daudets and the Bérauds were godfathers to a whole generation of mediocrats who are still on active service and many of whom were formed by that far-right press.[31] Periods of social crisis bring out the truth, stark naked. The direct articulation of literary 'Parisianity' with the national and international class struggle has rarely been as obvious as it was during the thirties. The Popular Front was no more a 'Battle of the Books' than was the Dreyfus Affair, even though it set the intellectuals at one another's throats before, during and after the clashes between classes, leagues and parties. The battle between the newspapers probably carried more weight than the street-fighting, and the 'cultural' weeklies were in the front line.[32] The battle was obviously fought on unequal terms, as we can see if we compare the circulation figures for November 1936: *Gringoire*, 640,000, *Candide* 340,000; as against *Marianne* 120,000 and *Vendredi* 100,000. But the battle was materially possible and the numbers involved on both sides were of similar proportions. Ideas, ideologues and publicists have no more disappeared from the scene than have their aims and the issues at stake. What is tending to disappear is the weapons and the logistics. The battle died for want of a battleground. What, forty years ago, could be done by a publisher or a group of independent writers—the launch of a 'serious' national weekly—can now be done only by a group like Hachette or L'Expansion or by a great accumulation of capital.[33] But the things that a publisher of a group of independent writers might want to say are the very things that a group of

[31] The best known were Thierry Maulnier, Pierre Gaxote (*Le Figaro*) and, formerly, Kleber Haedens, Barjavel, Michel Déon (*Le Journal du Dimanche*). Before he joined *Paris-Soir*, Pierre Lazareff worked on *Gringoire* and *Candide*.

[32] Or did they perhaps carry the decision? Shortly after May 1936, Gide and Duéhenno were summoned by the new President of the Council, and Blum told them something to the effect that 'In this country, where right and left are very stable, majorities depend on three or four thousand floating voters, who vote one way and then the other. Thanks to *Vendredi*, we got the floating voters this time. That is why we carried the day and I want you to know that I know that' (Lucie Mazauric, *Vive le front populaire*, Paris 1976).

[33] In view of the post-Resistance period, the time-gap really should be reduced. Witness the adventures of *Combat* (Camus, Pia, Bourdet) and *France-Observateur* (launched by Claude Bourdet in 1950 with a capital of five million old francs).

financiers cannot and will not have said and done. This is the bind. Full speech is hollow if it has no support; empty words that command support ring out loud: for the last ten years, the small proportion of distribution networks that have yet to bow before the promotion-management-sales system have been dominated by a disappointing dialogue between gagged intellectuals and talkative financial backers. To jog our memories, let us recall the publishing genealogy of the most committed of the media of the previous period. *Candide*, 'France's first politico-cultural weekly', was started by Fayard in 1924. Later it was joined by *Gringoire* (Carbuccia) and then in 1930 by *Je suis partout* (editor, Pierre Gaxotte; literary critic, Brasillach). On the other side, Gallimard (Gaston in person) launched *Marianne* in 1932, and it was the selfless devotion of a handful of left-wing writers that got *Vendredi* off the ground with savings, legacies and gifts. The unforseeable rise in fixed costs and production costs (given comparable print runs and pagination) has perhaps made such artisanal methods out of date. Yes, but the positions of literature, of intellectuals and of publishing (respectively) in the 'thought network' of the modern computerized city have also changed radically. What publishing house of any substance would risk starting a politico-cultural weekly these days? It would be risking no more than its capital, but nothing less than its professional 'credibility', which is much more important. The new social position of publication and distribution precludes extremes, demands eclecticism (the golden mean is where extremes meet) and allows political commitment only on condition that all the forms of the apolitical are respected.

The Media Cycle
(1968–?)

The intellectual micro-climate cannot escape the macro-mutations of societies and states. A caricature, sketch or picture of the French intelligentsia, as of any other social institution, category or function, can be understood only if it is placed within the following framework.

Of all the 'State Ideological Apparatuses', the Third Republic placed the educational *apparatus* in the dominant position, giving it the place and position of the Church. As a result, it dominated the intelligentsia, making the high lay clergy of the University the ruling stratum within the intellectual corps. Although the authority of the publisher was able to displace the centre of gravity of power within the literary intelligentsia, it did so on the basis of a compromise with the previous equilibrium. We are now witnessing the rise of the information apparatus to the dominant position, to the place and position of the Church. There may be some debate as to cause and effect, but not as to what is happening—it sticks out like a sore thumb. Anyone who fails to note this new order in the ideological apparatuses is laying himself open to a comfortable but dangerous archaism. The information apparatus has outclassed and therefore subordinated and restructured the pedagogic, religious, trade-union and political apparatuses—and a fortiori, the cultural apparatuses.

This sudden rise to power of an apparatus that was formerly subordinate or peripheral has had the side effect of shattering the coordinates of the 'intellectual field', taken here to mean 'the system of social relations within which creation takes place as an act of communication'.[34] The order of its coordinates has changed, but inversely. Spatially, there has been a broadening of the base; temporally, a

[34] See Bourdieu, 'Champ intellectuel et projet créateur', *Les Temps modernes*, November 1966. The problematic of this text, which I discovered only recently, is so close to my own that I have gone over certain of my formulations and clarified them as a result of reading it.

narrowing. Increase in the potential audience; decrease in creative intensity: is it possible that the modern humanities have lost comprehension and gained extension, like the concept in classical logic? Depending on whether they take the x coordinate or the y coordinate, Paul will say that 'French intellectual life' is becoming richer, and Pierre that it is becoming poorer. Pierre and Paul may both be right, because they are not talking about the same thing. Pierre says: 'One showing of *Tartuffe* on television gave it a bigger audience in one evening than it had in three hundred years on the stage'. Paul will say that the three million viewers were watching TV, not a play by Molière and that it could equally have been showing Roussin.* Pierre says, 'In 1934, *La Condition humaine* won the Goncourt and sold 30,000 with great difficulty. Forty years later, a Goncourt sells 300,000 without any difficulty'. Paul points out that people no longer buy a particular novel or author, but the Goncourt wrapper, which can go around anything. It's an old argument and they are constantly talking at cross purposes. The argument has to be taken up from a different angle.

The new internal composition of the modern intellectual field derives primarily from the new position of the field itself in relation to others. Its autonomy has never been absolute, but its relative autonomy has been considerably reduced in that it no longer includes or produces its own sanctioning instances. The author's potential readership is his prize jury. And the intellectual is the one human being who, as we have said, spends his entire life on trial, whose every word, article or book depends on the verdict of others and constantly hangs between life and death, between acclaim and oblivion. This independent character 'who seeks his happiness in others' opinion of him' (Rousseau) does not have his centre of gravity within himself; both essentially and existentially, he is dependent upon others. The quantity of 'others' will determine the value of his 'ego'. That is why the public information system is even more dominant for the intellectual creator than for any other productive species. We know that no one ideological apparatus is equally dominant over all social classes and categories. For the worker, the productive apparatus of the factory, with its rules, its organization of tools and its internal hierarchies, incarnates an ideological power that is obviously greater than any other: the newspapers and the TV cannot be the alpha and the omega of his life. Whatever he sees on TV or reads in the papers is filtered through the grid of his day-to-day experience of social relations. How are we to explain the fact that there is

*Roussin: popular dramatist born in 1901.

still such a thing as a workers' movement if there is not, somewhere in day-to-day experience, a kernel of reality that resists the formidable power, built up over more than a century, exerted by a mass of social ideas and images in which the word 'exploitation' figures as merely an invention of embittered ideologues? But what objective reality can an intellectual fall back upon? How can he look on indifferently while his product is pulled to pieces in public or simply destroyed by critical silence? He is in the same position as a comedian who cannot make people laugh. There is no point in the comic saying that his audience has no sense of humour; ultimately, it is not the actor who decides the value of the audience, but vice versa. There is no appeal against their verdict, for the comedian's purpose is not to confirm his own opinion of himself but to be reassured of what he *believes himself to be* by those who watch him *act*. A modification of the instances of admiration could therefore not fail to affect in their very project those whose vocation is winning admiration: artists, intellectuals, show people. By extending the reception area, the mass media have reduced the sources of intellectual legitimacy, surrounding the professional intelligentsia, the classic source of legitimacy, with wider concentric circles that are less demanding and therefore more easily won over. Hence the possibility of playing off the wider circles against the narrower, the exoteric against the esoteric, the amateurs against the professionals. Or, for example, the weekly against the specialist journal, or even the popular daily against the cultural weekly and, in the last instance, the TV against the daily. By definition, the law of the market is on the side of the biggest circle, so the smallest has to fall in line with it if it is not to see its market disappear. The mass media have broken down the closure of the traditional intelligentsia, together with its evaluative norms and its scale of values. Logically enough, this move towards a mass audience is accompanied by the atomization of the intelligentsia. Whatever its degree of geographical or social concentration, a milieu loses its social density when it is broken up and dispersed, when the internal links and relations between its members lose their former strength. Groups are dissolved, families scattered, communal rituals (letter writing, reading aloud, the cenacle, the review, and so on) disappear. This removal of constraints has two aspects: the products become insipid, but the producers are given a new lease of life. It is always easier for a professional to seduce amateurs than his colleagues. By cutting themselves off from one another, the professionals increase their chances of breaking through to the outer circles, not to mention the reverse effect and the possibility of an increased pay-off at the centre of the circumferences. In that sense, exclusion and dissidence are the *nec plus ultra* of profitability. If laws and communities are still tolerable, it is because they are pads for launching rebels and outlaws into promotional space. The mass media run on personality, not the collective, the sensational, not the intelligible and the singular, not the universal. Henceforth, these three innate characteristics, which ultimately boil down to the same thing, will dictate both the nature of the dominant discourse and the profile of those who bear it. They introduce an individual strategy and the break-up of collectives. No more need for *schools*, *problematics* or *conceptual systems*. Mick Jagger has prolonged the life-span of the Rolling Stones all by himself, but the Beatles signed their own death warrant with their 'It's the four of us together or no one'. A President of the Republic can do without a party, but all it takes to make a political party credible is a potential presidential candidate; whether the party does or does not have a programme, a world vision, or some idea about society is unimportant in comparison; such superfluities might get in the way. 'Lots of dynamism, little sense of direction' was how one old observer of the Holy See described the *style* of Jean Paul II, the first pop pope, who will set the seal of the Vatican on our long *fin de siècle* with a weekly news flash—which sums up the whole period and reconciles the sacred and profane worlds. If there is a canonic model of identification valid for both intellectuals and politicians, it has to be admitted that it is the Supreme Pontiff, in whom the two functions merge.

We will not take issue with the derisory poverty of the schools in literature and philosophy, with their little popes, their anathemas and their index; nothing dates more quickly than these ostentatious avant-gardes, which are more concerned with their coats of arms than with the meaning of the mottoes. The school derives less from the field of knowledge (or creation) than from the repetitive libido of power—the one being a parasite on the other. The fact remains that wherever there is a school, there is an objective division of the field, which is organized as a totality around an ideal unity of the objective type. A school of thought may give rise to the phenomenon of a fashion, but it is the thought that is fashionable rather than one person, or a certain number of singular individuals borne along by a thought whose generality goes beyond them and englobes them. The fashion groups of the contemporary intelligentsia, however, have to do without fixed points, definitions or logical articulations, as the truth-value of the statements disappears behind the show-value of the subjects of the speech-act, the content of the theses behind the faces and the idea behind its 'impact'. If, for example, the New Philosophers, as they call themselves (or the new whatever it is), had been obliged to organize themselves into a school and provide themselves with a review before making themselves known, they would have had to invent a philosophy, no less. Which would, *ipso facto*, have made them non-profitable in the eyes of their backers. The fact that the sphere of legitimation can retract in this way promotes the transgression of censure and vaguely recalls the way the sophists outflanked the philosophers in the fourth century BC. The sophist is not defined solely by his mastery of discourse as a power technique, as opposed to the slow establishment of knowledge. He puts truth to the vote, with the agora as judge. He backs quantity against quality, finesses his neighbour and crowds out the expert. By diluting the collective ego of the old intelligentsia, the mass media have broken down the old collective super-ego of its members. In 1950, no philosopher would have dared to publish a work like those that have been all over the magazines of late for fear of being ridiculed: the academic environment was still sufficiently compact to exercise self-censorship. It had not yet been dissolved into the second circle of authority, whose existence now allows the first to be short-circuited and circumvented. Even Camus, with all the advantages of integrity and of not being a member of the university congregation, did not succeed in getting *L'Homme revolté* accepted as a philosophical reflection; salvoes from professionals like Sartre and Jeanson were enough to deflate it in the eyes of well-read men (and it would be sectarian to reduce their reactions to sectarianism). In 1951, the journalists finally came round to the opinion of the *professeurs*; a quarter of a century later, the *professeurs* are coming round to the opinion of the journalists. It is not a question of deciding who was right or wrong, but of locating the inversion of the fields. Sub-contracting out a philosophical concept as a literary generality is a profitable option once more, since the inner court of popular ideological journalism has broken the chains of the former philosophical community. Given that the market rules and the university no longer has a monopoly over intellectual legitimacy, it is not at all unreasonable openly to finesse the opinion of 2,000 professionals by setting it against that of a million magazine readers or ten million viewers. By modifying the composition of the referential, the extension of both the jury and its competence has therefore had its effects on the function and the quality of the production. Not that we've gone from 'serious applicants only' to 'no serious applicants': each mediological epoch determines by consensus what is 'serious', just as each ideological epoch produces its reality by modifying the things than men agree to accept as 'real'. In the fifties, it 'wouldn't have looked right' for an academic to write a piece for *France-Soir* or for a writer to appear on a television variety programme. In the eighties, those who do not will probably seem suspect.

All intellectual universes have their own time-space. *Minority* and *posterity* are twin values, the latter being the support for the former. An artist can accept being put in a minority by the critics of the day in so far as he can presume that his work will survive the moment of publication. Stendhal found happiness by dedicating himself to the 'happy few', because he could entrust *Le Rouge et le Noir* to those who would read it in 1935. He withdrew his case in 1830, but appealed and was posthumously acquitted. What novelist ignored or scorned by his contemporaries in 1980 would dare to say that he was writing for the year 2080? In our mental space, 'few' rhymes with 'rue', for in the times in which we live there is no appeal against the passing weeks. Try as the writer may to convince himself of the opposite, the first judgment passed on his work is also its Last Judgment—and so he panics, pleads and crawls. In 1979, the Eternal Father of the French novelist is called Bertrand Poirot-Delpech, that of a political essayist André Fontaine, and that of a biographer or writer of memoirs Max Gallo.* We may have other saints, with their own angels and intercessors. But it is in the interests of mortals to work fast. We are all equally ephemeral and fallible? Of course. But 1. some judge and others are judged; 2. there are no written codes or tablets of law to refer to; 3. topicality moves fast, and there is another book on the heels of the last one.

In the eyes of the creators, the disappearance of appeals to higher courts and the shortening of suspended sentences completes the legitimation of a somewhat expeditious Justice who is blind and has a rather poor sense of balance. 'If I try to see what it was about Valéry, Proust, Suarès, Claudel and myself that makes us recognizable as belonging to the same age, I almost said "team", I think it must be that although we were all so very different we all shared a great scorn for topicality. Which shows the more or less hidden influence of Mallarmé. . . . That is the major difference between us and the leaders of the new generation, who judge a work in terms of its immediate effect. They seek immediate success, whereas we

---

*Bertrand Poirot-Delpech: critic and major columnist on *Le Monde des Livres*. André Fontaine: editor-in-chief of *Le Monde*. Max Gallo: historian and journalist, contributing to many newspapers.

thought it quite normal to remain unknown, unappreciated and despised until we were at least forty five. We put our hopes in duration, our sole concern being to produce a work that would last'.[35] Gide's fears again fixed a date—twenty years ahead. *Les Mots* and *La Chute* are adequate proof that topicality was not the ultimate horizon of the 'leaders' of 1948. They were two generations removed from the leader of the NRF, but they were still haunted by the same (puritanical?) notion of redemption through a message in a bottle and of the ephemeral as original sin. The break is between their endurance and our living for the moment, infantilized as we are by the false telepresence of a planet reduced to the size of a speck. Our ability to see the world from our living-rooms condemns us to inaction and the eternity of the moment, a privilege reserved for rogues, children and poets. There are few poets among us, and we have grown up. Camus's prophecy is coming true before our very eyes: 'If nothing lasts, nothing is justifiable'. And if nothing is justifiable, everything is permissible.

When the event deposes the work, the 'journalist' trumps the 'author'. The writers' monarchy could resist the horrors and squalls of the secular world so long as a certain idea of permanence prevailed and contingent history was less important than the meaning it sheltered and which outlived it. Dos Passos, Hemingway, Malraux, Vaillant, Cendrars: those writers of the first half of the century (which, given the famous fifteen-year time, lag takes us up to the sixties) who were most involved in Adventure pursued the event or the exotic only so that they could X-ray it and see the hidden sicknesses of man against the light. They were looking for myths and values on this side of all the violence—or beyond it, not that it matters greatly here. *L'Espoir* is a metaphysical report because in 1936, every man was, whether he knew it or not, fighting in the Spanish Civil War, simply because he was a man. They 'covered current events', not so as to discover themselves, but so as to track down what linked this 'me' with all others: there was a certain narcissism about these disaster hounds, but it was an ethical narcissism; poor journalism, but true literature. But journalism can only be itself against the backdrop of eternity, when, because of its accuracy and humility, observation becomes a poem once more. The witness who disappears behind his testimony makes its contingency disappear too: such is the paradox and the reward of those who are modest but observant.

[35] André Gide, *Journal*, Pléiade II, p. 322 (19 January 1948).

Twenty years. As it clouds over, the crystal ball of history shatters into current events; the crumbling of meaning gives off a dust of events and 'sensations' that owe their value not to their power of revelation but to the way they are staged and to their percussive force. The mythological rout of European Communism, which began with Khruschev's report, undid things that had until then been united: the intellectuals and the party, forms and forces, the written word and the lived experience. It reshuffled the cards of time; now, it is always now. Goodbye memory—if the present can do without memories, why should the future burden itself with a past? History ebbs and becomes an instant, the days wash each other away on the sands. When signification crumbles away, all that is left is 'news'. And news is the concern of newspapers. Information becomes its own horizon. No more coding, no more code-breakers; we record, shoot and take notes, full stop. Those who laboriously chiselled away at meaning, who worked with ciphers and secrets, are giving way to the lay-out artists, the curators of archives to the manufacturers of surprises. If there is no more to the event than what is on the teleprinter, what is the point of maniac cryptologists who translate the event into a work of art? Our brother paper, who hovereth just above the ground, give us each day our daily news and thy will be done on earth as it is in heaven; thy kingdom of nonsense come each day.

Let there be no misunderstanding. The cycle opened by the media does not announce the apotheosis of journalism, but rather its decadence. The mediocracy is not to be confused with the reign of professional journalists; first and foremost it means that they are crushed, so alien is the logic of the mass media to the process of uncovering the immediate real. The activity of the journalist represents the height of that intellectual function whereby the human mind accedes to what Hegel calls the dignity of effective reality by gradually rising from the abstract to the concrete, from the indeterminate to the singular, from the hollow to the full. A journalist does not 'betray' anything by becoming a journalist—he is realizing his essence by displaying an intelligence too demanding to be satisfied with rhetorical generalities and programmatic apriorism. It is no accident that the 'great intellectuals' who laid the foundations of the contemporary revolutionary movement—Marx, Engels, Lenin, Luxemburg, Gramsci—were not professors, but *journalists*, perhaps the best of their day, and were in direct contact with reality. Analysis of the concept and the practices corresponding to the term 'mass media' will one day reveal the radical heterogeneity of the universes in question, or at least it is to be hoped so.

To our eyes Albert Londres and Friedrich Engels, Kessel and Gramsci belong within the same space in civilization. All of them organized their existences around a common hypothesis that the new idealist technologies are inverting, namely that the real exists independently of anything I say about it, know about it or believe about it, independently of the titles I give it, the images I show of it and the commentaries I make on it. The category of the 'real' is no more than that 'independently of', but that is enough to establish the eminence of the journalist as of right, because it has as its corollary that it is always worth going there to see for yourself, with your own eyes. 'There' could mean a far-off country, a scientific domain, a nearby factory, a political regime, the place where a car crash happened, a prison cell, a salon, a file, a statistic, a porter's lodge, a village in Vietnam, a minister in Paris, a book in a foreign language—in a word, any object corresponding to some current topic, the very thing there is something to say about. But if we turn to the intellectual hierarchies of the land, we note the lack of consideration generally enjoyed by those who deal with the real and, in the media in particular, by the investigators and the journalists. The very basis of journalism is the dregs of the media. The 'thing itself' is never honoured in France; fine words get all the praise. Americanized, but ashamed of it, the heights of France, unlike those of North America, are not the paradise of journalism but its purgatory. Satellites take the worst from the metropolis and leave the best. The national 'news' has taken the management, the format, the laconic tone, and the glossiness, but forgotten the content: the accuracy, the feel for detail, the respect for the facts and disrespect for positions, the impudence and the stubbornness, that are quite rightly the pride of the wild adventurers of the American news. Falling between two stools, between America and the nineteenth century, trapped between his habits and his ambitions, the top French journalist has two strings to his bow, which he constantly gets tangled up and then trips over: the brilliance of his ideas and the materiality of events, commentary and summary, understanding motives and exposing facts. In the nineteenth century, Marx called France the land of ideas. The Atlantic world lives in the era of the scoop. Atlantic France has manufactured the ideological scoop. It teaches newsmen nothing, still less men of thought. But it satisfies a certain 'national intellectual personality' (and we have seen how much that owes to an educational system inherited from the nineteenth century and the values of scholastic excellence). The ability to speak brilliantly on a subject about which one knows virtually nothing derives from the bitter farce of the all-surface gymnastics (of scholastic descent) that Levi-Strauss describes at the beginning of *Tristes Tropiques*.[36] Even today, the French character is more inclined to judge rather than to look and prizes moralistic appreciation above concrete analysis. We have never seen so many triumphant ideologisms as since the officially proclaimed end of ideology. Which is why the leader writer has spontaneously taken the place of the publicist of the nineteenth century at the pinnacle of the journalistic hierarchy. He is the moralist of the news and his function, as everyone admits, is to enlighten his readers not about the ins and outs of a question, but about the position he personally chooses to take up on something or other. The man-who-is-supposed-to-know no longer needs to know, or rather he needs not to know, as vagueness about the factual enhances the glitter of the Idea and the style. This elevation of thought, adapted to a country with average resources, is proposed as a model for neophytes from below, all the more so because a good leader writer saves money. Field trips, travel, accommodation, checking information and researching documents all cost more and more—time and money—and bring in less and less—public aura and consideration from colleagues. So the reporters stay in their offices, investigating over the telephone and sending the researcher to go through the agency files. No wonder they're rarely in a good mood. Relate, describe, check, go over: no room, no interest and, above all, no *time*. Verbalizing, stigmatizing, congratulating, concluding: reserved for those upstairs. The outcome is that those who know least write the articles and those who know a little more stay silent. Articles are 'well brought up' and silences are not heard. We will have to come back in more detail to the objective laws that increasingly subject journalists themselves to a rigorous and aberrant logic, but it should already be clear that the term 'journalism' does not refer here to the intrinsic reality of a trade, but to the objective distortion of a status.

The coronation of the 'event' (and the consecration of all those in a position to manufacture it) was not, of course, an event. It was too decisive to be noticed immediately, too pregnant for its true relief to be noticed. It did not just take place one fine day, and any attempt to date it would mean forcing things. The critical threshold of the mutation does, however, appear to have been reached in or about '68. When history is voided, the event becomes master. Is it not somewhat paradoxical to trace the origin of

[36] See Pierre Bourdieu, 'Systèmes d'enseignement et système de pensée', *Revue internationale des sciences sociales*, XIX, 3, 1967, and Claude Lévi-Strauss, *Tristes Tropiques*, London 1970.

its reign to the fullest moment in recent French history? In May '68, the media *made* history 'live' for the first time ever; the fate of the country was decided on the radio and acted out on TV; the journalist, who was already distributing the prizes, turned king-maker: who made you a king? who made you a prince? Why not? The producers of material commodities are on strike; the political machine has broken down: someone has to step in and occupy the ground. The inrush of air brought to the fore those best qualified to go on the air. The masters of the air and those who wrote the headlines dethroned the masters of language and those who wrote the lectures. The Tarpeian Rock was not far from the Capitol. The only reason Sartre could triumph in the Sorbonne was that both Sartre and the Sorbonne were about to be cast down. In '68, the play was performed backwards, and afterwards the actors in the intellectual revolt (not all of them of course) started their careers backwards. They began by struggling against the 'corrupt media' in the name of the oppressed; they are now collaborating with the media to corrupt the struggle. Against all despotisms in the name of knowledge—they now constantly say that all knowledge is despotic. In the name of truth, against censorship; but they are as good as the next man with the scissors and the extinguisher. You see and hear them all over the state. In a word, they have won, but no one can rule innocently, least of all the mediocrats. The new lords of the news talk morals, not politics; but don't the means their lordships use—the media— destroy all intellectual morality?, some grouch asks. The brave reply that the old ethic is faltering because a new *ethos* is taking shape.

In any case, May '68 is the point at which an observer with retrospective binoculars cries: 'Nothing in intellectual society will ever be the same again'. In '36, Gide talked to Marceau Pivert* in the street; it was Gide who was news. When Aragon had a debate with Cohn-Bendit in '68, it was Cohn-Bendit who was news. A permutation of accents: the news goes to whoever is new, just as fame comes to the famous and money to the rich. The news was now the authority and it was driving out seniority. Henceforth, it would force itself on us as the only *valid point of view* on the old. The break-up of the university—a joyful and healthy explosion, but those who should have benefited from it were its first victims—helped to displace the centre of ideological gravity and psychological interest of young intellectual producers towards the media; it is as though they had sawed through the branch their social identity was sitting on. After '68 the university world and its like saw the appearance of a social type hitherto

* Marceau Pivert: leader of the leftist 'Gauche révolutionnaire' tendency within the SFIO.

known only in literary milieux: the *theoretical ghost*. Worse-treated, more ridiculed and less well paid than the literary ghost, he has to produce ideas (as a collective worker, but one who has no union rights) and pass them on to his superiors—the big names of research—who will rapidly feed them into the mass-mediatic network, *ipso facto* increasing their fame and therefore their credits and authority, their potential number of ghosts, colloquia, seminars, theses, research, working notes, trips, missions, translations and the rest. Every month these channels pour out a fabulous wealth of raw material for those who have the practical means to transform it into finished and readily negotiable products (articles, books, interviews) because they are close to the sphere of the media, whose gangways and decision-making centres remain inaccessible to the intellectual workers at the base.

As for publishing, it was trying to catch up with journalism at all costs, inventing the instant book, the poster-book, the tract-book, in a word, the book-as-event. The publishers wanted to be topical; they aped topicality by amplifying it and eventually frightened it off by chasing after it so much. It was a question of who could capture the feel of the times; in every publishing house a strong press relations department appeared in all its glory and soon became the main axis for the company and a strategic screen for the authors.[37] The first press officers in the world of books seem to have appeared in the early sixties (or slightly earlier in the case of Julliard) and the *Association des attachés de presse de l'édition* was duly and officially set up in 1971 (their status was defined by a decree from the Ministry for Information in 1964 which referred to 'the professions of public relations adviser and press attaché'). In late 1968, INSEE therefore adapted the relevant categories: advertising specialists were listed under the 'intellectual professions' in the new *Code des Métiers*. They were still there in 1975 and are unlikely to move. The middle-men—logically linked with the information apparatus—are the social stratum that has grown most rapidly since 1968: 'Middle-men in *animation*,* (130,000 *animateurs de formation*, a category introduced in 1975), in the press (sub-editors and journalists), public relations (press officer), decoration (designers, advertising executives, window dressers, set designers, interior designers) and advertising (heads of media studies, copywriters). All these profes-

---

[37] See Geng, *L'Illustre Inconnu*.

* *Animation, animateurs*: the terms are applied to a wide range of activities, from leading a debate to 'youth and community work'. *Animateurs de formation* are employed in adult education, retraining schemes and in-service training.

sions are growing very rapidly; the number of middle-men in the press and in public relations has risen from 17,000 to 23,000 in 1975. But it is the rise in advertising specialists that has been most spectacular: there were 5,000 of them in 1968 and 12,000 in 1975. When the *Code* was drawn up, these various intellectual professions were not well represented and the fact that they were classified together with teachers was not very significant. But now that they are classified together with comparable professions like the buyers mentioned above, it becomes more obvious that the number of teachers is remaining stable, the post-war bulge over, while the number of people in advertising is rising rapidly as a result of the extension of commercial and advertising services.'[38]

In 1975, the category 'journalist' was once more included in that of 'men of letters', from which it had been removed in 1954. It is obviously not easy to interpret the changes in INSEE's nomenclature, but they are not neutral; they may not look important, but they are a concentrate of the mood of the times and they are not without a certain malice. In their own way, they illustrate the chess game of hierarchical places: when one piece moves, the relative positions of all the other pieces on the board are changed. The permutations of the various elements of intellectual society is never mechanical (move over so that I can move in), but organic (all change at once). The synchronization of the moves may make each of piece think that nothing is moving, but that is an optical illusion.

To sum up: in the period opened up by May '68, two phenomena appear at the same time and each conflagration served as the other's detonator: 1. the distributors of thought become separated from the producers; 2. the distributors now determined not only the volume but the nature of production. The maximal separation between the producers and the distributors corresponds to the maximal subordination of the former to the latter. Hence the dialectical pirouette at the end of the assembly line: if the distributors are masters of the thoughts of others, why should they not distribute their own 'thought'? The two instances are finally merging, to the advantage of the more commercial of the two. Those who show us the world are only going to show us their own world vision, and it will come to be the final truth of this world. Gicquel and Zitrone*—the most widely seen and heard men in France—are in a position to thrust their own

---

[38] Laurent Thévenot, 'Les Catégories sociales en 1975: l'extension du salaiat', *Economie et Statistique*, juillet–août 1977.

* Roger Gicquel: presenter of the ten o'clock news on TV. Léon Zitrone: prominent news reporter on TF 1.

peculiar notion of the French character at us as a general theory. In the meantime, the latest 'new' school (the new romantics) is already announcing the game of the future: the new leaders of schools are chosen solely on the basis of and in accordance with their mediatic legitimacy. One has a widely-heard radio programme, another has a news programme and the third a weekly circus. Cultural production is becoming a tautological reduplication of its distribution.

What is giving way, almost without our realizing it, is, perhaps, a system of thought in which information could inform its supports rather than the reverse; a cultural technology in which the needs of production could still, at certain privileged points in the system, have the upper hand over the imperatives of distribution. One wonders what vectors the variety of positions, sensibilities and profiles, which made earlier periods so luxurious, will find to support it and what territorial sovereignty it will attach itself to. How will the richness of the old messages resist the homogenization of supports, which aligns the content of thought with the demands of a single market? The mutation may be the corollary of a global economic restructuring in the advanced industrial countries, where the sphere of circulation is becoming increasingly important and is turning the sphere of material production into its satellite. But the nature of what is at stake introduces a comic note, so great is the *contradictio in terminis* between the principle of individuation, which is basic to the 'creations of the mind', and the principle of profitability, which is basic to industrial production; between the principle of information, which is differential, and the principle of the information market, which is identity. The permutation of instances within the intellectual corps has done more than simply invert the relation of forces between the review and the magazine, books and the press, 'writers' and 'journalists' (there is a delightful sketch of this in an unpublished and privately-circulated article by Gilles Deleuze[39]). The new social supremacy of the distributors over the

[39] 'Journalism, along with radio and TV, has become increasingly aware of its ability to create events (controlled leaks, Watergate, public opinion polls?). Since it needs to refer less and less to external events (because it can create so many of them), or to people like 'intellectuals' or 'writers', journalism has discovered an autonomous and adequate thought within itself. Which is why, ultimately, a book is worth less than a newspaper article on it or the interview it gives rise to. This is a new type of thought: interview-thought, conversation-thought, instant thought. One can almost imagine a book on a newspaper article rather than the other way around. The relation of forces between journalists and writers has changed completely. It all started with the TV and the interviewers making consenting intellectuals go through their paces. Newspapers no longer need books. I'm not saying that this reversal, this domestication or 'journalization' of the intellectual is a catastrophe. That's simply the way it

producers translates the constraints inherent in distribution into cultural programmes. As those constraints are the same for all in a given place and time, the uniformity of the channels will eventually absorb the multiplicity of the forces to be channelled. Thought has always been a matter of extremes. The mediocracy is, by its very nature, centripetal, since maximum profitability is to be found in the centre. France not only wants to be *governed* from the centre, it wants to be *thought* from the centre, to be debrained in accordance with the lowest common denominator, which allows the distributors to add up all their potential audiences and make off with the licence fees, budgets and clienteles. The mediocrat is overjoyed when he can simultaneously put left and right out of action—that is the guarantee slip that certifies him not only to be in line with sound reason and human nature but also to be on his top industrial form.[40] The philosophical and political comedy of Human Rights, which has been running for so long amongst the mediatized intellectuals—'we're all Human, aren't we?'—is probably only a curtain-raiser before the race for a guaranteed maximum audience and guaranteed credit in advance.

Perhaps we should invert the adage of classical Reason: truth is simple, error multiple. In her day, Simone de Beauvoir added: 'It's not surprising that the right professes pluralism.' The monism of the true idea is perhaps the ultimate truth of idealism: in which case, falsity ought to be scattered. But is it not in the theoretical that we find multiplicity? Perhaps it is of the essence of ideologies to be unique when they are dominant. In contrast, dominated ideologies appear to be scattered, refracted, proliferating, for many reasons, the most important, if not the most recent, being no doubt that their supports and means of transport are scattered, in no fit state, too expensive and therefore non-conformist and non-standardized. Media which have to work upwards, from lower to higher, are technically marked by heterogeneity, in accordance with their vocation of conveying the heterogeneous. Only those which work downwards can bundle themselves

---

is: at the very moment when writing and thought were abandoning the author-function and when creation no longer went via the author-function, it was taken over by radio, TV and journalism. Journalists have become the new authors and authors who want to go on being authors have to work through journalism or become their own journalists. A function which had fallen into disrepute has found a new modernity and a new conformism by changing its place and its object. It was this that made intellectual marketing firms possible.'

[40] From a four-page advertising leaflet for *Le Point* (1978): 1. *If you are looking for information from the left* (a sieve); 2. *If you are looking for information from the right* (a sieve); 3. *If you are looking for real information* (images of plenitude, five *Le Point* covers; 4. *Le Point, the weekly which owes no one anything.* Page 5 is missing: *Because is has nothing to say, it can say it to anyone.* This rhetoric is typical.

together (and probably have no alternative); their future lies in amalgam-
ation and it is their fate to be amorphous. Truth is multiple, error simple.
The mass media are a machine for producing simplicity by eliminating
complexity. In our societies, it is the right which enforces uniformity
whilst professing to do the opposite: pluralism may be its faith, but the
mass media are its practice. And, ultimately, its social being will determine
its political practice. Today, pluralism has changed sides, both in theory
and in practice. Mediologically, it is on the left.

'The public may believe that there are several papers, but there is really
only one newspaper', noted Balzac in 1840 as he left the little office run by
M. Havas, a former banker whom all the papers 'use as a source'. The joke
has become a reality, the witticism the death of all wit, both private and
public. It is a fact, both at the national level and throughout the wealthy
countries, and it is not simply a result of the world monopoly enjoyed by
four news agencies (UPI, AP, Reuters, AFP) who all copy each other, or of
the national monopoly of AFP, the former Havas, the source from which
the country's press takes 75 per cent of all the news it prints. What Balzac
could not foresee was the 'intellectual' consequences of his axiom one
hundred and fifty years later. Today's public may believe that there are
several intellectuals, but there is really only one. The matrix of the
mediatic system will print as many copies as are needed—only the mould
is original. Since there are no frontiers or customs posts between
L'Express, *Le Point* and *Le Nouvel Observateur* (or between *Newsweek* and
Time), between the three television channels or between *France-Inter*,
Europe 1 and *Luxembourg*—which allows freedom of movement between
them without any need for moral, aesthetic or political identity cards—
one can move from one to the other, by way of a third, (the Club does not
have that many members), from one political extreme to the other, without
ever for a moment feeling lost; one always finds the same round tables, the
same air-time, the same discourse, the same score of equidistance,
innovation and commotion, though the colour may vary a little; the same
supports, personifications and characters. One paper, one idiom, one Jack-
of-all-trades. But it is the Voice of the People in its various registers that
creates a collective Master who speaks with several voices.

Teaching Staff in Universities
1976–1977

	Disciplines						
	Letters and Human Sciences	Law and economics	Sciences	Medicine	Dentistry	Pharmacy	Total
Professor	554	538	767	806	—	163	2,828
Senior Lecturer	1,168	831*	2,445	2,220	—	322	7,436
Junior Lecturer	3,395	1,078	6,709	—	—	577	11,759
Head of Laboratory	—	—	—	1,138	—	—	1,138
Assistant	2,624	1,845	4,794	4,826	448	594	15,131
Professor Exceptional category	—	—	—	—	22	—	22
Grade 1	—	—	—	—	134	—	134
Grade 2	—	—	—	—	231	—	231
Language assistant	853	—	—	—	—	—	853
Total	9,044	4,292	14,715	8,990	835	1,656	39,532
Other teaching staff							2,373
Total							41,905

NB. These figures including staff teaching in Guyana (77) and Réunion (62).
* including 823 *agreges de droit*.

Three

The Logic of
Power

Morphology: Overview

From the air, today's intelligentsia stands out against the French countryside as a clearly-defined triangle—the university, publishing and the media, the area known as the intellectual milieu.[1] It is a *logical* area defining a certain class or set of beings with the same attributes: any individual who makes a living from at least one of these branches of activity may be said to be a member of the intelligentsia (the number of attributes is the measure of the internal hierarchies inherent in a class). It is a *social* area, characterized, apparently, by a certain community of interests, habits and idioms. And finally, it is a *territorial* area delineated by an urban perimeter in the heart of the capital (the fifth, sixth and seventh arrondissements) where the population density is highest. As everyone knows, the concentration is historically and materially determined by the surplus of intellectual plant in Paris, which has the most prestigious universities, as well as the best libraries and art galleries, the *grandes écoles* and the research centres (CNRS, Maison des Sciences de l'Homme, Ecole Pratique, Fondation Nationale des Sciences Politiques, and so on), the main publishing houses, with their respective dependencies (cultural reviews and periodicals): 300 of the 400 publishers in France have their registered offices in Paris. And, finally, all the important media with their peripheral annexes and circles: the weeklies, the big dailies, the radio (France Culture), the television. It is the same for ideas as for the manufacturers of ideas: there is no salvation outside Paris.

The intellectual milieu is an environment, in the sense given to the word by Vexkull and the ethologists. At first sight, this specific *Umwelt* has all the appearance of the bush, if not the jungle. But despite the disconcerting opacity, certain laws of order and regular patterns in the professional, sexual, feeding and martial activities of the species soon become apparent

[1] See Claude Sales, 'L'Intelligentsia', *Le Monde de L'Education*, February 1977.

to an observer armed with a little patience and a pair of binoculars, as do its daily and seasonal rhythms and the routes it takes to go to its watering places. For display purposes, it has been noted (for example), the predominantly academic branch tends to frequent the *Balzar*, the journalistic branch the *Lipp*, the publishing branch the *Closerie des Lilas* and all frequent the *Coupole*. The bars and public places used for fighting, predation and mutual exploitation are close to the family habitat: the Gallimard branch controls the *Pont Royal* bar, Grasset *Le Twickenham*, Le Seuil *Le Pré aux clercs*, and so on. Display and predation culminate in the lunch, when the contract is discussed, the programme, article or review prepared, and the title and layout negotiated between copious draughts: this is an indispensable rite which also has its settings, its protocols, its longueurs and its high points (all strictly timed). If this gastrography, which gives a specific space a very subtle but definitely structured order, channels the most obvious aspects of the motor activity, the neuroendocrinal system is governed by temporal rhythms. Summer and winter correspond to a normal nerve tone, but autumn (September-October) and spring (March-April) are periods of stress: for these are the months when the product is publicly launched. On the weekly scale, the chronic appearance of strong reactions to high-intensity stimuli will be noted on Thursdays, when the weeklies are put to bed and *Le Monde des Livres* is published, and on Saturday mornings, when the three politico-cultural weeklies—the most important being *Le Nouvel Observateur*—go on sale. There is a strong discharge of adrenalin at 9.30 on Friday evenings, when most of the species are either in front of or on a luminous small screen. As for the daily rhythms, there is a general and pronounced tachycardia between 2.00 and 2.30 each afternoon, except on Sundays. Use of the computer has allowed a strong correlation to be drawn between the unusual tracing on the cardiograph and the appearance of *Le Monde* on the news-stands in the area under observation. Please excuse the summary nature of these studies in ethnophysiology; this is due mainly to lack of funding and the ageing of the laboratory, from which the researchers are the first to suffer.

Anatomy: Transverse Section

A transverse mediological section allows us to abandon the idea of a triangle, which is a platitude and therefore an illusion, and to replace it with the more adequate idea of a pyramid of levels. Three sedimentary strata overlap in the contemporary intelligentsia, three instances of legitimacy, three successive historical periods, each corresponding to a different mode of production/distribution. These different levels of organization are arranged in tiers under the dominance of the most modern, the most recent, which has the highest functionality and which therefore serves as an 'element' or 'atmosphere' for the other two. Increasingly, the organic stratum of the media supports, structures and promotes the formerly dominant strata, which are now dominated or subordinate. The intelligentsia of the late twentieth century is a social microformation in which several modes of production of differing ages and with various internal relations coexist under the hegemony of the most advanced, just as they did in the great historical societies of the late nineteenth century. And just as ideological institutions outlive the historical situations that gave birth to them, so each institutional level within the stratum of the ideologues lives on when it has been functionally relegated, by adapting itself to the demands of the level above, on which it depends for its survival. After all, the Catholic clergy has outlived the landed aristocracy and the Communist parties of the West the revolutionary industrial proletariat that gave birth to them. Mutatis mutandis, the university and publishing now exemplify this negotiated survival, bought on certain conditions from an instance that was once subordinate but is now dominant. In France, this ability to linger on, which is inherent in all institutions, has given us an intellectual corps at once uniform and composite, conservative and modernist, in which everything is still in place and nothing is what it was.

The cell is made in the image of the body. Just as each age of the intelligentsia contains within it the other two, but in a different hierarchical order, so every organic intellectual in a given period is a real *écorché* of hegemony, displaying the organs of influence accumulated over the past century like so many layers of sediment laid down in their order of appearance: the university, publishing, the media. Although he is a walking pyramid, today's big-wig claims to be simply one of many producers of texts, possessing nothing but his intellectual labour power and putting his copy on the market punctually once a year just like everyone else. Let us go beyond appearances. Our leading light is a tenured professor, a senior lecturer or a director of studies in a teaching or research centre; he is a literary adviser, the editor of one or more series, and a member of the readers' committee in a big publishing house; he is a journalist, critic or leader writer on a popular weekly or daily. He has a good old-fashioned spread of titles. And the new 'New whatever-they-are', those pariahs who are hounded by all the authorities, have been careful to add a regular debate at Beaubourg, an event at FNAC,* two or three TV programmes and as many radio slots. Times are hard; we're never persecuted enough. Be they big or little, these individual pyramids are all built to the same plan: legitimacy (knowledge) at the bottom and effectivity (making it known) at the top. The important thing is not the title or the diploma, but the ability to put it to work. The *cursus honorum* of university degrees gives me the right to speak, but it is a purely abstract and honorary right if I do not have the ability to make myself heard, in either the written press or, better still, its audio-visual equivalent. A mediatic position is, logically, the crowning glory of an intellectual career. That is what now maintains principalities and makes kings.

Feudal lords had their houses. Now mother companies have their subsidiaries. The old fiefs have become firms; the industrialization of the intellectual has preserved the prerogatives of intellectual feudalism. Every Intellectual Prince is a *Konzern* in himself, vertically integrating all the stages of the process of production, from publishing to distribution and promotion. He is more than a *cartel*, in that all the firms really are integrated, but less than a *trust*, as the organic intellectual often has difficulty in imposing any really unified management on his complementary activities (internal splits are common)—let us say, a *group* of companies represented by a single chairman and managing director, or a general-staff-cum-soldier. He has three officers, three secretaries and

* FNAC: large record and book shop in Paris; also used as a setting for cultural 'debates'.

three telephones, for the various moments of the day or the days of the week, three sources of income (salary, royalties, fees), three concentric spheres of influence integrated to produce a personal and material authority, and therefore an ideological and moral authority that is, to say the least, worthy of respect. The professor chairs the thesis jury, confers degrees, unblocks funds if need be, selects candidates for the posts that depend upon his, votes for or against coopting a colleague: this is the first circle. The series editor accepts or rejects manuscripts, gives orders, influences projects, decides (or suggests) advances, publication dates, print runs, the extent of the publicity, the advertising package, the number of display advertisements and where they are placed: the second circle. The journalist agrees or refuses to write up a friend's book or thesis (or asks the editor to let so-and-so do it instead), decides between a major article, a short report or a mere mention under 'books received', gauges as he sees fit the level of enthusiasm, respect or polite interest to be shown: this is the third circle which englobes the first two, in terms of both the audience it finds in the outside world and the chain of reactions it may or may not instigate for the beneficiaries within the milieu itself, at the publishing and the professional levels. Such a man accumulates both functions and clienteles. He has *his* pupils in the school or the laboratory. He has *his* authors in his stable or chapel. And to top it all off, he has *his* audience: readers, correspondents, those in his debt. He is a guardian three times over; he patronizes, supports and sweetens. If relations of order (transitivity, asymmetry, non-transitivity) define relations of power, this figure concentrates three of them under the hegemony of the most profitable, that of the media, where the asymmetry and the non-reciprocity between the sender and the receiver of messages are at their greatest. Fifty students can ask their teacher questions. Five hundred actual or potential authors can make complaints, either in writing or in person. A million listeners or ten million viewers can only receive: mass communication is a one-way process.

The social capital a high-ranking dignitary in his forties has accumulated gives him such capacity for mobilization, fire power and range of action that he is a *political and military power* to be reckoned with by friends and enemies alike. The heavy weaponry is not visible; it consists of purely non-material connections. The platform of cultural power rests upon commercial, industrial and institutional props whose tangible materiality usually escapes those they support. But anyone wishing to enter the hegemonic battlefield and to fight there on more or less equal terms needs those supports. It is already under siege and the occupying forces are so thick on the ground that he needs to be wearing good armour if he is to carve out a place for himself, or to win even a minimum of consideration, human respect or—and why not?—friendship from his neighbours and competitors. *Si vis pacem para bellum.* States do not take up arms for the sake of it, but to defend themselves against other states. In intellectual as in international relations, necessity rules. And in the last resort, even the heaviest expenditure on arms can be justified in terms of self-defence. The mediatic arms race between the great intellectual powers of the day may well have started with each of them recruiting a personal militia for the purposes of self-defence (the editorial board of a specialist journal, a publisher's reader, a freelance working for a provincial newspaper). But the stakes get higher all the time. If I do not occupy the commanding heights from which I can pound the enemy positions and cover my infantry as they advance, my own troops will come under heavy fire. I have to attack simply to protect my men and keep down my losses. And so I merge several journals into one, break through to the heights of a big daily and consolidate the freelance's precarious position by entrenching him as a leader writer, integrating him into a larger unit on a full-time basis. The ground on which the forces meet is never empty. It is, by its very nature, always already occupied and any attempt to establish a political and intellectual hegemony can therefore be made to look like resistance against an existing hegemony. Imperialism can be justified only if it can be seen as anti-imperialism. Put into practical application, this general rule is not without its comic side, as when on the current French ideological scene, the general staff who have taken control of the main lines of communication and of the very flow of communication can claim to be a pathetic handful of partisans, down to their last bullets and fighting bare-handed and backs to the wall against the heavy battalions of dogmatic-and-totalitarian-Marxism. They have convinced themselves of this, even though they would be hard pressed to find a sole survivor from those battalions who is still on active service and threatening the places where political power is seized, so heavily have they been bolted up by the heralds of the anti-power. Strategists are well aware of the fact that all successful offensives are launched as counter-offensives with purely defensive aims. Today general officers are all resistance fighters and surrender is subversion.

There is a political morality, but no one has ever transformed the law of the heart into civil legislation. Machiavelli does not contradict Kant; he speaks a different language. In order to translate from one to the other, one has to learn both languages and then learn not to confuse them. Intellectual society is slightly more political than most, and the social moralist a political animal like any other. There are good and bad intellectual policies, but there is no politics of good and evil. There are intellectuals of greater or lesser intellectual value, but no great intellectual fails to observe certain tactical rules in the expression of his thoughts and in relation to his peers. As a whole, these tactics do admit to a moral judgment, but they do not submit to it. Moral judgments apply to the judge as well as to the accused, and the behaviour of a social species does not derive from the 'laws of conscience', still less those of the civil code, but from the objective and constraining laws specific to a given field of activity.

Just as the high intelligentsia does not constitute a moral or immoral person, the individual integrity of its members is not a pertinent criterion for analysing their social strategy. There are some intellectuals of integrity—we have met some of them[2]—who, in the very heart of the high intelligentsia, use their military equipment equitably, decently and even altruistically. But that is scarcely relevent to our present concerns, which are descriptive and not normative. We are concerned here with the logistics of hegemony and not with its tactical or political uses. The question of transport and supplies is equally important for all the warriors of the sign, image or sound, be they on the right, the left or anywhere else. In industrial culture, the role of logistical services becomes as important as it already is to industrial warfare: that is, vital. In modern times, management cannot come ʼlast: it must precede the shock troops. Qualitatively and quantitatively, ideas count less than their vectors. From Machiavelli to Trotsky, there have always been two kinds of prophet in the West: the armed and the unarmed, the fortunate and the unfortunate. Today, weapons are the priority: prophecies can be invented later, as and when required. The man who sits in the corner polishing his intellectual missiles without first getting a gun is dead before he has even fought. He is either a madman or an idiot. An intellectual without media is no longer a general without troops, but a laughing stock.

[2] The distinction between the position and the person is the ABC of any political and intellectual moral philosophy. Without it, we would be in hell.

The curious thing, in these conditions, is the hegemonic experts' prickly intolerance of professional politicians. Given the virtues the intellectuals demand of the politicians, how many of them would have gained their present positions? All the political *savoir faire* in the world seems to have been granted to the French high intelligentsia—just think of the paradox that the very men who politicize everything they touch (from sexual life to art criticism) *ex professo* refuse to have anything to do with professional politics, even though one of its little failings draws all their sarcasms: the accumulation of municipal, departmental, national and European mandates. On the other hand, they have never been known to fight for incompatibility of titles within our own profession, where there are so many hats for so few heads. The inconsistency is logical in two ways. In the military logic of the old world, the balance of fear and mutual deterrents were the only practical equivalents to the impossible goal of general, controlled disarmament; one had first to join the club of the heavily armed to have the right to negotiate conditions for disarmament. The family circle is a planetary system in which gravitation balances out and in which everyone supports everyone else. 'Hasn't his authority become weighty of late: three editorial boards, a fourth collection published and regular work on the paper.' 'Yes, but we simply had to do something about so-and-so. At the rate things were going, we wouldn't have heard or seen anyone else.' The mechanism is timeless, but it is still too abstract to explain the new configurations of intellectual power *hic et nunc*. The logic of the New World lies in its economy: its servitudes affect the moralists as well as the generals.

3

Economy:
The Infrastructure

We should not be fooled by words; figures do not speculate. Nowadays, the cover price of a book (excluding tax) breaks down by professional groups as follows (and the proportions are unlikely to change in the near future): manufacturing costs (printing), 20%; production costs (publisher+author), 25%; distribution costs (distributor+retailer), 55%.[3] That simple analysis conceals a great economic complexity, and the complexities of the intellectual world conceal a very curious simplicity. The proportions themselves establish a hierarchical order, indicating both the average rate of profitability in the various firms grouped together in the *konzern* and the recommended rate of activity for each. The ideal ratio between investments in labour time and volume of energy for each author breaks down as follows: one quarter for producing manuscripts (work in the study at home), one quarter for office work at his employer's (editing, relations with other authors) and the remaining half for promotion and sales (promotion of the product and the producer). That half may be divided in varying proportions—which themselves do not really matter—between lunches, TV appearances, interviews, articles, round tables, polemics in the press, press statements, appeals to the nation, being photographed or filmed, televised arrests, manifestoes, disorderly behaviour in the street, and so on. All the data provided by empirical observation of 'intellectual life' confirms the conclusions reached by inductive reasoning. It is an objective fact that the mediatization of the product on the market is now more important than its production, and the diaries of the big companies operating in this sector reflect this permutation in the relations between distribution and production in the

---

[3] ASFODEL (Association nationale pour la formation et le perfectionnement professionels en librairie et papeterie), *Le métier de libraire*, Paris 1978, p. 28.

cultural industries. What is chonologically the last stage in the production process is logically the first; down is up, the strategic link is at the end of the chain. In concrete terms, and at the individual level, this means that articles about my book are more important than my book, that the adman in me has to take precedence over the writer. Creator, save yourself, be your own journalist. Any serious management stipulates: finish first. Be someone before you do anything. Get yourself talked about before you utter a single word. A good author takes care of the after-sales service *before* the work is done.

The restructuring of the intellectual corps has thus imitated that of industry. In the latter, marketing has become the key sector; in the former, the key sector is the media. This is especially so in the book sector (and the sector of the printed word in general), where the strategic site is no longer manufacturing or publishing, but distribution. You can set up as many publishing houses as you like (concentration at the top does not prevent small artisanal houses proliferating at the bottom or on the fringes), just as the citizens and printers of France can write as many manuscripts and print as many books as they like: he who laughs last laughs longest. There are almost 700 publishers, but four mother companies control half the book market. In publishing, as in creation, pluralism below is subject to the monopoly above. The publisher decides where to place the book, but it is the bookseller who decides how to turn it to good account at the point of sale. Bookshops are increasingly being pushed out by supermarkets controlled by the distributors, or reduced to being mere agents. It is the distributor and not the publisher (assuming they are not the same person) who negotiates discounts with the bookshops. Hachette and Presses de la Cité thus have every reason to be courted by publishers who, unlike the big four (Gallimard, Laffont, Le Seuil, Flammarion) do not have their own distributors, just as those who control the mediatic network are courted by the authors, all of whom depend upon them for their self-realization as authors in search of an audience, be they major or minor, sociologists, or novelists, buddhists or monarchists. If the fate of creation, like that of intellectual production (of books, records, cassettes and prints), lies in the hands of a diminishing number of decision makers, then both intellectuals and entrepreneurs need to be where the decisions are taken, physically and mentally. The publisher's criteria (for selecting manuscripts and allocating advances) have become those of his filters, just as the author's criteria have become those of the media, and for the same reasons. 'Sorry, my friend, your book just isn't up to it,' says the publisher to the author as he hands back his manuscript. 'True, my last book got no press coverage, but I'll be on target with the next one,' says the author. The publisher is not being cynical, and the author is not being opportunistic, or if they are they have every reason to be. Basically, both have suffered the same *diminutio capitis*, one *vis-à-vis* his·distributors, the other *vis-à-vis* the mediocrats. The revolution in distribution methods has turned publishing a book which sells with difficulty (or simply getting it stocked in a bookshop) into an act of philanthropy: the faster stock rotation, the cost of stockage and accounting, and the imperatives of circulation have a stranglehold on publishers and booksellers alike.[4] An author who is ignored by the media has become an economic disaster (for his publisher), a social disaster (for those around him) and a medical disaster (dyspepsia and coronaries). Having a book turned down by FNAC, which already accounts for one-third of the turnover in bookselling in Paris, will soon be disastrous for any publisher. Will FNAC, as some people fear, soon be in a position to make or break certain titles and certain names? Once, a publishing house could live off a backlist of titles that sold slowly over a period of years. Today, books that move slowly do not even cover the cost of the shelf-space they take up in the bookshop. 'It is said,' according to ASFODEL, 'that a title that is not reordered at least four times a year not only fails to make money; it costs money'. The publisher's profits depend on those of the bookseller. Since it is the backlist that costs most, and since everyone has to live, the only way to make a living is to pull off stunts, which are now the common practice (because in the common interest) of publisher, authors and booksellers alike: only the successes of the moment are profitable (unless of course you stick to dictionaries, cookery books and the Bible). As it becomes more and more concentrated, the book trade concentrates more and more on them and consequently forces the publisher to do the same— *and* the author, who lives on what the publisher gives him, or rather, gives him back, and, ultimately, the reader. For the publisher, the economic optimum means maximum sales, so discount supermarkets are ideal for him, as they claim to give the reader the widest possible choice at the lowest possible price. But thanks to a classic mechanism—clearly explained by Jérôme Lindon, incidentally—the monopolization of distribution ultimately and paradoxically leads to the narrowest possible choice at the highest possible price. Whether the prognosis is gloomy or

[4] See Jérôme Lindon, *La FNAC et les livres.*

not, there is no doubt as to the diagnosis of the phenomenon: concentration at the top—functional in the case of the managers of ideology, economic in the case of publishing companies—is the perverse effect of distribution on production. In any case, whilst the inevitability of industrial concentration is a fatal virus for small-scale artisanal production, it has stimulated the nerve tone of the intellectual world, which is both much less archaic than it might appear and very sensitive to the new. A hundred years from now, it will be apparent that the modest artisan-owners of late-twentieth-century literature were further ahead of their times than many employers in textiles or steel. By deserting the abbeys, seminars, cenacles and salons of the past and taking to programming and leading the FNAC debates, to take only one example, they have shown a very sure instinct in matters of industrial redeployment and competitiveness. A firm that draws a third of the clientele of Paris is one of those 'important nodal points in social communication' where cultural *animation* becomes a necessity. In a society where the circulation of commodities regulates communication between men, the acceleration in stock rotation determines the acceleration of modes of thought.

The rhythms of culture are as slow as the rhythms of nature: it takes a novel ten years to grow, a concept flowers after ten years of study; the rhythms of the commodity are becoming faster and faster and have caught them off balance, and the uncontrollable turmoil of the cycles of profit is having the same devastating effect on the landscape of culture as on the rivers and forests of a country. When distribution takes command of the economy, it transforms the producer into a commissioned labourer. There has never been any more demand for novelty in the artistic field than there has been a social demand for truth in the theoretical (religions and mythologies give more imaginary satisfaction, by definition). Literary or aesthetic innovation meets with hostility or indifference from its immediate audience, just as a scientific discovery is greeted with hostility or indifference by the priests and sorcerers of the day. If audience response is to be the measure of the nature of the questions artists, creators or philosophers can ask themselves and others, if the only form in which symbolic values can circulate is a commodity-form that gives immediate and therefore massive and punctual profits, then an entire civilization is swinging on its hinges, sacrificing innovation to safety, conquest to the protection of acquired values, the future to the past—and the living to the dead. In 1952, Beckett sold 125 copies of *Waiting for Godot* (Editions de

Minuit). If the profitability of a book is to be calculated over the first year—or the first three months to be more accurate—after its publication, all that will come out is worn-out things dressed up as something new. 'Newest' does not always mean 'most profitable', and the book trade has its steady earners. There is, of course, no mechanical correspondence between real best sellers and the extent of public acclamation. Quite apart from the mass media's box-offices of scarcity, there are fixed readerships and monopoly markets. Druon, Cesbron, Pauwels and Des Cars represent reliable product lines that are unaffected by conjunctural market fluctuations, and it is mainly in the middle ground of 'ideological' production (mid-way between truth and fiction, the imaginative and the scientific) that mediatic arbitration comes into play and separates the 'dated' from the 'innovatory', the 'archaic' from the 'modern', the chaff from the wheat. The problem is that, because of a law whose effects are well-known in the public domain, the authentically new is always late in arriving, and if big business is to set the norms for small-scale literary production, there will soon be no literature except in schools (so long as there are still schools), no catalogues except in the libraries (so long as . . .). 'It has to be said that most titles in the list of any major publisher of general literature sell no more than three copies a year world-wide . . . it does not make any difference if it is Faulkner, Georges Bataille, Valéry or Conrad' (Lindon). Just as surely as free economic competition eventually suppresses competition, the commercial imperative for novelty eventually leads to the mechanical repetition of the old, as we have seen over the last few years in the French ideological market, where every leap backwards in the exhumation of ancestors is presented as a step forward in the seasonal invention of something new.[5]

Let's be quite clear about this: there is never any *incipit*, either in the life of a people or the life of a person, and a culture is a slow weaving of renewals. The new intervenes in history only through the repetition of the

[5] Here is an example of these leaps backwards in 'political thought'. 1976: the right thunders that 'Marx is dead' (for the fourth time since his physical death) and that the 'new philosophy' has discovered the productions (themes and styles) of the 'non-conformists of the thirties'. 1977: under the label 'a new political culture', the left invents an equation that was banal in 1910: (Sorel + Péguy) ÷ Proudhon as a reply and alternative to Leninist 'barbarism'. 1978: Clavel and his friends hit the headlines every week with anathemas and sarcasms from Bonald and Joseph de Maistre, whose fears of the French Revolution, abstract Reason and the Terror become the latest fashion of the 'intellectual' avant-garde in France. The hurricane of the eighties will probably be 'empiricism as organizer'—Maurras has been forgotten so far.

old: both Marx and Nietzsche have, in their different ways, established this as a definitive law. But a culture involutes when the repetitions cease to be cumulative and become regressive through successive impoverishments. For some time now, the French cultural spectacle has been host to the alarming scene of a retrograde sequence of unwitting pastiches. Given the imperatives of commerce, one might accept their claims to be innovatory, but not their bowdlerization of the originals, or that they set our present back from our past. Repetitions are liberating when they are experienced as such and know themselves for what they are; every revolution in the western world has aped its predecessor, but it would have been no more than its ghost had it not known it was doing so. What is worrying about our annual ideological revolutions is that they do not reveal their sources, through carelessness rather than design. Hence the mixture of fury and marking-time in the articulation and the feeling of prophetic *déjà vu* in the statements. This is not plagiarism, but the clumsy exploitation of a lucrative seam: the lack of historical culture and the ideological amnesia that have come to characterize the society of the ideologues thanks to the reign of the topical. Far from lessening their importance or hindering their work, the increasing illiteracy of the dominant society facilitates and valorizes the work of its intellectuals by constantly lowering the level of qualifications. An ideologue who, thirty years ago, would have looked somewhat dated in the eyes of his fellows now looks like an innovator to the general public. Having had to abdicate before public opinion and having been dispossessed of its institutional means of existence, the old community simply no longer has a say in the matter, unless it buys its survival by joining the choir of the mediocrats.

In culture, spontaneous attraction to the side of the new is the act of a shopkeeper, not an innovator. In politics, spontaneous adhesion to the side of the majority is the act of a collaborator, not a democrat. Just as in history, it is the resistance and the minorities—and sometimes even the terrorists—who reinvent democracy, so each spring sees the dustbins filling up with the winter's best sellers and the autumn's latest fads. What is called public taste is what those men of taste who are the arbiters of the moment force upon us as natural, just as the 'public opinion' of the polls is an artefact constructed by the pollsters, where the answer given by those polled is already present in the question. Whilst those who resist the culture of their day are the very people who advance it, the new economy of cultural production gives conformism, preferably disguised as dissidence, an incomparable position and weapons without compare. Everything from the technical conditions of distribution to the conditioning of the public by advertising is programmed for immediate recognition at the lowest possible cost. It is a golden age for the intelligentsia—every intellectual relies on being recognized by the rest—and an iron age for creation; the mark of the masterpiece is that contemporaries fail to recognize it. Prognosis: products will proliferate and works will disappear. It is the eternal dilemma of having to choose between being someone and doing something. It is going to become more difficult to choose import rather than importance, non-recognition rather than cash payment for recognition. We know that the 'someones' of a given period never coincide with the 'something', but how are we to keep our distance from the times? It was not the great writers of the early part of the century, the Popes and Princes of Youth—an Anatole France, a Paul Bourget, a Maurice Barrès—who refashioned the literary field of their day, nor the great scientists with their titles and chairs who refashioned its discursive field. A list of the misunderstandings whereby the great scribbles of a period are mistaken for its great writing (or its ideology for its theory) would be both interminable and hilarious. What future Martian will be able to escape the classic optical illusion of contemporaneity that makes dwarfs look like giants and vice versa? And what if there is being set up before our very eyes an economy of misunderstandings and an optics of oversights . . .

4

New Scarcity, New Power

Europe today is suffering symbolic famine and cultural force-feeding. Far from being paradoxical, this situation confirms a rule with which all historians are familiar: periods of decadence are always plethoric. When the value of values collapses, values multiply, and the proliferation of cells bodes ill for an already mature organism. The devaluation of meaning corresponds to the inflation of signs, the devaluation of representation to the over-abundance of spectacles. The crisis in the theatre, the cinema or painting that we hear so much about—and rightly so—has never meant that there were not enough plays, films or paintings to satisfy public demand—on the contrary. But here we are concerned only with books.

'The wealth of societies ruled by the capitalist mode of production can be seen in their immense accumulation of commodities'—and it is even more conspicuous to those from societies that do not have them. Finding yourself on the streets of Paris after having been in a third- or fourth-world country is a shock bordering on panic. In the proliferation of objects, the printed word stands out: papers, periodicals, magazines and books. The window displays make you dizzy: a forest of titles, the splendour of the jackets, the wrappers wink at you. And everywhere you hear the groans of professionals begging for mercy—victims who were supposed to be beneficiaries. Booksellers are collapsing under the burden of their duties, publishers beneath the weight of manuscripts, newspapers beneath the weight of requests from authors in print, critics under the weight of the day's review copies, the literary juries under the weight of the autumn novels, the window dressers under the piles of books, and readers under an endless avalanche of writing. Literary Paris is no longer a feast, it is a fair—Gutenberg with a hangover.

The number of titles has, then, doubled over the last twenty years,

Number of titles registered by publishers[6]	1962	1969	1970	1976
New titles	6,019	9,464	10,924	10,729
Reprints	6,603	10,370	9,241	11,310
Total	12,622	19,384	21,571	23,363

although it levelled out somewhat in 1970.[7] The numbers had remained stable for the previous hundred years, after the upturn brought about by mass education and industrialization. In Balzac's day, just under 5,000 works were published in the kingdom each year; 8,000 under the Empire (1856); more than 14,000 under the Republic (1889), a level which, with some variations, remained constant until half-way through our century. In terms of numbers of copies, production has risen from 180 million to 325 million in 1976, and turnover in publishing has quadrupled over the same period. The total backlist of French publishing now includes 220,000 titles in print. The figures must, of course, be examined carefully and adjusted in space and time in accordance with their various categories.[8] The 'general literature' category (excluding the paperbacks and thrillers normally included in it) represents a stable level of production, but it is proportionally the largest category, both in terms of the number of titles (an average of 4,500) and in terms of copies (35 million) and turnover. Within this sector, the rise in books on history and current affairs compensates for a slight fall in 'belles lettres' (novels, poetry, plays, literary criticism and essays). But between them the categories of 'literature' (thanks to the print runs for the prizewinners) and 'encyclopedias and dictionaries' still account for almost half of all turnover in publishing (45% in 1976). In terms of percentage of turnover, handbooks

[6] ASFODEL, *Le Métier de libraire*, p. 20.

[7] In comparison, the UN Statistical Yearbook (1976) gives the following figures: USSR—80, 196 titles in 1973; USA—83,724; Great Britain—35,177; West Germany—48,034. The figure given for France is 26,247 in 1974. The figures are swollen by the imprecise nature of the criteria which in some cases distinguish between books and brochures, commercial and non-commercial publishing, but sometimes not.

[8] SNE statistics divide books into the following categories: text-books; scientific; professional and technical; human sciences; literature; encyclopedias and dictionaries; fine arts; childrens' books; handbooks.

have come third since 1975. That is a sign of the times; before then it was text-books.[9]

Could it be that French society is producing more books than readers each year? Don't worry, 'France is starting to read'. A headline in a weekly unhesitatingly puts its faith in a survey carried out between September 25 and October 6, 1975', using a national sample of 2,000 people representing a cross-section of the population over the age of 18. 'The conclusion is final, surprising, even amazing; the number of people in France who read has risen by 15%.'[10] Since when, which people, and what are they reading? A young executive in a hurry has no time to bother with such minor details. Even if the figures—which cannot be checked—are taken at face value, the implication is that over a period of twenty years, the production of books has risen ten times faster than the number of people who read books. Whether or not the 1960 survey carried out on behalf of the publishers, and showing that 53% of the population of France never read books, has or has not to be corrected downwards does not alter the basic fact that a mere quarter of the population of France—the 22% (1960 and 1978) who 'read a lot'—absorbs most of French book production. The national capacity for intellectual production has risen (thanks to the democratization of education, extended leisure and cultural activities, adult education, the bad company adults keep, the titillations of the environment) at a very different rate from the capacity for consumption, to which there are natural and social limits. Given that they are not all philanthropists, however, publishers would not have increased production without a market outlet. What has changed over the last twenty years is therefore not only the volume, but also the internal balance of the market. A relatively stable number of readers is buying a greater number of books, which in fact means that more copies of fewer books and fewer copies of more titles are being bought. Increasingly, writers are being read by other writers (if they are not best-sellers): there is a tendency towards a

[9] These figures make sense only if they are viewed from a certain distance, and it should not be forgotten that the overviews and false extrapolations that the specialist institutes make each week on behalf of the media are based upon a cavalier view of statistics, which reduces them to perfectly abstract results by separating them from the processes whereby they are established.

[10] *L'Express*, 11 November 1978, p. 152. 'Investigation by Janick Jossin, survey by Louis Harris' was splashed across the front cover. The magazine is overjoyed that only 43% of the population of France does not read. A SOFFRES survey carried out in 1972 put the number of people in France who do not read books at 41%. Are we to conclude that France stopped reading between 1972 and 1978?

superimposition of readers and writers. As practical activities, the drama of reading and that of writing are mutually exclusive. It is physically and mentally impossible to read and write at the same time. Writers are the last people to be able to read other writers, but if they do start reading each other, they are no longer writers; the aporia sums up the neurotic relationship between every writer and his friends in the trade. He expects them to criticize, appreciate and encourage him . . . who else can do it? But they in turn expect him to do the same for their latest book—which I have had neither time nor energy to read because I am busy writing my own. This farcical vicious circle leads to an unfortunate confusion amongst the members of the brotherhood. Friendship between writers is impossible—as it is between intellectuals, but for different reasons. Peers do not form couples. When a professional seducer meets a professional seductress, anything can happen between them, but not love.

When publishing statistics put the average total print run of all books at 15,000 and the average print run for a book in the 'literature' category at 8,000, they display the same comic seriousness (or vice versa) as the UN Statistical Yearbook when it assesses per capita income in Columbia at $515 (1975) or that of India at $136, the difference being that the gulf between the highest and lowest per capita income is a permanent feature of Columbian and Indian society, but has not always been a feature of French literary society, where the gap between rich and poor widens every year. In the world of books, as in the world at large, the strong are getting stronger and the weak weaker. Inequality, that accursed younger sister of liberalism, is growing all the time. As a modest publisher recently put it, 'the annoying thing is that books which used to sell fairly well are being squeezed out' (J.C. Fasquelle). We are all agreed that it is even more annoying for the writers than for the publishers. The distribution curves for printed matter are like an inverted Gauss jar; the convex has become concave, with a dip in the middle and a bulge at either end. Publishing now runs on best-sellers. Companies spread their risks by publishing lots of authors, one of whom will have huge sales and nine of whom will not sell at all. Everything in between is disappearing—the huge spread that once (and particularly between the wars) included all those that sold 3,000 to 10,000 copies and everything that mattered in terms of essays and literature. For a long time, our finest flowerings and our long-term classics were in this honourable middle category. Now everything is either a best seller or a flop. Such is the effect of the homogenization of a branch of production subject to the laws of distribution. Why? Because the selection made by the media in aesthetic and ideological production is brutal, final and directed towards a mass audience, and because *there is no middle way in the sphere of the media*, where the law of all or nothing works without any feel for detail or subtle distinctions. It is a strange fate for an intellectual work to have to choose between 'selling very well' and dying as soon as it is born. To be more accurate, it either takes off and snowballs—it is talked about because it is talked about because it is talked about and so on; the medium comes to the medium, just as fame comes to the famous and money to the rich—or nothing happens. The simple reason is that unlike Buffon's Nature, which does everything by degrees, or Constant's Truth, which lies always in nuances, the media know nothing of graduations (positive or negative). Competition leads to uniformity, not diversity. When an author is 'in' *L'Express*, he is almost certain to be 'in' *L'Observateur* and *Le Point* too, for the other of the media is itself: *L'Express*'s only horizon is *L'Observateur*, and vice versa. For the media, the objective world—the thing there is something to speak of—is what the other media are saying. Be it hell or heaven, from now on we are going to have to live in this haunted hall where mirrors reflect mirrors and shadows chase shadows. Here we see the perverse effect that mediatic dominance has on the media themselves. Slaves to their own mastery, they involute and become totally wrapped up in themselves: they implode. In the previous age, it was normal for a journalist to hear his editor-in-chief say 'Hey, you should do something on that; it's interesting and no one has mentioned it.' Now, the same journalist suggests a piece on 'something' that has not been covered and the editor says 'No, it's not interesting. No one's talking about it.' Or 'Wait and see what happens.' Any mediological fault turns the old world upside down, without even seeming to touch it. 'How to orchestrate unison and vary the tone at the same time': this remarkable treatise on harmony has everyone dancing to the same tune on the same dance floor, and leads them from affair to polemic, the programme of the week to the revelation of the day, by way of the book of the month and the man of the year, under the baton of a conductor who left the platform a long time ago. It plays all by itself, out of inertia. Those who are too proud to join the dance are in the same position as those who have to 'watch the draw in a lottery for which they do not have tickets' (Chamfort).

Aside from the probabilities, one thing is certain: in French society, where twice as many books are being produced as twenty years ago, only half as many newspapers are being printed.[11] Ideological-cultural production is flourishing, but the organs of criticism and diffusion are disappearing. There is more and more to go through the funnel, but its mouth is getting narrower and narrower. Hence the functional hypertrophy of middle-men. Whether the producers work well or at a loss depends on whether they put the funnel in the right place at the right time. One writes in order to be read, as widely as possible and by as many different people as possible. But the already limited audience of available readers—those who buy books—is increasingly turning towards particular products because the centralized sorting and channelling apparatuses with which they are in contact either daily (radio, TV) or periodically (weeklies, magazines), and which they therefore trust, tell them they meet their needs. In the most recent of our three periods, the mechanisms of those information apparatuses capable of channelling social demand for one or another cultural commodity have been subjected to such draconian concentration that the choice to be made among the works of the mind—between those that will live by finding an audience and the rank and file that will die in silence—is also becoming draconian. Forty mediocrats (at the very most) have the power of life and death over 40,000 authors. For the latter, publishing a book means being brought before the Court of Forty; the silence of the jury is a death sentence. The jurors have neither the time nor the space to give an individual verdict for each of the accused. The disproportion between the number of channels available and the volume of production to be channelled, between the ever greater supply and a demand with limited growth, between the number of works received and the restricted space (or time, on TV and radio) devoted to book reviews and articles on authors means that the principle of selection is unavoidable. 'We can't talk about everyone at the same time.' But the agents who put the principles into action have the real power in their hands. They are the sieve through which all works have to pass, that separates events from non-events, being from nothingness, the useful

[11] That's one way of putting it. Here are the figures for Paris: between 1960 and 1975, the print runs for the serious Paris dailies fell from 4,068,304 to 3,116,235 and their sales fell from 3,309,753 to 2,364,424. With 9.6 million copies, the French daily press has yet to return to the lowest point on its distribution curve since the Liberation (1952), but since 1945 almost 70 out of 203 papers have disappeared. In 1914 there were sixty dailies in Paris, in 1939 there were thirty and now there are a dozen. The Hersant group alone controls more than half of the national papers.

from the absurd. More than ever before, those who decide decimate. Placed at the head of the new 'apparatus of discernment' (Péguy), those who belong to this micro-milieu occupy the strategic dispatch department and have the two-fold function of breaking down barriers between the professional micro-milieux of the intelligentsia (science, arts, theatre, or, to be more accurate, mathematicians, doctors, philosophers, biologists, novelists, and so on) by ensuring that messages pass between them, and of removing the barriers that separate the micro-milieux from the audience of honourable citizens (and in a given time and place, with the televised medium, from the widest possible audience). In a word, if, for an author, publishing a book is like posting a letter to his contemporaries, it is the media sorting office that decides whether or not it will reach its unknown addressee—or, to be more accurate, whether the address on the envelope is written in or left blank. At its own level—the highest—*Le Monde* serves the twofold function of *Bulletin Officiel* of French society and a box for letters between the high intelligentsia and the senior personnel of the State; they use it to ask after each other, make requests and reply to them. Anyone in France who enjoys the status of being a political, intellectual, scientific or artistic personality (or anyone with pretensions in that direction) knows that events, clarifications, statements, communiqués or demonstrations do not exist until *Le Monde* has given them their birth certificate in print. *Le Monde* is therefore the registry office for all the symbolic productions issued in the country (or which immigrate in the shape of translations). Whoever controls *Le Monde*—and especially the *Le Monde des Livres* and *Le Monde des Spectacles* supplements—has partial control over all who aspire to live. Ten men and women decide for 5,000 by choosing or not choosing to take an interest in their fate. There is a lot of wastage. In 1976, about 6,000 new books were published (human sciences and literature) and almost 4,000 were sent to *Le Monde des Livres* for ratification. Articles (full birth certificates) were written on 881 of them; 768 were given short certificates ('just published'). The rest ended up in the crematorium. *Le Monde des Livres* has a full-time staff of seven (the head of department, a regular columnist, section editors and sub-editors), plus a score of columnists and regular contributors selected from within the high intelligentsia. The most select of sieves is not, however, the most selective. The TV is more vulgar, but it is infinitely more efficient—there is scarcely any possibility of having a best-seller without its help—and even more strict. There, anyone who wins through does so by climbing over the invisible corpses of nine of his dear colleagues.

Power lies where scarcity is greatest. The rarefaction of the means of mass communication—or in plain language, the bottleneck—has inevitably displaced the site of intellectual power into the sphere of the mass media. There are 15,000 assistant lecturers in the universities, 300 literary advisers, attachés or series editors in the publishing houses, but only thirty important leader writers, columnists and critics in the mass media, and these are recruited through 'contacts', not competitive examinations. Each post is therefore expensive, all the more so in that its cost is established not by arithmetic but by the algebra of strategic calculation. Academics produce manuscripts, assistant editors proof-read them and turn them into books, but the media determine their market chances. The bigger the crowd at the entrance to the system, the harder the struggle for influence and control over the sluice gates and the exit. The whole process of valorization is decided *in extremis*, and as there is less and less room in the lifeboat, people fight to the death to get into it. The saturation of the intellectual market, and the exceptional density of talent, competence and ambition that characterizes a highly civilized country (or a metropolis) create the conditions for an unprecedented savagery in the manners of the intelligentsia. The more cultured the country, the more savage its intellectuals. Only the great carnivores survive. If I do not suffocate others, I get smothered. In this jungle, survival means killing, climbing means pulling someone else down, and making your way means pushing someone else aside. There has never been enough room in France, or anywhere else, for 20,000 famous authors, for if there are 20,000 celebrities in the same place at the same time, no one is famous. The means to fame have become very scarce and the stakes very high. The intrinsic nature of the media, which work on personality and therefore exclusivity, on originality and not therefore on the solidarity of a collective, combined with the typically French concentration of these apparatuses into a small area and into the hands of a few (contrast the USA's one hundred television channels or Italy's 150 private radio stations), turns the eternal struggle for recognition, which is the destiny of the intellectual, into a fight to the death for a little piece of the media. Such is the career of the intellectual in France today. 'Since it is based upon inequality and constantly aggravates the desire to "possess", but does not give everyone the opportunity to do so, it inevitably produces delinquents', said Maschino of consumer society. He was referring to petty crime. Given that the mass media too are based upon inequality and that their function is constantly to reproduce and exacerbate the desire to be seen, but that they do not give everyone the means to realize that desire, it is inevitable that these institutions secrete their intellectual delinquents, forgers, crooks, plagiarists and sophists. Apart from the fact that the intellectual delinquents promulgate the laws and dictate the norms, the same thing happens in the suburbs and in the centre; as their numbers increase, they lead one another on.

Writers have never been known to come to blows in order to see their name in a publisher's catalogue or in the *Bibliographie de la France* and the electors have never been known to fight to be on the local electoral roll. But they have been known to make life a misery for themselves and for their fellow citizens to get on to the list of candidates, and although those who stand in elections do not fight over school yards, they will fight day and night for two minutes on the ten o'clock news. For similar reasons, the things you can see every day in the intellectual milieu, when it is a question of a name in capitals on the front page or a television appearance, do not bear thinking about. It would give Candide pause for thought.

The yearly catalogue or monthly newsletter that a publisher uses to advertise his list is not a limited space; it can be expanded to infinity whenever a new genius appears to join the others. He has only to add another page and there is another place in the sun. That, presumably, is why no author feels that he has been promoted when he sees his name or his photograph in an alphabetical list of authors. The mere fact that all his colleagues are there too means that it is of no interest to any of them. For the moment, the printed surface is neither prize, means nor power. It would be if ever there were a shortage of paper or ink, as there is in certain underdeveloped countries, socialist or otherwise, where the objective limitations (shortage of competent technicians or the very high cost of paper) on the productive capacity of the printing industry make the appearance of a collection of poems a hierarchical symbol for the intelligentsia, a mark of favour and a sign of success. In an advanced capitalist society, anyone can have whatever they like printed to give to friends or to impress the family, even if it is printed at the author's expense. Equality of opportunity at this level means that the demarcation line has to be displaced: none of La Pensée Universelle's* authors have ever been asked to appear on Pivot's programme or to write the cultural page in the front of *Le Nouvel Observateur*.

Regardless of the external factors of scarcity—in the present case the

* A Paris publishing house, specializing in publishing at the author's expense.

scarcity of influential popular media—competition within the intelligentsia will never come to an end, even if the media proliferate. For, in the last analysis, there is 'always' one thing at stake: time. Cultural power, like any other form of power, is the power to take up other people's time. And for what is called cultural consumption, time is a natural condition that is by definition scarce. Its relative elasticity is one thing, but the absolute limits on it are another and there is no contradiction between the two. The ratio between free time and labour time has always varied and it will continue to do so in the future in accordance with technological progress (rises in productivity) and the class struggle (negotiated reductions in working hours). The more socially available free time there is, the more outlets there will be for cultural production. But even the most perfect affluent society will never be able to add a twenty-fifth hour to the day, make it possible to watch two video-discs at the same time or enable the enthusiast to watch two top quality TV programmes at the same time. It can introduce a tenth television channel in addition to the existing nine and thus increase the potential choice, but it cannot increase the time available for consumption. The most liberal television system in the world can never do away with the need to share out air time, which is by its very nature unequal and in short supply. Even when all creators have access to the screen, someone will still have to decide who gets the 8.30–9.30 slot, the prime time which has most influence and is therefore most coveted as a prize and an instrument of supremacy. The odds are that no open democratic discussion between authors and producers will ever resolve the question of how to share equally a commodity that recreates inequality the moment it is shared out. Penury and authority are correlative. Total penury leads to 'totalitarianism' and relative penury to authoritarianism tempered by the trades unions. There will never be a surplus of time and there will never be an end to the struggle for power—least of all between the producers of goods whose value can only be realized through the consumption of considerable amounts of free time. The moon still goes around the earth and the earth around the sun, as though to mock the idiocy of all the so-called programmes for the audio-visual revolution, the total democratization of information and free access for all to the small screen as the key to the emancipation of the human race.

Four

Acoustics as Conductor

The Technology of Influence: 'Ambition'

Hong Kong, 1978. A young Chinese refugee meets a Western journalist.—'I was about to go the university when the Cultural Revolution came along. I was a very active participant in it. When it ended, I was sent to the countryside to work in a village in the back of beyond, like most of the country's educated youth. That means that my education ended when I left secondary school.'—'So you don't think of yourself as an intellectual?'—'Yes, *because* I try *to influence* people through what I write.'[1] Admirably concise—it is the truth of the West spoken at the antipodes. For it is not his level of education that defines the intellectual, but his project of 'influencing people'. This moral project is essentially political: it aims to direct others and to correct the directions they have taken from elsewhere. Being a *Directoire* of opinion, the high intelligentsia finds itself in competition with other political powers, no matter how apolitical it would like to be. Here are two cases in point. In China (and similar regimes), the de facto unity of the leadership means that the Party-State is the only possible *Directoire*. The intellectual is therefore by his very nature an adversary to be silenced, as he sows the seeds of separatism and division. In the West, where the state relies on a division of the tasks of direction, it is (from the last historical period onwards) possible to develop an intellectual territory with a system of internal authority within the limits and on the conditions set by the sovereignty of the state: a federal solution that permits coexistence but does not remove tension.

So there could be a geography of the world's intelligentsia, with political and institutional determinants. Within a given geographical framework it might therefore be possible to write a history of the intellectual, a history

[1] Henri Leuwen, *Le Monde*, 26–27 February 1978.

of the means of influence available to him in a given period: such would be the object of applied mediology. In order to influence people, one must first be able to make oneself heard (or seen), which means having access to the place and the forms with the best audience, other things being equal. The desire to 'speak' to men is timeless, but public speaking has a history, that of its successive echo chambers. Zoology ends where mediology begins. It is through acoustics that the intellectual species comes into its own and gains the right to leave the zoo—whereupon it heads straight for the battlefield. The ivory tower exists only in the imagination of artists. The history of acoustics is not the history of music. It tells of the sound and the fury: of the best channel of speech in each historical period, the one that will facilitate the loudest sound and the greatest fury. The man of influence is one species within the genus 'man of action'. The use of symbolic violence is a substitute for violence itself. In wartime, man acts upon man by following a chain of command and the outcome is decided in a physical confrontation. In peacetime, it works through 'persuasion', prestige and authority, and the outcome is decided on the battleground of intellectual confrontation. The will to reach the institutional sites where the outcome is decided is called ambition.

Now those sites are, by definition, crowded. Hence the melée, the wounds, the kidney stones and ulcers. In general, there is always a crowd around the highest sites of influence. Even in periods of calm, there is a bustle. Logic would suggest that struggles for influence will be much more intense in peacetime than in wartime, and the history of France confirms that this is indeed the case. If struggles within the intellectual tribe have now become so oppressive, it is because Europe, and France in particular, are going through an abnormally long period of internal and external peace. There is no longer any external outlet for the violence, so it is bottled up at home and minor questions become crucial. The men of action champ at the bit and the men of influence take their place at the front of the stage (or become king of the castle)—to say nothing of the movement in the opposite direction: lots of men of action and organizers are using influence to compensate for having nowhere to go and are throwing themselves into the intellectual battle for lack of anything better to do. Is this the ghost of a battle or a battle between ghosts? Probably the latter, but the dust flies nonetheless (it gets everywhere and dirties everything), for, if wartime strengthens cohesion by raising the stakes, it also revalues community and trans-individual values. Peacetime compartmentalizes and atomizes by making the individual fall back on himself. And the value of intellectual individuality therefore rises on the stock exchange. Wars and revolutions alike bode very ill for the intellectual species, not only because anything that reinforces the cohesion of the social body reduces the margins for individual tolerance, but because it loses its monopoly over symbolic functions, which are confiscated by others. Peacetime and dull periods of reaction, on the other hand, give the species the best possible environment in which to grow and multiply. Then the men of influence can fight openly, each under his own banner, with no uniforms and with no unpaid labour or unfair competition. They are sole masters of the field, since the word rules. At such times, they are the important men. At last they can fire their own weapons at point blank range. No one is a better shot with words than the man of letters. They often get drunk on their own credit, forgetting in their drunkenness or *hubris* that the state is simply lending them credit by delegating authority to them, for the means and vectors of authority are state-controlled (in France today, radio, TV and written media). Those who have franchises in influence naturally see themselves as sole owners, but their assets are rediscounted on the Banques de France and they prefer not to know about it. These transitional periods, when the centre of gravity moves from coercion to hegemony, do not mean that the state is retreating, that the monster is being driven into the shadows by thousands of white hands; it is functioning in a different way. As a certain statesman said on the radio in December 1978, appealing for a new, intellectual mobilization of Gaullist forces, 'since 1968, the state has had to seduce and convince; it can no longer give orders.' To seduce and convince: these are the very tasks of the men of influence. The professionals have rarely been in so enviable a position. Given that they are in the government, it is only logical that the last thing they want is a change of government; no regime could be more favourable to the *Directoire* of opinion than the present bourgeois regency. The regime does not have the intellectual means to put its policies into effect because of the ruling political elite's lack of symbolic resources. It therefore has to live on credit. Hence the complementary tasks, the delegation of powers and the exchange of courtesies; never before have the great mass-mediatic apparatuses (radio, TV, magazines) opened their doors so widely to the French high intelligentsia. Political ambition exists only in so far as it is intellectual. It follows that intellectual ambition has never been so immediately political as it is now, both in terms of its origins and its effects. Cultural technology has rarely been so closely super-imposed upon the political technology of the day. If we 'talk technique' or 'technological history' we are still 'talking politics', but when it comes to the root of things, words mean nothing.

A history of hegemony could well be written as a history of personal ambition throughout the ages and their respective cultures, and it would in part be a history of the state. Shortly after the Napoleonic wars, young Julien Sorel was still hesitating between the Scarlet Empire and the Black Restoration—cavalry lieutenant or an Abbé at court? Several wars later, other young men of the same age would wonder: pilot or novelist? The answer to such anxieties comes as much from the nature of the times as from the nature of the individual. What ambitious young man would now dream of 'the fine career of a priest, which leads to all things', as Julien did in his Franche Comté? Twenty years after Mme de Reynel's lover, it was already more natural for a young man in a provincial town to dream of being a writer: it had become a career (one might live by one's pen) and a (privileged and disputed) position. In the meantime, the priesthood had become a narrow way. While still a poet in Angoulême, Lucien dreamt of being Victor Hugo in Paris. The dream burst; he became Walter Scott and wrote a bad historical novel. But never mind the failure: he would be a literary critic on a popular newspaper—naturally. D'Arthez had already warned him while he was still hovering around his Şaint-Simonian cenacle: 'You would so much like to have power, to have power of life and death over books that you'll be a journalist inside two months. A journalist ranks as a pro-consul in the Republic of Letters.' Given the tight deadlines he had set himself, his inability to stand loneliness and his neurotic anxiety, literary journalism provided Lucien with the greatest possible social power, all other things being equal. But things change—and so do career profiles, renumerations and scales of influence. The demand for a magistrature may remain constant, but the supply varies over the years, depending on the material means of the magistrature. That is the matrix of the most secret projects of adolescents, the plot-line for the imaginary scenes of unrecognized talents. The power dreams of the men of the sign are channelled through the networks of social communication and, without being aware of it, they come up against certain thresholds of acoustic capacity (which in turn are dependent on the productive forces of the day). But they go beyond them in the next period. 'The repression of culture by technology' (Aron) is an indestructible cliché. No technical system represses a cultural project: it organizes it.

Which threshold do they cross and which rooms do they enter? Ask the intellectual: he always homes in on power. When it comes to tracking down the site from which the ideological direction of a given society can best be exercised, the watch-dog is the best of all hounds. The tribune from which the word rings out loudest and carries furthest, from where the master of discourse can address the prince on equal terms; the place where the assymmetry between the sender and the receiver of messages is greatest—that is the site of power. Go there: you are sure to find the 'great intellectuals' of the moment, the most widely seen and the most widely heard, for this site combines the greatest social visibility with the optimum resonance. In 1680, it was the preacher's pulpit; in 1750, the stage; in 1850, the professor's dais; in 1890 the bar; in 1930, the front page of a daily; in 1960, the editorship of a news magazine; in 1980, the producership of a television programme. The periodization is arbitrary and more symbolic than descriptive. Every system of political domination has its megaphones and its favourite speaker systems: *religious* so long as *omnis potestas a deo*— the church, cathedral or monastery where the word of God exhibits its omnipotence, and reflects upon its bearers; *ethico-juridical*, when the legal state is established—the lecture theatre where the spirit of the laws is enunciated, the chamber where they are passed and the court where they are applied; *mass-mediatic*, where both God and the law have to bow before the market of quoted opinions and ratings, when an economy based on commodities, services and performance sets the norms for political decisions—there, power, like influence, is won and lost on the small screen.

Each type of acoustics has its corresponding scale of cultural perform-ances, the front row being occupied in turn by sacred eloquence, drama or tragedy, the lecture, the leader or the column, the televised speech or debate. There is an index of performances, to which each epoch pins a name and a face, a model with whom whole generations of *clerics* or intellectuals identify: St Thomas or St Bernard; Bossuet or Bourdaloue; Beaumarchais or Voltaire (who was first applauded in the theatre); Villemain, Guizot or Michelet; Zola, Clemenceau or Daudet; Sartre, Malraux or Camus; today's media stars. None of these sites, genres, or symbols destroys its predecessors or its competitors; it displaces and relegates them. Necessarily so, because there is not room for everyone in the place with the best acoustics. The possibility itself of getting there works as principle of a hierarchical discrimination within the order, as the object of inner struggles, as a criterion of success and as a membership badge. Intellectual power is the fact of being there, controlling access to the site and keeping a monopoly over it. If everyone in the intellectual world could be there, the place would not play that decisive role. It is therefore, ipso facto, the place where selection is at its most draconian, where the audience is largest and the reception clearest. It is the pole of attraction that structures the intellectual force-field of the moment. Everyone who matters is called to the meeting place of the hegemonic apparatuses, precisely because few are chosen. Everyone pushes and shoves to see, read and listen to those few. In 1680, they fought to hear the Lenten Sermon at Saint Germain or the funeral oration for Henrietta of England in the Louvre chapel; in 1770, the same people were at the Paris Opera in the evening; in 1850 at the Collège de France; in 1890 at the Palace of Justice; in 1950, in a certain editorial office; and in 1980, in a certain TV studio on Friday evenings. The studios in the rue Cognacq-Jay are the latest place to rub shoulders and exchange witticisms with archbishops, lawyers, generals, ministers and actors. The unifying point for the symbolic field in France today is the meeting place known as Bernard Pivot, the only man, apart from the Presidents of the Republic and the National Assembly, who can bring together ministers of state and managers of minds, the *tout-Paris* of the moment. As the *tout-Etat* and the *tout-Esprit* coincide, the dialogue can take place only with the head of state (at the Elysée) or with the head of the spirit (on Pivot's programme). Those who frequent the one are also to be found on the other. But if, tomorrow, it turned out that the best place from which to be seen and heard by the greatest possible number of French speakers was the moon, the interplanetary rockets would already be fully booked.

Elements of a
History of Literature

If these hypotheses are not totally without foundation, a number of lines of research, or at least a few supplementary hypotheses, can be derived from them.

The first touch upon the history of literature. This usually boils down to a history of literary doctrines and genres, as though they contained within them their own laws of succession. But does that not mean getting hold of the wrong end of the stick, mistaking cause for effect and unnecessarily prolonging the idealist reversal that explains ideology in terms of ideology in the artistic field? Is it impossible to imagine a political science of literature that would go beyond the sociology of literature and form part of a strategy for the fine arts? Mediology may one day be able to pose, if not answer, such questions in a rigorous way by drawing up a *mediological table* of the period for each epoch and culture, or a table of the comparative profitability of one or another vector or form of expression as a support for influence. In general, the influence a given genre has over the intellectual creators of an epoch should be correlated with its index of *resonance* at that time, taking into account the size of the potential audience and the practical possibilities of entering into relations with it, given the technical level of the communications networks of the epoch.

Let us take the example of the theatre. 'The crisis that has affected the theatre throughout the world since the appearance of talking pictures and television has taken a more acute form in France than in the English-speaking countries', notes one specialist.[2] 'Paris has lost its reputation as the theatrical capital of the world to London and New York', precisely because Parisian authors and intellectuals are more concerned with their image than their counterparts in London and New York and because they

[2] Georges Versini, *Le Théâtre français depuis 1900.*

have a political function here that they do not have in those cities. There being no politics without a politics of grandeur, the theatre has lost its former prestige because intellectual politics no longer have to be presented on stage. French authors have a long range and do not like to waste their ammunition. The word 'range' is used in acoustics, politics, ballistics and moral philosophy, and it can be described as good, long, wide or high. All its meanings come down to the same thing: the ability to have an effect by hitting a target or goal. The disappearance of 'first-rate authors' is said to have occurred about twenty years ago (1955), at the very time when television and *cinéma-écriture* appeared, giving the 'new theatre' (Beckett, Ionesco, Adamov) time to slip in. Until then, what the French call works with a major moral and philosophical import often took dramatic form, and literary authors who were quite unsuited to the stage felt themselves under a moral obligation to write a play or two (Mauriac, Gide, Romains, Martin du Gard, Camus, Thierry Maulnier . . .)—the acoustics were still worthwhile. The directors of consciousness now turn elsewhere, because the square stage and the semi-circle of seats no longer provide the best possible resonance for their words. The stage is no longer a profitable hegemonic investment. Only the professionals are still interested in the theatre. Most of them are foreigners like Beckett, Ionesco and Arrabal or Frenchmen who do not belong to the French intelligentsia, like Genet, Audiberti and Rezvani. Indigenous authors with a message to put across, be it political, religious, philosophical or moral, used to employ the genre of the play, less as a specific art than as the most generic of all forms. Better platforms have since appeared and guarantee an infinitely wider audience for a relatively less expensive transmission. What is the point of throwing out witty comments, when they can no longer be heard because they do not carry far enough? Miraculous staging, fine playing, excellent companies, brilliant producers, sumptuous sets . . . the French theatrical world has never had so much talent on the production side and so few playwrights. The kingpin is missing: the spectator. When he left, the author left with him. The great warriors of peacetime, from Molière to Sartre, from Beaumarchais to Voltaire and Hugo, wrote for the stage in order to 'conquer' the public or 'win' an audience. No more audience, no more plays: the smell of powder has gone from the dress rehearsals, and the battle has lapsed for want of repercussions.

So long as it represented the best point of contact with the widest (and choicest) possible audience, the theatre remained the main axis for symbolic influence. But would anyone still write that 'the theatre is a melting pot of civilization. It is a place of human communion. The soul of the public is forged in the theatre' (Victor Hugo, *William Shakespeare*). The theatre was a place of *communion* in that it was the nodal point of social communication, with only the church and the cathedral to compete with. A theatrical performance was therefore 'the Mass of the fashionable and profane world' (Jean Giraudoux) because it was the most public operation in which an individual could legally participate. The crucial fact here was that the theatre was a place of assembly. Hence the precautions taken by the monarchical state, the clergy's old distrust of it—and the role it can still play in liberation or national resistance movements as a practical way of overcoming bans on public meetings or assemblies (the Italy of *Senso*, Franco's Spain, contemporary Chile).

The return to the oral should have reactivated the oldest (and most recent) form of oral literature. But no theatre can bring together one-hundred-thousandth part of the audience for a television play. The paradox is that the numerical increase in the size of the audience is equivalent to its break-up, as it is atomized at home, and to the disintegration of a public soul which can no longer take on a body and see itself doing so (as in civic ceremonies and revolutionary festivals). The physical segregation of those who watch from those who officiate is completed by the audio-visual media, which mark the end of the 'mystery', as though there were a critical threshold to the audience for the rite, beyond which the effect fades and the energy is lost. That timeless pathos once survived, in a degraded form, in the thrill of the fashionable dress rehearsals, when a contagious joy circulated between the stage and the audience, the wings and the corridors, the joy of being brought together for once because we were united in something greater than ourselves—a joy that now resembles penitence, for many reasons and not least because of the downgrading of such small, formal assemblies. The stage is therefore no longer a political issue. What was in its heyday a centre for cabals and plots remained so until it was put into its subsidized iron lung. The cinema and then TV replaced it in its role as the art-that-kills, and with reason: a good play is seen by 20,000 people (over several months), a film by 200,000 (over several weeks) and a television play by 10,000,000 (in one evening).

At the opposite extreme, the decadence of poetry—concomitant with that of the theatre—does not relate solely to the disappearance of the 'people' in western society, together with its gestural language, its sense of the oral and its ritual pleasures. The poets are dying between the pages of their slim volumes because public readings have disappeared. Poetry is still alive in the Soviet Union, not simply because the Russian people still exists, but because a poet can draw an audience of 10,000 for a recital in a university lecture theatre in Moscow, Kiev or Minsk. Similarly, readings keep it alive in the United States, and in the Caribbean and Latin America, *el recital* is a popular and hallowed ceremony (or was—until television). For decades, Neruda went backwards and forwards between the capitals, towns and villages of his America, attracting crowds of young people wherever he went. Going to see the poet was like going to see a film. In France, the disappearance of listeners led to the disappearance of readers and then publishers—a process that finally dries up the lyrical vein, something unthinkable a hundred years ago. Auditorium, influence and audience are synonymous. There are fewer poets in Europe than in Latin America because, amongst other reasons, in an advanced capitalist society, a good poem confers less prestige on an author than a 'good' appearance on television. But in 1850, the desire for hegemony in Paris was encoded as a lyrical vocation, and some admirable poems came into being as a result. Who wrote *Le Lac, Les Châtiments,* or even *Le Balcon*:* the poet or the *other.* Or was there really no difference between them?[3]

Do we mourn our dead heroes any the less because the genre of the funeral oration has disappeared? No. The homily and the sermon are no longer dominant cultural genres and sacred eloquence is no longer the supreme flowering of literature because the *volume of the social audience* reached from the pulpit is close to zero compared with what can be reached with a radio microphone or a television camera. The decline of the Catholic Church and the withering away of religious feeling within the

* Lamartine, Hugo, and Baudelaire respectively.

[3] Poetry has found a new form of existence, and a new audience, in popular music. Dylan may be our Lamartine. As for the traditional written form, the last revival of poetic creation dates back to the Resistance and relates to historical factors. Language is the very substance of the being of the nation, and poetry, even more so than prose, which stands in a purely instrumental relation to language, is the religion of language. The religion of poetry is essentially a national religion and a decline in national feeling necessarily leads to a decline in lyrical interest, just as a revival leads to a renewal of fervour. The poets of the Resistance were militants in a battle that fused the national and the social: hence their numbers and their splendour. At that time, poetry really was a symbol of legitimacy and a vector of influence. To try to distinguish between the poet and the militant (the good and the bad, the eternal and the contingent) in the Aragons, Eluards or Chars of the period is to miss the organic link between militancy and poetry, the coherence of national ego and lyrical ego.

ruling class are not in themselves enough to explain the disappearance of certain canonic forms, certain rituals of public expression.

'Ambition' as the force behind artistic innovation: to carry the theme over from moral ideology into cultural theory, we first have to do away with the ready-made couplets that give 'politics' connotations of utility and 'beauty' connotations of selflessness. In any case only hypocrites will cry scandal before adding a codicil to the late debate between formalism and positivism in aesthetics. The autonomy of the *literary* has nothing to fear from mediological approaches adequate, apparently, only to the procedures of 'political' hegemony. It might at least allow the history and the etymology of the word 'authors' to be restored to their concordant truth.

History: literary expression had never achieved such efficiency as a political weapon or such awareness of itself as an instrument in the struggle for hegemony as when—at the end of the eighteenth century—it gained an autonomous status. Historically, the birth of 'literature' from the ashes of belles lettres coincided with the birth of *politics* from the juridico-ethical ashes of *the art of government*. The professionalization of the writer, a complex process that followed on from the birth of literature and which (in France) occurred between 1830 and 1880, was concurrent with that of the politician. The Société des gens de lettres appears at the same time (1838) as the first parliamentary groupings, in a logical and chronological concurrence that would in itself be an interesting subject for research.[4]

Etymology (digest of a more ancient history): the word 'author' has nothing to do with 'audience' or 'auditorium'; it is connected with 'authority' and 'authorization'. It is in fact the same word. *Auctor*, from *augeo*, one who increases, who adds something. To what? Initially to public confidence: the author as guarantor, source or guardian. Later, to collective enterprises founded on trust: the author as instigator, promoter and founder. Finally and necessarily, to language and to the accumulated writing of the past. The different meanings followed logically and chronologically from one another; the juridico-moral acceptation preceded and provided a basis for the politico-moral, which in turn provided a

[4] The basic work on the professionalization of the writer in the nineteenth century appears to be Gérard Delfau and Anne Roche, *Histoire Littérature*, Paris 1977.

basis for the literary. Before it came to mean 'one who composes a literary work', author meant 'one who inspires men to act', and before that again it meant 'one who increases confidence'. By giving the hegemonic primacy over the directive and the literal—even within the hierarchy of authors— contemporary Western society may be going back to its roots. The city is founded upon trust and trust is founded upon the written word. An author is one whose revealed word allows towns to be founded, wars to be declared and trials brought to a close. In the juridical language of Rome, *auctoritates* meant the authoritative opinions of the jurisconsults. In a different language, authors of authorized opinions, authors whose opinions have the weight of authority and individual authors whose opinions represent jurisprudence are grouped together by our term, 'the high intelligentsia'. Their responsibilities would appear to be radically 'political', always assuming that the roots of words do indeed point to the roots of things.

The prognosis that derives from these hypotheses is reassuring. The fate of the *littérateurs* is not necessarily bound up with that of literature. They may outlive it, just as writers may survive if writing goes under. So many of them are already beginning to distinguish themselves by their audio-visual vitality. They have rapidly compensated for the dislodge- ment of the written word from its social pedestal by physically putting themselves on pedestals as the stars of a second-rate, but still (already?) profitable show-biz. At the turn of the century, Apollinaire was already noting that 'typography is ending its career brilliantly just as the cinema and the phonograph are coming into their own'. It is only natural that those for whom writing was a means to a career should now be haunting more profitable places. Which is more important in an intellectual 'vocation': the strength of the call or the need for an answer? If there was still an audience in our society for epics in decasyllabic verse, there would be no shortage of Valéryiads or Songs of the Gulag, but the rhetorical essay in prose seems more in keeping with the times. In the contest to gain public marks of individual difference, the deal is less important than the stake. That is why Minerva's owl is a phoenix: it pretends to fly at dusk, but each new technological morning sees it spring to life again from its ashes. Although determined by it in practice, the magisterial function transcends the magisterial organ and the self-same reasons that inspired a poet to dedicate a madrigal to the Prince de Condé in 1670 inspired his 1970s counterpart to send a script for a serial to the programme director of

TF 1. In 2001, their descendant will be recording olfactory tacto-video cassettes.

No social species is better equipped to keep up with the times than the knights of the intemporal. The clerisy always find their way in the profane world, and if they look like getting lost, they immediately pick up a new compass and find the road back to power. Today, this is called 'the new responsibility of the clerisy' or the 'challenge of modern technology': when it comes to choosing formulae we can rely on the common sense of those whom Benda thought were devoted body and soul to the clerical values (truth, reason, justice). 'This class of men whose activities do not pursue practical ends but who find joy in the exercise of art, science or metaphysical speculation, in, that is, the possession of intemporal wealth', is forced by its function, and not by some vice or congenital defect, to adopt the procedures of subjection of the society in which its members practise. The function is permanent; its practice varies; the means of the clerisy are transitory. In short, there are as many priesthoods as there are betrayals. The lever behind every betrayal is the infrastructure of the function as the organic intellectual necessarily evolves in line with the technical organization of social domination. Those whose trade it is to relate God to Caesar, abstract reason to the city of men, values to facts, rulers to ruled are an integral part of the apparatuses, instruments and institutions through which ideas and values circulate in a real society. If they were not, how could they carry out their twofold mission of (dialectically) idealizing society by socializing ideas and vice versa? The audio-visual is the lever behind today's betrayal because it is the main instrument of domination.

It is becoming clear that this centralized machinery, with its terminals plugged into our nervous system, is establishing a new social relation to truth and to history. As a curious gentleman (to whom we will have to return) said, even if it is all he did say, 'with the coming of television, a number of things no longer function as they once did' (MacLuhan). These include that 'class of men' who stand at the intersection, so crucial in the west, between truth and history, and whose mission is to administer the former in—and to—the latter, a class which, ever since the Catholic Church ceased to wield temporal power, has been known as the 'intelligentsia'. In a society where anyone who does not appear on TV does not 'exist', with political hierarchies in which those who are 'best on TV' are put in command, it comes as no surprise to see the big cats of Arts and

Letters turning into TV animals in order to maintain their supremacy within the pride. Not without impunity is the intellectual animal a 'beast of power'. He now has to pay tribute to a new type of *medium* which, not content with transmitting influence, superimposes its own code on it. If the inner rationality of the mass media is the very rationality of bourgeois domination, the intellectual animal who fails to transcend his specific animality in the name and by virtue of a non-specific moral imperative will not be able to renew his own dominance without reproducing and extending that of the ruling class—without, that is, becoming its servant.

The Dynamics of Influence: Corruption

If a history of ambition could stand as a prologue to an applied mediology, a treatise on corruption could well form its epilogue—or table of contents. Human corruption has a history; if not History itself, it is at least the history of the intelligentsia, and follows the rhythms of its avatars and the scansions of its means of influence. When domination comes under a new sign, so does corruption. That is not—I must insist—to be taken as a moral aphorism, but as a historical index and a political criterion. 'Putrefaction is the laboratory of life' (Marx) and, as we all know, the compost that produces the finest blooms of the Mind. From Imperial Rome to New York City, from Quattrocento Florence to the Paris of Parisianity, it is well known that good morals do not make for fine cultures. Everything, from cheese and wine to works of art, confirms that civilization and fermentation are synonymous. When we say 'germs of intellectual power', 'seeds of putrefaction', only the relation between the two is worthy of study. Organic corruption follows the lines of the genetic mutation. Tell me, intelligentsia, where the rot is, and I will tell you what you are thinking.

If the intellectual is indeed the *mediaman* and is required by his function to serve and be served by the existing means of communication, he would appear to be the most exposed of men, or the most easily seduced. Tell me, party, regime or system, what your capabilities for communication are and I will tell you what your intellectual equipment is. Whoever controls the media system will see the mediamen come under his control sooner or later: the axiom applies to all epochs and all regimes. Whoever controls only part of it will lose them all. If, for example, the French left still wants a few intellectuals on its side, it should start by providing itself with a paper, given that it cannot have a radio or TV station—and if it wants top intellectuals, a popular newspaper. If it doesn't want any intellectuals at all, then let it stay as it is and die with dignity. It is the natural reflex and the vocation of the intellectual to be on the side of those who own the papers (and/or the microphones, screens, concert halls, galleries . . .). The problem is that reflexes often replace reflection and that this professional tropism is not always without its risks, depending on the epoch or the regime.

The legend is again spreading that the intelligentsia of France 'paid very heavily' during the purges of 1944. To judge by the dossier, it got off amazingly lightly. For apart from the big industrialists, no social category rallied to the German occupation regime in such strength. Drieu and Brasillach now eclipse Decour and Politzer in the firmament of our memories. Every age has the stars it deserves. But none of them (and they have not been bracketed together for the sake of *balance*!) can eclipse the terrible truth of the night: until 1943, the Germans and their collaborators could count on the support of almost all of the high intelligentsia of France. Let those who think that is an extreme statement browse through the 'cultural' papers and reviews of the time. From *Comoedia*, a weekly dealing with 'theatre, art and literature,' to the *Cahiers franco-allemands*, from the flimsiest to the most forceful organs, which of the big names did not answer the call? Let them read Gide's *Journal* (1940–1945) more closely—and Gide was one of the most distant. Let them ask why the best known publishers (Grasset, Gallimard, Fayard) had to disappear briefly at the Liberation, so that their houses could be reborn from oblivion.

Someone once said that the great intellectuals of the establishment had never felt so 'free' as they did during the Occupation—which also means so pampered, so supported, and so listened to; more sociable, more productive, more full of their own importance. What a flowering of papers, reviews and titles! The facts suggest that it was a splendid time for publishing (the number of titles was higher than before the war, despite the restrictions on printing), for the theatre (packed houses), for painting, which sold better than ever (to the Germans), and above all for literature (more books were written, and more works went out of print). In journalism, censorship was light-hearted and, at the beginning, even encouraged an amazing variety in the range of titles. We will not go through them page by page, for it would take a whole book to do so. As it happens, that book has already been written; here is the conclusion of the chapter devoted to the 'intellectuals of the new Europe', the professionals of the word. 'There is a story that when the first German military governor came to Paris, he had a letter in his pocket telling him that two non-military objectives were to be taken as a matter of priority: the Hôtel de Ville and the NRF. As we have seen, the second part of his programme was carried out quite literally and without any major difficulties. If one goes from part of the French literary world to the whole, one might well ask if he wasn't even more successful'.[5] But we must understand the intellectual vocation. Apart from a few crusaders, who never returned and a few rogues hiding behind their baseness, the French intellectuals— journalists, writers, theatre people, and so on—did not go over to the Germans out of any predilection, and still less to make money. They went over to them because the material and administrative means of communication were in their hands: paper (the prime problem for journalists, writers and publishers) was rationed both by material shortages and by the Control Commission of Newsprint; titles (the 'Otto list', censorship); authorization to publish (both newspapers and books, issued by the Propaganda Abteilung). They frequented the German Embassy, dined, inaugurated, speechified, lunched, lectured, made lecture tours. Was this the thoughtlessness of fashionable Paris? No, it betokened conscientiousness. A writer has to write and get himself talked about, just as an actor has to appear on stage, a musician to give recitals, a composer to have his compositions played and a painter to exhibit. What have politics and morality got to do with it? The newspapers may well be subsidized, but at least they exist. Censored plays may well be admirable, but they are not performed. So let's collaborate with the newspapers and ask for a visa from the appropriate authority (the foreign section of the Reich's Propaganda Ministry). These are the minor servitudes of the profession; only its splendours should be remembered. As Amouroux rightly points out, there was no particular feeling of embarrassment in the world of the arts, letters and the theatre in the occupied zone, nor even any feeling of collaboration: 'Those whose vocation it is to appear, appear, the writers write and the actors act'.[6]

Today's vocations are much less onerous and more easily satisfied, but equally unconcerned about their material supports or the real meaning of the compromises they reach with the new masters of paper and

[5] Pascal Ory, *Les Collaborateurs* (see Chapter X, 'La Figure', p. 235), Paris 1976.
[6] H. Amouroux, *Les beaux jours des collabos* (see Chapter XIV, 'La gloire et l'argent', p. 495).

authorizations to publish. The new masters seem to demand nothing and to give all without asking anything in return. They are not in uniform and do not belong to any order, ideology, party, system, or even class. They are simply individuals who happen to be there. If the bourgeoisie had to say on stage that it was the bourgeoisie, it would lose all credibility. It has to disappear as a social subject and pass itself off as a mere agent carrying out technical operations whose automatism in some way guarantees their neutrality. It controls operations (extraction of surplus value on a world scale, ideological inculcation at the national level) simply in so far as it seems itself to be subject to them. As for the latter operation, it appears even to leave all the initiative and control to the professional themselves— the teachers, journalist, writers, artists—and to let them do what they like, where they like and as best they can. The French ruling class is like Victor Hugo: it prefers influence to power. It exercises power by sheltering behind those who exert influence. A system of domination that works through communication works through the intelligentsia. And so it puts it on the highest possible pedestal. Bourgeois society's over-estimation of the value of intellectuals is the other side of its under-estimation of the value of peasants and workers (and this is particularly true of French bourgeois society). It is not simply a picturesque aspect of its folklore but a functional requirement of the system. No social regime has ever flattered the intellectuals as much as ours. It does not just pay formal tribute to them. It serves the intellectual as much as it is served by him, but on certain conditions. Those who occupy our minds are our fellow-citizens and, basically, this is an occupation we want—for many reasons, and not least because they have control over the heirs to the NRF.

It is time we rid ourselves of an outdated and therefore naive imagery of corruption; the mythological or terroristic use made of it deserves to be greeted with mockery rather than with the anger of the past. It no longer takes money to corrupt an intellectual—his pride is enough (and precludes under-the-counter payments or backhanders). No one is paid by the Comité des Forges or the Ministry of the Interior nowadays, but by *Paris-Match* or by what used to be the ORTF. Consciences are now bought under the spotlights—in front of at least five million witnesses. In a society that crossed the threshold of survival two hundred years ago and in which the same standard of living—well above the living minimum—is gradually being imposed on everyone, the reproduction of the differences characteristic of the social logic of needs lies no longer in *having* but in *being.* And that means being *seen.* In a village, you become *someone* by having your picture in the paper; in a town, by being seen on TV. And as the village has been annexed by the town and the local paper by the national TV, the second process has replaced the first, even at the local level. No intellectual longs to have a more powerful car than his neighbour (all cars, from the cheapest to the most expensive, can now reach the speed limit and that is all there is to it), four bathrooms rather than two, or an alarm clock coffee-maker with scented FM stereo keys. In a 'mass' society where all consumer goods and services are in theory available to everyone, individual distinctions can no longer operate or be graded in terms of the quantity of what I *have,* but only in terms of the quality of what I *am.* How can we evaluate a quality that unfortunately and by definition cannot be measured, even if it is tangible?—by counting the number of those who do not have it. The quality of what I am is inherent not in what I am, but in the quantity of those in whose eyes I am what I am. Being means counting for others: being a little for a few other people, being a lot for many other people. So I have to know how to count—print runs, audience ratings, time slots; the lead story or a short paragraph on page 8? How many of us will there be around the table, my dear Pivot? What is my position in the hit parade?

In a proletarianized intelligentsia with a mass audience, anonymity is the stigma of powerlessness, and powerlessness the punishment for anonymity. Making a name for oneself is fine, but who creates the demand for interviews? Making your face known is even better—but who decides whether or not to print the photo? Today, the bourgeoisie no longer buys men with cheques but with newsprint and electronic images, with *their* images (physical and trade). It controls the material means of reprography, the stocks of paper, the administration and the editorial boards of the illustrated magazines, the doors to the television studios. It controls them but it does not mark them: on the surface, all images are 'innocent', reproductions of things and people who are there. That they are selected in the production department, that those that are kept are edited and have captions added: all this is concealed by the glossy surface of transmission-publication. It is as though it were all done by machines, without anyone knowing, for the last thing machinery looks like is a machine. The true magic of our societies is to show everything in such a way as to make the absolutely visible relatively invisible. The corruption of the high intelligentsia is invisible because it is all we can see.

The members of the high intelligentsia are dependent on their image, and the dependence often becomes an obsession. For the professionals of the idea, 'Is my image good or not?' is a much more pressing (and frequent) question than 'Are my ideas correct or not?'. My image is primarily, but not only, my TV appearance, my picture in a display advert (preferably on the front of *Le Monde*). That appearance is my substance, both in the metaphysical and in the economic sense. We touched on the metaphysical side with Hegel, the first philosopher to explain the brute fact of *homo sapiens* as animal-ready-to-do-anything-to-get-his-photo-in-the-paper. This specific pruritus does not, as we have seen, derive from a weakness of character, but from a structure of consciousness, a destiny. We will come to the economic aspect in a moment. But mid-way between Hegel and Marx stands Jean-Paul Sartre and the phenomenology of lived experience. We have already seen something of the material insecurity of the high intelligentsia, an insecurity due to its insertion into the uncertainties of the market and political fluctuation, the ebb and flow of ideology and the fickleness of the clientele. Its insecurity is also, or therefore,[7] existential. Basically, everyone is afraid that he does not really exist—since he exists only in so far as he is recognized by others as worthy to exist. He exists only in so far as others talk about him—or watch, quote, criticize, slander or praise him. Does the echo make the voice, or the image the body? No echo, no voice; no image, no body—hence the strongly reassuring effect of the media in the intellectual world: they provide a convenient scale of hierarchical insignia. Souls are ranked in a hierarchy in accordance with their typographical bodies, the lay-out reveals their rank to the naked eye, and the media give the whole corporation a table showing the prices at which their individual values are being quoted.[8] Lack of

[7] I prefer 'also': it may be vague from a methodological point of view, but it is more reliable from a philosophical point of view. A strict Marxist would say 'therefore', which sounds more serious. We have already demonstrated the want of seriousness in these determinisms 'in the last instance'. In our view, the existential instance has a real and philosophical autonomy.

[8] The simplest way to find out what your name is worth is to send an article on the current intellectual debate to *Le Monde*; you will immediately discover how far you have or have not gone down the road of the combatant and, unfortunately, how far all your competitors have gone. Will your piece be on the centre of the front page or in the bottom left-hand corner; will it be by itself on an inside page or merely a 'point of view' on the left-hand side of page 2, along with five others; is your name at the head or the end of the piece, is it mentioned in the title? It is dangerous if you find yourself in 'Letters to the Editor' a month later; but if your text is politely returned for 'lack of space', you can reasonably assume that your (civil) life is in peril.

modesty has its advantages: it gives an objective guarantee of existence. A photo, a name, a title in print—these are tangible and palpable: they really exist. No one can take them away from me, not even the doubt inside me, not even the inner nothingness that gives me my being. Compared with a consciousness, a broadcast is something solid, whatever else can be said of it. The worst misfortune of the intelligentsia in the advanced capitalist countries is not the unhappy consciousness or the pain of existence, but that modern capitalism has invented the best possible instrument for soothing both.

Everyone loves to be loved, but the intellectual—outstripping even the artist in this—is the one who cannot exist without being loved. He came into the world qualified not to speak, but to be *listened to*; not to see the world around him, but to be seen by it; still less to know it (that is the task of the scientist), but to be known by it. Now the channels of communication, the instruments of social visibility and the practical means to recognition, belong to the masters of our world (those who legally own or have technical control over them). If they financed the digging of the channels, it is only right that they should control the taps of the public-image fountains—the media as public service—or the fire hydrants of the 'private' press. The rebel who thirsts after fame cannot slake his thirst without alienating himself, without serving the faceless master he wants to denounce. The Leviathan of the West, more welcoming than the other one, has two profiles: state and capital, administration and industry, but only one face and one body. And in order to be loved—which is a legitimate desire—I the intellectual must first satisfy the appetite for legitimacy of the very small number who rule over all.

'I need love', groans the intellectual in silence. 'Do you really love me', the echo returns. The bourgeoisie loves to be loved too, and has every right to do so. But there is no symmetry between these two demands for love, and still less any reciprocity, for the bourgeoisie controls the energy reserves and the organic channels of love. 'Whoever controls the energy controls the code' (Michel Serres). Without a channel, there can be no transmission and, a fortiori, no reception. The intellectual and the artist can no longer make love to the audience (reading as coitus, the show as relationship, as they wish—directly—without permission from the masters of energy and codes. Intimacy is impossible. If I want to make love to those below me, I first have to swear that I love those above me. I am in their power; they are not in mine. With all the good will in the world, I can do nothing: I have no TV station or mass circulation magazines and even if I do cobble together a pirate station, I cannot even get through to my next-door neighbour (who cannot stand the interference and prefers Luxemburg anyway). What is to be done? I might reply to the ambient demand for love, physical security and pleasure echoed, amplified and produced by the fifty mediocrats whom capital, the state or both has put in a position to make decisions; or I might adapt my little ideas to the great ideas put about by the linotype and the airwaves, the ideas that cause storms, scandals, heresies, explosions, sacrifices and major quarrels, the ideas that are brought to me each week for the greater happiness of my friends and colleagues, the kamikaze pilots of moral courage and thought, though God (and failing God, their friends and colleagues) knows they are not particularly heroic. It would be so easy to be like them, wouldn't it? Better different; but to overtake them, you have to fall in line, follow suit, run in the same direction. The debraining machine grinds on, come what may.

Amor con amor se paga, runs the Spanish proverb. Hostility too is paid for with hostility. If I cannot bear this oppressive system and try to explain to it why it makes me suffer so, it is only fair that it should refuse me the means to make myself heard or seen, without giving any explanation. *Paris-Match*, *L'Express* and *Le Point* will not print my photo, except to insult, slander or mock me. *Le Monde* will not publish my article, and my publisher will turn his back on me. It is neither his fault nor mine. No one is being unpleasant: there is no plot, boycott or cabal. The media work automatically. But the programming of the programming machines is pure politics or, in other words, concentrated economics. Don't mention oil, or Africa, or immigrant workers, or unequal exchange. Everyone, either in his own career or that of others, has been able to test the reflexes of this rigid machinery by applying different stimuli to it.[9] Like a rat trying to find his piece of cheese in the laboratory, the intellectual animal in the

[9] Compare the reviews that Jean Ziegler, the author of *Une Suisse au dessus de tout soupçon* (a relatively restricted demystification that did not touch on any national interests) got in France with the reviews that the same Jean Ziegler got with *Main base sur l'Afrique*, a battery of capital and very wide-ranging questions pointing towards the very source of French interests and the prosperity of the West in general. Conversely, one might compare the minor coverage the post-'68 leftists got—and with such difficulty—when they took oppression in France here and now as their target and the coverage the same people got when they discovered the Soviet 'Gulag' a few years later. On a minor scale, the author of these lines had the opportunity to calculate the comparative mediatic profitability of two 'investigations' bound and printed with six months between them: one dealing with the French Communist Party and one with the French imperialist party.

labyrinth learns (by the so-called method of trial and error) which buttons to press to get the right response: those which give material rewards (photos, interviews, invitations, reviews, debates, polemics, TV appearances), financial rewards (sales volumes, royalties) or compensations (calming inner anguish). A 'left'-wing intellectual who is concerned about his good image (being asked to appear on *Questionnaire*, *L'Homme en Question*, *Apostrophes*, *Les Grilles du Temps* or other Debates and Soapboxes) might find it worth his while to wonder why it is that, in all left-wing organizations, what we call the right creeps into our minds via the media and what we call the media all creep in from the right.[10] And he might remember Spinoza's old axiom: 'We desire nothing because we deem it good . . . but, on the other hand, we deem a thing good because we desire it.' If the media do not desire me, it is not because I am better than others—I will be the best when I desire them and all they convey very strongly. Woe to the worried, the impatient and the humiliated. Woe to anyone in the metropolis who wants to be intelligent, just and handsome. For the social power that sifts the candidates and tells the majority who is most intelligent, just and handsome cares nothing for intelligence, morality or aesthetics. But it does have an infallible flair for knowing (from a distance) where the danger is coming from and what will succour it.

The revolutionary militant does not rise up where the Great Medium has gone before him. But he who goes 'there' and he who watches others grovel gets across as best he can.[11] 'You don't agree with us? Good. Come

[10] A banal comment, but one which can be extended to infinity: when there is a choice between Rocard and Chevènement, Ellenstein and Althusser or Fabre and Crépeau, the hero of the media is always the former and never the latter. When Mitterand and Giscard meet face to face on TV, the TV acclaims Giscard. We have here a necessity intrinsic to the logic of the mass media (see *Traité*, tome II).

[11] A Communist journalist recently expressed his surprise that a 'Communist' and presumably Marxist intellectual could talk about everything and anything on TV for an hour without once mentioning the class struggle and capitalist imperialism, the *raison d'être* of Marxism in general and Communist parties in particular. I'm surprised he was so surprised. If Jean Ellenstein talked about such 'old-fashioned notions' more often, we'd probably see less of him on TV. For similar reasons, Althusser, who has never been on TV, is less likely to be asked to do so on those conditions. On the other hand, if Ellenstein did not so often appear as a special guest-star at peak viewing time he would not have become 'the leader of the CP dissidents'. Fair's fair. The fact that only one in ten of the dissidents would recognize him as one of them and that the other nine would laugh at the very idea won't stop them laughing on the other side of their faces soon enough. Given the present state of affairs, what is there to prevent the opinion and the practice of the mediocrats forcing itself on the opinion and practice of the *militants* of the two surviving parties on the left (the Communist and Socialist parties)?

here and say so'—'here' being *RTL*, *L'Express* or *Antenne 2*. You start to surrender when you say yes. Going 'there' to explain that one disagrees means agreeing with the implicit idea that disagreements have to be channelled through the conduits of mass information, the best means the (feedback) machine has to keep individual desires in a state of equilibrium. The content of what I say, scream or whisper is of minor importance; what matters is that I say it there. What matters is that every possible message is immediately overcoded by a grid of equivalences (the programme schedule is its physical counterpart) that makes any thesis one opinion amongst others (all equally valid), all truth a point of view (all defensible), any contradiction a mere difference (all admissible). They are all valid, and, in other words, worthless. Resistance? Collaboration? Please, no manichean visions of the world. Of course not—so vulgar. The great family of men . . . the great fraternity of the intellectuals. So vulnerable, these crucified, abused victims of History. . . . Let's sit down and talk. About each other? With one another. Drieu was as good as Politzer, who was as good as Brasillach, who was as good as Aragon, who was as good as Maxence, who was as good as René Char. . . . The only man who is better than the rest is he who puts the equals sign between them, the man who knows that it will all be settled over a drink with Pivot on TV. That is, Pivot himself: the columnist of the Eternal, who has transcended History because he enjoys all histories.

Five

Hierarchical
Signs and
Insignia

If the darkest spot were not always beneath the lamp, and if the intellectuals of the West had as adequate a knowledge of their concept as the exiled Chinese worker in Hong Kong, they would stop being fooled and thrown off the scent by outdated insignia. We need not worry. In this war of everyone against everyone, access to the media is indeed target and touchstone, prize and apple of discord. Will I have access to the maximum means of influence or not—in a universe of communication where optimum and maximum have become synonymous? Will you? Will he? Will we? Where? How many minutes? With whom and against whom? Which channel? Front page? Mentioned on the cover?

It is a classic case of retinal persistence: the features of the old hierarchies blur those of the new. An understandable flickering. What appears in the remoulding of the masters of public language, in the new way they distinguish themselves from one another and, collectively, from their subjects, is a new regime of discursive production with new procedures of exclusion and distribution, and new institutional divisions—and not only techniques to administer speech, but a very different position of discourse as object of desire (for the opportunity to speak, to reach the site of social speech), which probably makes it a different desire and a different discourse. Why the malaise—and the mistakes? Probably because we continue to apply an old grid to a system of political and cultural domination that has rearranged its blank spaces and the places to be taken, its access corridors, its inner allegiances and solidarities. The malaise is sometimes moving, sometimes openly comic, like those posters of ambitious young wolves masquerading as sheep, Cauchon dressed up as Joan of Arc and witch-hunters disguised as witches[1]—like the recent revelation (1977) from a high dignitary who said, with a perfectly straight face, that the tribunes of a certain late political programme contained no intellectuals, in an attempt to make us forget not only the death of the schoolyard and the wooden dais, but also that the true political tribune is not the one from which he was speaking and that it, on the contrary, is not short of preachers in his image. Is this the cynicism of the new lords, and the jeremiad of displaced colleagues? No. Perhaps it is more than that: a chronological overlap between modes of resonance, a technological junction between the tribunal capacities of two apparatuses, a reversal of dominance within the equipment of public discourse. The outcome is a complete turnabout in the mist: before our unseeing eyes, the aristocracy is being unseated by an intellectual mediocracy. The change also has to be viewed etymologically: functional domination by the most mediocre is passing itself off as the institutional rule of the best. Yes, the darkest spot in modern society is a small, luminous screen.

For every new mode of production of consensus, there is a corresponding new mode of promotion for the functionaries of the consensus. In the present case, the NCOs of the old symbolic order have the edge over the old staff officers. In terms of academic qualifications, a working journalist is probably the equivalent of a sergeant and a top mediocrat the equivalent of a subaltern. In the popular press, state doctorates are very rare and *agrégations* exceptional. It is not that journalists are not cultured, but that modern culture does not use the same paths as yesterday's hierarchies. Of the 183 journalists on *Le Monde*—the most academic of newspapers—175 have higher education diplomas. In the vast majority of cases, on *Le Monde* and elsewhere, that diploma is a first degree (in arts, philosophy, sociology, law, economics, or whatever). When whole classes from Saint-Cyr depend upon middling officers risen from the ranks for their promotion, something like a captains' revolution is taking place. The old ideological high command goes on issuing and signing written orders in the shape of theses, essays and academic research. But in every army in the world, an order has to be *transmitted* to the personnel and other units if it is to be carried out, and that transmission depends upon the operational intermediaries who effectively command the units and who are in direct contact with the troops. They are now the 'intellectuals' intellectuals' and

[1] Cf. the title, *Faut-il brûler les nouveaux philosophes?* (Paris 1978; a 'dossier' compiled by the new philosophers themselves)—an everlasting cliché with a brand-new future ahead of it.

the others depend upon them. Their promotion does not suggest any greater creativity, but a greater capacity for practical organization (or a sphere of influence englobing that of the others); or, to be more accurate, the subordination of creativity to organization, of the 'spiritual' to the 'material' or, as 'they' are beginning to put it once more, of higher education to primary education (they being the new intellectuals). Being functional, this subordination is invisible. All that can be seen is a strange amalgam in which juxtaposition conceals integration and the merging of strata conceals the direction of control. Since Gramsci, it has been normal to describe a stratum of intellectuals as organic when it assimilates and promotes within it 'élites originating from the classes below it' (the Catholic clergy creaming off rural youth, the party the young workers). But a new stratum of organizers can also assimiliate and promote the cream of 'higher' élites when their functional support (in this case the university) has lost some of its functionality. In that case, the young select their elders. To take the example of *Le Monde* again (an example which is far from amenable to our thesis, given its elitist and deliberately classical nature), the most numerous generational category among its journalists is of those between 31 and 40 years old. Ninety-four of its staff journalists are between 20 and 40, and only eighty-nine between 40 and 65. The average age of technical, commercial and financial executives in industry is much higher.

No review of the multiple indices of the new hierarchy in the intellectual corps—and its very diversity indicates its internal coherence—will give eyesight to the blind, but it is worthwhile to glance at them out of curiosity. In this chapter we will move from the anodyne to the serious, from the scale of prestige to the scale of incomes (the two are very close together). The division between the sexes, the steps on the career ladder, the degrees of allegiance and gastronomic demarcations are all of a piece.

I

New Prestige

In 1950, I say to a gathering of friends that 'Gallimard have accepted my manuscript'—and I am immediately different, acclaimed, put on a pedestal. In 1980, no one even raises an eyebrow at the same piece of news, with all its false nonchalance. In this world, everyone has contacts with a publisher, big or small, and a manuscript 'on the go' somewhere or other. To spark off the same reactions of love, spite or rivalry now, I would have to say something like 'I'm going to be on the front page of *Le Monde* next week', or 'Jean-Louis Servan-Schreiber has been in touch about next month'.* And instead of passing around a letter of acceptance from Raymond Queneau, signed and on headed notepaper, I give a blow-by-blow account of the lunch with Viannson or repeat Chancel's phone-call word for word. Signs of the times.

In social terms, snobbery is as precious as a compass in the woods. The intelligentsia's criteria for prestige are displaced together with the centre of gravity of the social markets. Prestige is an economic indicator—of the new frontier dividing public from private, recognition from anonymity; of the rising threshold of publication, which has moved from the editorial level to the level above. This brutal shift has changed not only the way reputations are shared out, but the very way publishing functions. It has raised the level of both the inter-individual battle for selection and the inter-company struggle for profitability. The emblems that distinguish intellectuals from one another are indexed to the hegemonic apparatus of each period, even though the desire for distinction itself is part of their very nature.

At what point does someone who enters the profession of letters become

---

* Président directreur général of the Expansion publishing group; producer and presenter of TF 1's *Questionnaire*.

certain that he will 'pull through', with the added bonus of some hope of standing out? In 1890, it was the point at which I entered ENS as a student. In 1930 it was when I was already a teacher and joined a big publisher as a literary adviser or a series editor. In 1970 it was when I was already a series editor and joined a big newspaper as a columnist, leader writer or regular contributor. For what is the point of being a series editor (apart from the useful 2% commission) if you do not have access to an important medium? What makes a series take off is not so much the quality of what is published in it, especially if you want to work fast, as the editor's ability or inability to make what he publishes really public. Since anyone can now print, bind and sell a typescript (thanks to the 700 marginal publishers in Paris and the provinces and the increased volume of production), the material act of publication has lost all discriminating value. Just as the intellectual no longer feels that he is 'realizing' himself simply through the books he publishes, but through everything that is published 'about' his publications, so booksellers are convinced that a book no longer realizes its value on the book market but in the 'mass media' that now regulate it. In a word, publishers fold if they do not have top journalists working for them, journalists who are capable of talking to their colleagues as one power to another. It is they who give their employers the benefit of their personal social capital by integrating them into the cycles of the influence market. To be able to return favours— something that neophytes ask very lightly—you must at least have a foot on the ladder: a column in a daily or a weekly, a regular hour-long slot. 'The small favour' ('Right, we'll talk about your book on next week's programme') is the prerogative of those who hold a lease. Failure to return a favour is not necessarily bad manners: it may be a question of inferiority. The direct favours that publishers can do one another are limited; those that journalists can do for them are considerable, and those that they can do each other through journalists connected with the company are extraordinary. In other words, between 1930 and 1980, the media-publishing link has been reversed. For example, in unofficial but functional tandems like *Opéra-Mundi—France-Soir, Laffont-L'Express, Grasset-Le Point, Le Seuil-Le Nouvel Observateur*, the publisher is much more dependent on his chosen medium than is the medium on him. Revel, Nourissier and Julliard contribute much more to the publishing houses because of their positions on the three big weeklies than they contribute to the latter because of their functions in publishing. Increasingly, the profits of a publishing company will depend on the number of media under its control or, in which it has contacts. The future belongs to the tricycle, but the big publishing houses already have four wheels. As for individuals, their influence (and therefore their productivity) will depend on the number of journalists they can count among their personal friends, unless of course they become journalists themselves. The future belongs to the multimedium, but the great intellectual animals of the moment will soon be going on all fours.

The New Logistics

The source from which social ideas radiate appears to be at once the home port for the bearers of ideas, the launching pad for the product and the logistical base of the producer. The leading intellectual producer of the moment (the big name) usually finds his safest haven and his main source of income in the most profitable institution. The same man who made a very poor living out of the university in 1890 did fairly well out of publishing in 1930 (and 1950) and very well out of the media in 1980. And the author, or the current of ideas, launched by the university lecture theatre in 1890 was launched by a review in 1950 and by a weekly or a TV programme in 1980. The instances are not juxtaposed; they move within a sphere of influence that provides them with a frame of reference. Ideological 'fashions', for example, are inseparable from their mode of transport or the vehicle that launches them. Bergsonism spread to the literary world, the salons and the stage, but was still based in the university sphere (as did its refutations and its counter-attacks). Existentialism spread to the university and to the timid mass media of the day, but remained deeply rooted in publishing. As for the New Philosophy—so baptized by a headline—it appears in its essence to be a *new logistics* (in that it is not known to have any specific theoretical essence or even ever to have needed one, which is quite in line with the mediatic canon).

Observing the metamorphoses of a recognized discipline such as philosophy—whose effects cut across the fields of pedagogy, publishing and politics—is like watching a spectral band unwind: each period brings its own logistics; the lecture/discourse system for the first, the book/review for the second and the press/TV system for the third. Each dominant support has its individual paradigms: Bernard/Bergson; Sartre/Camus; our theoretical serial-writers. In the present mediological age, it is not necessary to *teach* philosophy to 'be a philosopher', nor is it necessary to carry out philosophical *research* and submit it in published form for the professional approval of the philosophical community. What is necessary in one period is optional in the next. Yesterday's canon is today's eccentricity. That does not mean that there will be no more teachers or books of philosophy, but simply that these will no longer be the owners of the patent or social image (the standard vehicle). The persistence of cultural signs on the social retina means that they go on acting long after they have been worn out, just as the organ outlives its function, the description outlives the practice and the qualifying term the substance. In the New Order, it is no longer necessary to think anything to be a thinker or even to write books to be a writer; but to have all the marks of a *writer* or *philosopher* (in order to demarcate oneself from the non-writers and non-thinkers) is still a social necessity. It would be a mistake to conclude that the modern mediatic network is incapable of breaking the symbolic systems of a culture by hawking the legacy of the past.

3

The New Strategies

'Why buy an umbrella for twelve francs when you can buy a beer for six sous?' Why invest ten years of your life in writing a thesis that will give you a state doctorate and a life sentence in a provincial university (where students 'ripen' and lecturers rot) when it takes a month to vitriolate an ideological pamphlet on the subject of the day (The Gulag and Destiny) and make your name in the popular press, or when sparkling on TV for an hour will make you a national hero? It is well known that the law of value appears not to apply to intellectual and artistic production—or at least every producer is free to think that it does not apply where he personally is concerned.[2] There would seem, rather, to be an inverse ratio between labour time and the volume of renumeration. A novel that cost me three months' work may sell one hundred thousand copies and give me enough to live on for three years. A theoretical work that cost me ten years' work will sell one thousand copies, all but ruin my publisher and reduce my family to living on bread and water. It is not surprising that more people have vocations to be novelists than to be theoreticians, even if theory does help people form the world while novels help them dream it. Nor is it surprising that authors 'rarely make any connection between their work and their financial renumeration', as Sartre put it. If they did they would soon lose heart. Culture—by definition a selfless activity—is also a school of cynicism for those who work in it, for if others enjoy it, 'men of culture' have to make a living from it. For many reasons, and subsistence is not the dominant one, an intellectual career is now the best professional training

[2] The question of the price of works of art in particular and the market value of the products of intellectual labour in general calls for a much more complex analysis, which might lead us back to the labour theory of value. On this question, see the forthcoming works of Michel Gutelman.

for the practice of immoralism. The theory is open to everyone and recommended to none; some virtues are better practised if one does not know what they are, or that they are virtues. Immoralism is one of them.

Courteline's observation does not only apply to base material things. It can be turned into a model of the objective economy of the cursus, based upon the comparative profitability of the various sectors of professional activity in terms of hierarchical promotion and valid for the whole of the intellectual corps in a given society at a given moment. Someone will say that the best careers are those that follow no plan, that the best regimes are those that are not guided by a political doctrine and that the best revolutionaries have never read *Capital*. It is a familiar argument. There is little point in sailing into the wind when pragmatism has the wind in its sails, so we will simply point out that, to use Madame de Cambremer's expression, those who scorn the outside world most are never the last to carve out a place for themselves in it. There are career guides for executives in industry, so why should there not be one for executives in Ideas and Letters? One's life is organized very differently, depending on whether one is ennobled by going to ENS, or joining the NRF or *L'Express*. If the main advantage of hereditary monarchies is that they restrict power struggles at the top and that of caste societies that they stifle the class struggle as much as possible, the advantage of republican civil societies with high social mobility is the opposite (and the intelligentsia is one of those states where the hierarchy of members is both more pronounced and less palpable): the struggle for promotion is constant and involves everyone. The competition is so merciless and the slightest navigational error so irrevocable that one cannot afford to play around with the New Order of investment priorities. Hindus have metempsychosis, but we live only once.

The classical university cursus still represents an essential outlay on equipment, but it should be kept down through restriction to the lower echelons, like fixed costs that cannot be reduced any further. The important point is that investments in diplomas can no longer be redeemed adequately on the ground where they are made, namely in higher education. There is a glut on the upper floors (professors, senior lecturers) and overcrowding in the basement (assistant lecturers): the stairs are blocked. Even if the administrative (or generational) block were by some miracle to be removed tomorrow, the university would still be a promotional blind alley, as it has been for some time. Once it has been acquired, academic capital must be invested in the sphere of publishing as soon as possible, since that is where it will make the biggest profit, both economically and socially (it is typical of the period that there is no longer any distinction between the two). On the one hand, knowledge is transformed into a commodity form (books, encyclopedias, albums) and on the other, which is more important, the author is put on show for the first time: this is a precondition for his subsequent exploitation, but he will really be turned to good account only when he is promoted to the upper and decisive levels of *social visibility*: radio, TV and the magazines. Three remarks are called for: 1. for every input made at a given level, the maximum output is obtained at the level above; 2. accumulation of profit works retroactively; 3, each level of activity can, at its own level, make a profit from the level above, provided that the latter makes a still greater profit from it. In plain language, a good position in the media guarantees the journalist a better position in the publishing world, which in turn guarantees the graduate access to or promotion in the university apparatus—with, of course, a little help from the interests of friends. Theoretically, the cursus moves upwards (in accordance with the criteria of the previous period), but in fact it goes downwards, as can be seen from the slowness and hardships of the reverse journey. Similarly, it has become much easier and more profitable to make a book from a film than a film from a book. It is the mediocrats (working or retired) who obtain by far the best advances for their authorial projects and the highest positions when they go to work for publishers; there is no comparison between their audience, and therefore their influence and salary, and that of the great teachers or writers. Or again, a publisher will give a writer of fiction a much better advance if he can count on a serial adaptation. If the serial is made, both author and publisher will feel that they have used the TV medium on behalf of the book: the TV has used both of them by imposing its criteria of choice on the professionals of the book. It is a law that whoever uses an inferior medium can never use a superior medium without being used by it.[3] In the immediate, and to take only the most blatant example, it is well known that TV does not serialize just any contemporary novel (D'Ormesson is much more likely to be chosen than Claude Simon). The orientation of production follows the hierarchy of the producers: the *media* control *publishing* and publishing controls the *university*.

The stronger the social command, the higher the individual demand.

---

[3] For the meaning of 'inferior' and 'superior', I am obliged to refer the reader to the *Traité*'s concrete analysis of the media in and for themselves.

Those who were once at the bottom of the ladder (the journalists as intellectual proletariat) are now at the top; the highest finality corresponds to the strongest causality. The mediological break we are witnessing has permuted the content/form ratio in the various circles of the intelligentsia. In 1955, towards the end of the second age of the French intelligentsia, Raymond Aron could still place novelists in the 'inner circle', immediately adding; 'Below them we find those who work on the press and the radio, those who maintain communications between the elite and the masses. In this perspective, the creators would be at the centre of the category and its boundary would be that ill-defined zone where the vulgarizers stop translating and start betraying. Being concerned solely with success and money, slaves to what they imagine to be public taste, they become indifferent to the values they profess to serve.'[4] But when, twenty years later, he became chairman of the editorial board of *L'Express*, Raymond Arom did not feel that he was coming down in the world; on the contrary, he quite rightly felt that he was moving to the heart of the inner circle— because over the same period, the first and second circles had changed places. This particular ideologue deserves the greatest respect for his ability to home in on the best acoustics: a mandarin when there was still an echo in the lecture theatre; pontiff of the pen so long as there were attentive readers; and now head of the most audio-visual of all news magazines. There is nothing accidental about this rise. The odds are that when the old man granted his patronage to the only Anglo-Saxon paper written directly in French he felt himself grow younger. Glossy paper feeds on young blood.

In the process of valorizing intellectual productions, the mediatic apparatus is the most dynamic of all factors, and this is why it is so economical to begin one's career 'at the end'. Fortunately, the climb back along the chain of causes from the most to the least profitable coincides with the line of least resistance. Hence the crush of young talent at the door to the mediatic sanctuaries and the youth of the intellectual 'elites'. No one has a chair in philosophy at the age of 35 and no one is a novelist at 25. On the other hand, it is in one's interests to save on life and studies, to become competitive with the programme producers and the leading lights of intellectual journalism; in these areas, seniority is a hindrance rather than a help. The intelligentsia is getting younger than ever in its old age. Michel Tournier's comment that 'seniority and hierarchy are almost always

[4] *L'Opium des intellectuels*, p. 285.

synonymous' was true of the old France, but now it is wrong. An Americanized intelligentsia in a Europeanized France puts the emphasis on smiles, good teeth, nice hair and the adolescent stupidity known as petulance.

4

The New Lunches

Mediology, which, in the absence of state subsidies, is forced to use the state as its laboratory is not shy of social experimentation either, and that, in its eyes, includes society news. The 'Horizon 2000 writers' lunch' at the Elysée Palace on September 7, 1978, is therefore worthy of attention. The ethnic ceremony of the lunch, celebrated on the plains as well as on the heights, calls for an ethnographic description all to itself. This lunch was exceptional, as all the media said both before and after the event. The Republic, which does not gather for lunch every day, spreads out its meetings, so as to keep their value constant.[5] It is not in fact good for the various fragments of political authority in France to have official meetings too often. The tenured men of 'influence' function best when both they and those they influence are convinced they are alone. What applies to the juridical and military apparatus applies also to the intellectual apparatus: it is politically more effective when it is seen to be apolitical. Too many meetings would damage the dialogue, in that intellectual dissidence would lose credibility if it revealed its political buttresses too often. Many people are aware of this, and the farce of the public polemics with which the intellectual milieu punctuated this summit meeting will no doubt provide inspiration for some follower of Molière (or Beaumarchais?). But the little man who simply wants to look at the times he inhabits in the hope of one day reaching that point in life normally known as wisdom, where laughter and knowledge cancel each other out, and who is armed with Spinoza's axiom ('neither weeping nor laughing: understanding') will be able to

[5] In the same period, a state luncheon on 9 December 1976, brought together both ruling Presidents (of the Republic and of the National Assembly) and a delegation from the high intelligentsia consisting of Le Roy Ladurie, Philippe Sollers, Dominique Desanti, Roland Barthes and Claire Brétecher. But that was a private function.

resist the giggles: you can recognize serious matters because they are carefully hidden beneath the ridiculous.[6]

'What is there to understand?' means 'Where is the unexpected', 'What is there to be astonished at?' Not simply that it happened: the occasion conforms to all the principles of state formations in general and the French state in particular. The prince and his scribes is the 'primal scene' of politics, but it is the only original sketch in the comedy of French power that distinguishes it from all its rivals. In Germany or the United States, the literary column of the day is on a different page from the political column. In France, those who write one act in the other and vice versa. It has been said that the interpenetration, so typical of French society, of the administrative and scientific elites sealed the fate of French science in the last century: it was sterilized in the egg and anaemic in its methods and principles. On the other hand the interpenetration of the literary and political elites stimulates the life of both. In that sense, when the high intelligentsia confers with the top personnel of the state, it is not simply enjoying one of the human rights that are so dear to it—the right to choose one's dining companions—it is giving in to the irresistible duty of its office. By sitting down at the Presidential table, it honours not only its concept, but its past. When one half of the state meets the other, should it not do so somewhere better than the dining room? It is true that in any other country, both would have gone into the office. But where else would such a conference have been of interest to the rest of the country? This masking of the gravity of an obligation with the splendours of fashion is a classically French ruse and an institutionalized paradox.

So what is new in this historically programmed and banal episode, whose only novelty is that it seemed newsworthy in 1978? For the historian of hegemony, the novelty lies in the new balance between parties traditionally opposed to one another, a new balance that is to the detriment of *potestas* and therefore to the advantage of *auctoritas*. Such a shift is normal in moments of symbolic depression and it should not necessarily worry the political power. On the contrary: 'the President seems pleased that in ideas and philosophy, France's trade balance is favourable'[7]—which makes up for the other balance. The decoder of the dominant

---

[6] André Glucksmann, 'Mon ami, votre injustice' (*Le Monde*, 6 September 1978), Maurice Clavel, 'Terreur dans les écritoires' (*Le Monde*, 7 September), Lionel Stoléru, 'Quel dialogue, monsieur Glucksmann?' (9 September), and so on. See also No. 722 of *Le Nouvel Observateur*, 'Les Hôtes du Président'.

[7] Conclusion of 'Les hôtes du Président', *Le Nouvel Observateur*, 11–17 September 1978.

discourse would prefer to see the strange paths that this compulsive constant of French history, which ties the intellectual to the ship of state and literature to political issues, had to follow to make its way through a conjunctural ideology that makes the intellectual an activist in permanent insurrection against the 'cold monsters'. The attempt to make sense of this nonsense and turn the fever of the moment into the rationality of duration would once have demanded a certain rhetorical ingenuity, whose tropes, now codified, would have intrigued the author of *Les Fleurs de Tarbe*.* How to turn deference into defiance, an invitation into an ultimatum and 'worldly' into 'worldwide'—since May '68 there has been nothing insoluble about this little technical problem: the stage-managers of the word resolve it every week.[8] The true novelty is of a mediological order, and is not, therefore, news to anyone: it is the very composition of the intellectual delegation, a real cross-section of the new intellectual power.

How does one bring together the whole state, and on what criteria? There is no problem on the *potestas* side: in the eyes of all, the regularly elected President of the Republic represents that fraction of the state known as political power. On the *auctoritas* side, it is an old problem. How and to whom is intellectual and moral power to be delegated? In the socialist countries, the Head of State and Secretary General of the Party is ipso facto the President of the intellectuals. This is why he so rarely invites them to lunch: it takes two to make a dialogue. And if he wants to send his congratulations or make some comment, the channel is obvious: the Presidency of the Writers' Union will transmit them. In France, the problem is more delicate. Our intellectual corps has too many heads for it to be able to elect a unanimously recognized collegial president—we will see why later. But there are only so many places around a table, even at the Elysée. How is the Republic of Letters to select representatives of the Spirit of the Laws? Twenty-five years ago, the secretariat of the Elysée would have consulted the Rectorate of the University of Paris or the Permanent Secretary of the Académie Française if it had wanted a

* Jean Paulhan.
[8] 'If I may be excused for bringing up the past, I did not resist both Nazi and Stalinist terrorism and intimidation by the conventional left to be intimidated by malicious gossips who are spreading an exaggerated version of an article by a very good friend of mine all over Paris and telling me to conform to the rule of appearances' (Maurice Clavel, *Le Monde*). The death of the theatre brought the show into the stalls and the death of the monarchy brought the court to town. But what stage can Beaumarchais use to bring Figaro back to life—and will he be up to these stalls and this town?

representative assortment from the bourgeois intellectual elites. The elite of the elite (from the Greek root ελεῖν, to choose) can by definition select the elite. Given that the third millenium is approaching, the President was not mistaken when he recruited his prefects from this new stratum of intellectuals made by and for the mass media, whose value lies less in their personal work (usually non-existent or reduced to the strict minimum of one printed work), still less in their research work, than in their emplacement at the key points of social *resonance*. They stand out against the background of their quieter colleagues because of their capacity for making an ideological noise: a capacity that confers upon a whole new caste of ideocrats a position midway between the networks that produce knowledge—and on which they are parasites—and the public broadcasting network, where they are known as 'producers'. It is no accident that the Ministry of Culture has been renamed the Ministry of Culture *and* Information; that conjunction, which contains all the mysteries of the day, is the true 'black box' of our political and cultural cybernetics. In the modernized Republic of Letters, the value of an intellectual is calculated on the basis of his power of social communication. Yesterday's intellectual leaders had literary productions, today's have broadcasts; in the future the number of printed signs will have to be reckoned in frequencies of audiovisual signals. His position as a radio producer on France-Culture and the fact that he has the ear of the favourite media of the intellectual milieu suggested Philippe Nemo as an agent for the Republic—for, to my knowledge, the 'little' Ecole Normale at Saint-Cloud and an apparently modest literary output were never sufficient reasons for anyone to be assigned to such a role. Aptitude and titles are less important than the truly non-transferable capital that gives the intellectual his real 'surface': a knack with decibels. That means not only familiarity with the labyrinth of offices, studios, corridors and editorial units in which the philistine gets lost and at the end of which glimmers the event, the polemic, the talking point; it also means familiarity with the code of contacts based on passwords, good fellowship or simply friendship, which allows a single individual to mobilize in just a few days the thirty men who, according to Balzac, tell 30 million what to think—and with dispatch riders, moreover, so that urgent telegrams can be sent to the top intellectuals (academics, researchers, essayists) and a really fashionable delegation put together. Most of those approached will simply shrug their shoulders and go back to work. A few, more at home with the parameters of the new age and second to none in terms of know-how, will catch the ball on the rebound and score twice. They make it officially known both that they were invited and that they turned down the invitation, combining the prestige of integration into the summit (I could have been there) with the incorruptibility required of those who serve the plebs (but I didn't want to go). It is an admirable family that can give all its grown-up children the advantages of dissidence without any of its disadvantages.

At the inception of the Fifth Republic, the technocracy could not raise itself to the summits of the state apparatus without taking along the politicians, jurists and parliamentarians of the 'regime of the parties', and today's new ideocracy cannot raise itself to the summits of the ideological apparatuses without an escort of eminent men from an establishment whose end it is hastening. What difficulties and delays our young Carnots of hegemony must have had before they could concoct a plausible amalgam of generations, levels, prestige, tradition and innovation! The legion finally consisted of two veterans, one half-pay officer and two raw recruits. But there is no correspondence between relations within the hierarchy and stripes and seniority; the two 'traditional intellectuals' on the delegation were in reality passively organized by the new 'organic' intellectuals risen from the ranks. If the Académie Française in the shape of Lévi-Strauss and the Collège de France in the shape of Georges Duby contributed the *legitimacy*, whose halo effect valorized the organizers, the operational conception and execution were in the hands of the newcomers (Nemo and Lévy). Clavel, the mediaman par excellence and mediocratic link between the Ancients and the Moderns, relayed the broadcast from his tallest mast.

The mass media have invented democracy within the aristocracy, just as the atom bomb invented it at the military level. The star system sucks up those who are promoted, abolishing the distance—political, social, geographical, moral and cultural—that once separated them. That is how a chosen club of intellectuals ('representing no one but themselves') could in only a few years turn itself into the privileged partner of the elected club of political leaders representing at least several hundred thousand militants (or millions of voters in the case of heads of state). Those thousands and millions no longer carry any weight, for the simple reason that they cannot be seen on the screen or be heard on the radio: the blindness of the political leaders of the opposition, trapped by the media, comes from the invisibility of their troops. This reduction in the differences of potential within the intellectual club is equivalent to the equalization of megatons between the members of the atomic club. When the flash-bulbs pop, Nemo becomes the equal of Lévi-Strauss and Duby, just as France immediately became the equal of the USA and the USSR when she acquired several hundred kilotons. French citizens have already had the privilege of seeing and hearing an honourable chemist (Robert Fabre by name) decide their fate every day for a year, because the TV promoted him to the status of one of the three important men on the left, even though he won less votes than the ecologists. If the mediatic Household Cavalry can shelter behind two great men of science, who are austere and somewhat absent-minded, but whose work and image one simply has to admire (all the more so in that their work is politically neutral and their image blurred), they can be sure of a monopoly over the outcome as well as the initiative. The three friends (who have already praised each other to the skies in the press a dozen times) keep the broadcasting service for themselves. Almost before they have put down their coffee cups, they are making statements to all the radio stations, to the three TV channels, to tomorrow's papers; an unsigned account here, a spot of rewrite there, not to mention the phone calls to their three hundred closest friends. This public sub-contracting of a 'private' meeting is of no interest to the two traditionalists, who leave the Elysée and go home without making any statements or giving away any secrets. The photo on the steps was enough; they are no longer needed. But what they will laugh about tomorrow, as though it were an unimportant side-effect, was in fact the event itself: the national and international stir. Their professional gravity would scarcely predispose them to guess the centre of gravity of the stunt they began but did not pull off. Hegemonic manoeuvres have always involved such little tricks. But the tricks might in future replace the manoeuvres.

5

The Pyramid of the Sexes

To find out what floor you are on in any profession, all you have to do is ask what is the proportion of women there. That is a general rule, valid for all activities, but especially for those of the intellect. Relegation means feminization; promotion means masculinity. There is no feminist parti pris in this statement: the figures speak for themselves—that is, when they exist. The higher one goes, the more evasive the answers to the questions (just as answers to questions about income become evasive as you move up the ladder of wealth). Statistics always start at the bottom. Their accuracy is no privilege: it is a punishment for being poor, and sanctions relegation. It is not surprising that the most accurate figures on the distribution of the sexes are to be found in education. Primary: 72.7% of the 318,379 primary teachers in 1977 were women—secondary: 54% of 202,000 teachers— higher: only 35% of the 41,905 staff employed in the universities were female. Naturally, the number of women in higher education falls steadily as one comes to the higher grades: most of them come into the categories of language assistant and assistant lecturer. We have no statistics for the staff of the Collège de France, the CNRS or the Ecole Pratique, but it is common knowledge that they are practically closed to women (apart from secretarial and library work). In the days when primary school teachers were the hussars of the Republic and not unskilled workers, the distribution of the sexes in that category was the direct opposite of what it is now.

For understandable reasons, there is little or no statistical information on publishers and authors. We will therefore have to restrict ourselves to making our own count on the basis of a limited but representative sample: the list of professional authors affiliated to the social insurance scheme through the Centre National des Lettres as of December 31, 1976 (persons whose main source of income is their writing). Of the 365 writers, 114 were women—almost 32%, but the figure would have to be revised downwards if we wanted to distinguish literary professional from 'writers' (of works which are not really 'literary') This is enough to show that we have moved up a floor. A century after George Sand, and despite the current vogue for the female product, a female author has a thousand opportunities a year to note that she is (much or slightly, depending on her sales) less respected in her milieu than a man. It is no accident that there is a woman (Marie Cardinal) at the head of an attempt to unionize the profession.

On the top floor—that of 'popular' journalism—the initial impression that the hierarchy is confused is destroyed as soon as we observe the number of women present at each level. It is more than destroyed: the mass-mediatic hierarchy will be translated directly into decreasing percentages as soon as the statistics become available. There are obviously more women in the press than on the editorial side in radio stations, and more women in radio than in TV (the number of women on each channel can be counted on one hand). The size of the audience corresponds to the scale of responsibilities—and therefore of salaries and male predominance. To restrict ourselves to the written press and to take as an example *Le Monde*, the central seat of French intellectual power in the written order— less because of the size of its readership (the biggest of any Parisian daily: 1,349,000 in 1977) than because of its sociological character and political function—45.1% of its readers are women. Yet the detective will only find twenty-three women journalists working on it, out of a total of 183 (the company as a whole employs 1,246 people) or roughly 15%. Most of these work in the relatively minor departments, such as the cultural and social pages. The distribution is similar to that of government personnel and again shows the extent to which the structures of cultural power are modelled on those of state power. There is not a single woman in the top editorial team, or in home news (11 staff journalists). There is one on general news (19), five on the foreign desk (total staff, about seventy, including correspondents, sub-editors, columnists and desk heads). Yvonne Baby does have the Ministry of Culture, Jacqueline Piatier the book department and Dr. Escoffier-Lambiotte the Ministry of Health. But comparison with Françoise Giroud, Alice Saunier-Seité and Simone Weil would be just a bad joke: governments come and go, but *Le Monde* is always with us. It is sometimes salutary to attack the government, but it is more dangerous than ever to attack a newspaper that is not only the best in the world, but quite possibly the last. No change of government is capable of making the people of France regress into barbarism, but the disappearance of *Le Monde* really would imply the end of a civilization and its probable replacement by one objectively regressive in comparison.

It goes without saying that the indices of segregation to be seen on *Le Monde* are even more blatant in other institutions. The descriptive side of mediology, it will be recalled, is not concerned with making value judgments, but with making hypotheses to be tested against reality; in that sense, it is neither feminist nor anti-feminist, neither favourable nor hostile to the organization of intellectual power as it functions in France in the latter part of this century (and the organigram of *Le Monde* is merely one instructive X-ray among others). It simply makes a correlation and notes that although the word culture is feminine and inclines to 'femininity', its upper spheres in particular are definitely male-dominated. Immortality is the prerogative of the male: there are no women in the Académie Française.* The high intelligentsia is a predominantly male society and the lower intelligentsia—where the stakes are naturally much lower—is a category with much higher female representation. This general rule produces the opposite effect at the individual level, as any schoolboy strategist could demonstrate. Male dominance does not necessarily preclude female leadership at the local level; on the contrary, it requires it as a legitimating exception to the general rule. The relative scarcity of women in the high intelligentsia creates a surplus of value for the few who do get there; if handled properly it can be turned into a comfortable income. In matters of strategy, 'properly' means politically. Those women versed in political practice who do enter the high intelligentsia are in fact experts at making discrimination an authoritative argument and persecution a supplementary claim for a legitimate audience, just as being a Party member and *a fortiori* an ex-member or an expelled member gives the victim a particularly advantageous position in the general competition for an anti-communist audience (and, vice versa, the ex-fascist for the anti-fascist audience). Being in the minority position of an excluded woman can be a favourable differential position. Anyone who combines both handicaps (female sex plus Communist past) defies all competition. Unfair competition, some will say; usually those who are not politicized and know nothing of modern market strategies.

* Members of the Académie are often referred to as the Immortals.

6

The Scale of Indulgences

The effect of the trade in indulgences, with its agencies, abuses and automatisms, was to cut the history of the West (and as a side-effect the history of mankind) into two by precipitating the Reformation and Protestant emancipation at the beginning of the sixteenth century. The effect of the uncontrolled rise in contributions and remissions among the French intelligentsia on the history of that corps remains to be seen. Unlike the Dominicans at Wittenberg, critics of books, films and plays do not put their eternal lives at risk, but only because eternity is dead. In the long run we will all go to hell, and none of us is any the worse for it. The here and now is ample compensation and the cultural market contents itself with the short term: the practical paradise. Our advantage over the sixteenth century is that those who control the symbolic keep their promises. They hand out fortunes as well as death. And not always symbolically: the fortune may be real—and the death physical.

The spectacle of the weekly jubilee, so characteristic of so-called Parisian social life, fills only the 'nothingologists' (Balzac) with jubilation, and they have been laughing the same dry moralists' laugh for the last three hundred years. The mediologist, on the other hand, uses the festivities and the vendettas listed in the repertoire of the *Gendelettres* to identify and combine the eminently variable factors that govern the distribution of intellectual power in each period. The scale of indulgences on the socio-cultural market shows the hierarchical coefficients of the various categories that go to make up the intellectual society of a given period—or, to be more accurate, the play of mutual dependence whose system designs the structure of order that in turn defines the relations of power: transitivity, assymmetry, non-reciprocity. One day it may be possible to study 'opportunism' mathematically.

The jargon is new, but the practice is old. It does not derive from a universal moral philosophy, but from what Rameau's nephew called *professional idiocy*, from the logical behaviour connected with a particular type of activity. The idiocy of the species whose trade it is to influence the opinion of others is its desire to please those whose position gives them most influence over public opinion. They would not be nearly so eager to do so if it were not their duty. In a letter to Madame de Recamier, Benjamin Constant put this in the form of an axiom: 'One must never be displeased with those one needs.' The 'must' is typical of unconditional morality—and the imperative merely indicates a certain state of morals more strongly conditioned among '*littérateurs*' than in any other human species. In that sense, Constant's motto is closer to Diderot than to Kant and its impertinence towards practical reason makes it all the more pertinent with regard to intellectual morals. This rule of conduct is never taught; it is simply part of the apprenticeship itself. The voice of conscience is a trademark. We learn La Fontaine's fables at school, but society forces our corporation to invest his fables: one always needs someone bigger than oneself. This moral curse is the price of professional success, and all it takes to find out who is biggest is a look at what satisfies the little man. If the little men swoon so regularly over the works of the directors, the editors-in-chief, and the editorial correspondents of the most influential media (listed in order of diminishing enthusiasm), if they make such an effort to quote them so often in epigraphs, chapter headings, in passing and in footnotes (an insistence which is all the more admirable in that colleagues tend to be mean to each other), and if they so often show their displeasure with foreign heads of state or the secretaries of the national political parties, it may also be because they depend a lot on the former but not at all on the latter. For the intellectual order, power does not lie where shallow people thinks it lies: with those whom everyone calls powerful (state, party, unions). It lies with those who control career prospects, increased print runs and greater social visibility: the great mediocrats. This amphibology as to the word power lies behind the many impostures that disguise flunkies (in the true, professional sense of the word) as insurgents (against a power that has no power over me, even if over millions of others). Political power gets a bad press amongst the intellectuals, but only because the (worst) press holds power, and because saving one's slings and arrows for the one is the best way to court the other. Failure to resolve this ambiguity means failure to understand why those who boldly take up arms against Brezhnev and Videla ('one struggle') in the outside world are so circumspect about criticizing some well-placed rogue at home. The strongest is the weakest? On the contrary: it does no harm to annoy Brezhnev or Videla (and it may even do you some good in terms of credit); but if you displease the rogue you risk having certain crucial doors slammed in your face. Constant's axiom may be philosophically dubious, but it at least has the merit of explaining why the fight for truth and justice so often stops at the doors of the profession. A rather witty contractor to the army once told Marshal de Villars that 'You can't hang a man who has a hundred thousand crowns'. You do not fling insults at a man with a million readers or ten million viewers, replies the supplier of new ideas, two hundred years later. Yesterday, gold was mightier than the sword. Today, the audience is mightier than the pen. The media have displaced the axis of need.

This is an analysis, not a pamphlet. If a study of modern times resembles a history of infamy, it is not the fault of the student of mediology, who is not interested in *fama*, because he finds it more interesting to make an objective examination of the public causes and effects attributed to individual fame by the society in which he lives. The power to kill at a distance, without touching anything or even knowing about it, is an old typographical feat. Far from wearing off, this magic has been rejuvenated by new printing techniques and the increased circulation of periodicals. It is not necessarily connected with an obvious state of foreign oppression (the Occupation press) or the savagery of political struggles (the Popular Front). It does not lead to other techniques being forgotten: silence is a civilized form of genocide (it is often committed, all over the world, behind our backs and partly thanks to us). There are now clean, neutral routine executions. For example: on 26 June 1976, *Le Point* appeared with a black cover: 'The head of the terrorist support networks'. 24 October 1977, brought an article in *Der Spiegel*, 'Led by an Egyptian . . .'. Then, on 25 October 1977, Henri Curiel was put under house arrest by the Minister of the Interior. On 5 May 1978, he was assassinated. 6 May 1978: 'It's nothing to do with me' (Georges Suffert). An epistemologist would say that 'consecutive' does not mean 'as a consequence of'. A technician in 'psychological action' would see this press campaign as a model. The sociologist of hegemony would reflect on the power of influential people. An expert in journalistic deontology would begin to wonder about his trade. As for the French intellectual who took the French intellectuals in 1978 as an object of study, he merely had the misfortune to see the editor of a very powerful magazine, the man responsible for that cover and the author of a despicable, unsigned dossier, as ill-informed as it was abject in its intentions, surrounded by admiring authors and conversing very seriously about Christian humanism on TV shortly afterwards. He heard the deafening silence with which this areopagite of moralists, not one of whom ever let a humanitarian manifesto that was to be published in the next week go by without adding his signature, greeted the body of a militant without an audience or a newspaper, who had never been on TV. And he simply felt ashamed. Not of 'Man'—that capital letter has enough franchise holders—but for the dignity of a corporation. Like many others, he had felt ashamed of belonging to it before; but never so much as on that evening . . .

François Mauriac used to say that, in the eyes of the world of letters, the world of politics was a school of indulgence. Being a Catholic, but an upright man, he certainly meant no harm to the Catholic meaning of the word 'indulgence'. The world of letters is, in effect, more cruel than the world of politics; for many reasons, the most obvious being that in it dependency works from above to below. Hence the temptation of demagogy in the one and of elitism in the other. The electoral mandate places the elected member under the control of those who mandate him. A *député* who wants to stay a *député* has to drink with his grocer and smile at his secretary; the party secretary who wants to be returned to office cannot turn his back on the branch or federation secretaries, no matter how lowly they are: they hold the votes and at the next congress, every one counts in the balance of forces. Within the high intelligentsia, *cooption, recommendation* and *nepotism* invert the modes of selection and promotion. Hence the cruelty of its politeness and the very different orientation of human relations there. In the world of letters, great men despise little men, tolerate their peers and have eyes only for the eminent men. For all that they may be the best men in the world, professional idiocy ensnares the most generous of men.

It is *non-reciprocity* in relations that allows a distinction to be made between 'above' and 'below' in any social apparatus. It creates the dependence of the latter on the former. This complex banality is worthy of attention, as its effects vary over the years. In 1849, Balzac dreamed of devoting a column in the *Revue Parisienne* to a 'review of the periodical press': it was not his fault that he could not bring his project to fruition.

The press, by its very nature, precludes any reciprocity of constraints; the tendency may be corrected here and there, but it goes against the grain and costs great sacrifices of time, space and charm, at least if you want to get beyond 'letters to the editor'—always a flattering mirror. 140 years later, it may be urgent to put Balzac's mad idea into practice, as the pollution of the atmosphere (surrounding consciences and practices) has gone beyond the danger mark, if not the point of no return. As we can show by examining the *content* conveyed by the media in the areas of politics and culture. But the greater the necessity, the greater the impossibility. There would be so little profit in such an organ that no investor would take it seriously. For the moment, let us stick to the *form* of the relations that unite (dissociate) the senders and the receivers, the subjects and the objects of public commentary. Essentially, nothing has changed since Balzac's day: 'In France, the press is a fourth estate within the state: it attacks everything and no one attacks it. It spreads blame here there and everywhere. It claims that politicians and men of letters belong to it, and does not want there to be any *reciprocity*; its own men are sacred. They do and say incredibly stupid things: it is their right to do so. It is high time that we discussed these unknown and mediocre men who take up so much space and control presses which in terms of volume put out as much as the book publishers.'[9]

A 'top journalist' is the only man in a position to humiliate, mock or denigrate any one of his fellow-citizens without the latter's being able to reply on equal terms. The law does provide for the defence in cases of gross defamation, slander and libel and its provisions are not without their effect, but high court costs, the slowness and the complexity of the process, on top of self-destruction by numbers, make legal action a bad business reserved for a caste of publicists who are sufficiently well provided-for elsewhere to be able to work at a loss. As for the right of reply, which fans the flames rather than extinguish them, very few papers respect it and the few readers who know how to take advantage of it usually belong to the profession; its mysteries and quibbles are closed to non-professionals. The flamboyant slanders of the pre-war press have given way to unanswerable perfidies; distortions and savage attacks are more in tune with the insipid conformism in which all social communication now wallows. The verbal outrages of the past at least had the virtue of being frank. Like everything

[9] *Revue Parisienne*, 25 August 1840. So we see, among other things, that the American metaphor of the 'fourth estate' was born on French soil and is far from new.

else, destruction can, in extreme cases, now do without a text: it is still easier to destroy with a title, a caption, or a choice of type face. In reality, miscarriages of justice are so much froth: the crime makes the law less flagrant and allows it to be forgotten. In cultural society, journalistic immunity is an unwritten law based on an internal solidarity encompassing all members of the corporation. In that respect, the fanatical egotism of the 'authors' puts them in a weak position vis a vis a 'tribe' that is completely fragmented yet has very strong totemic cohesion: there is a confraternity among the gentlemen of the press, but not among men of letters.

No sooner has the general law been stated than it has to be modified. There has never been a complete divide between the two groups, and it is now smaller than ever. The post-war period was characterized by the entry of the *professeurs* into literature in force; the post-'68 period has seen the journalists do the same. There are two reasons for this: sociological overflow (shortage of jobs) and political legitimation. In so far as the media assumed not only cultural but political power as a result of '68, and in so far as the instance of literature still confers legitimacy on the exercise of political power in France, top journalists owe it to themselves to write great books, just like the marshals, lawyers and political tenors of the past. If the Académie Française once had the right to pre-empt the latter, it now has the same rights over the popular press. There is therefore some interpenetration of the two traditional categories. It is true that people rub shoulders more on the journalistic level than on the literary: all the editors are on first-name terms, they phone each other every day, dine together and travel in groups together. In their younger days, they often worked side by side on the same papers; they meet at all the big press conference and the same events; foreign heads of state invite them all together to collective interviews, conferences and visits. Annoyance, bad temper and dirty tricks do not damage a solidarity that is existential as well as professional; but they do divide writers from one another, because they have no practice in common. It is therefore in the interests of men of letters, ideologues and intellectuals to reach the level of the gentlemen of the press so that they too can benefit from a social code that guarantees individual immunity. One of the tacit rules of the confraternity is to keep quiet about any book that puts an important colleague on an important editorial board on trial (or into perspective)—provided the favour is returned, of course. Hence the self-censorship of authors and the impunity of journalists. Any writer who breaks the rules knows in advance that this book will fall flat, killed outright by the silence of the media, and that his publisher will have to bear that in mind when they are negotiating over the next manuscript.[10] Here we see the naive, outdated cruelty of institutions like the Index (the Holy See), the Otto list (the Third Reich) and the central censorship office (the socialist countries today), which correspond to rudimentary forms of political domination. There are no black lists in advanced countries, because they are in the hands of the authors themselves. Anyone can put himself on the black list or take himself off it at will. Always ahead of its time, the intellectual corps is already under workers' control in the matter of fame and taboo.

The lines of communication between the different points in a network are the best indices of the relations of dependence that link them. Any editor can contact any other editor at any time provided they are both on the same level. On the floor of 'journalism', communication works horizontally in terms of titles and function, cutting across the vertical divides of political affiliations or leanings. Serge July can call Jean-François Revel direct, Leroy can call Fauvet and Chevrillion can call Viansson*—or vice versa. Similarly, in the eighteenth century it was easier for a French prince to contact a Polish or Spanish prince than a French knight or baron. And if the French baron had ready contacts with the Polish prince amongst his acquaintance, it was in his interests to use those contacts if he wanted to ask a favour of the French prince. The cost of communicating upwards is out of all proportion with that of communicating downwards, but horizontal communication is still profitable. If a contemporary author with an average reputation thinks he has been wronged or offended by a medium on which he is not directly dependent, he must go through his prince in order to address his petition to the neighbouring or enemy fief—if, that is, he expects an answer. Andre Fontainé phones Olivier Todd, or vice versa, to obtain redress for the man or woman in his court who thinks (s)he has been offended. Such detours are good strategy, given the inequality in the relation of forces between an empty-headed little baron or baroness and the prince who can, with one

[10] There are, of course, exceptions on both sides. Think of the courage and stature of *Le Monde Diplomatique*, the best periodical in France; and of the independence of mind of certain recognized loners like Jean-François Kahn. Despite themselves, they confirm the rule.

* Serge July: editor of *Libération*. Jean-Francois Revel: Editor of *L'Express*. Georges Leroy: news director of Antenne 2. Jacques Fauvet: director of *Le Monde*. Olivier Chevrillion; leader writer on *Le Point*. Pierre Viansson-Ponté: leader writer on *Le Monde*.

word, set the presses rolling, make a name familiar to two million people and change the cover at the last moment. The system of communications between the different strata of intellectual society is moving in the direction of a rectangular tabulation of lines and columns, a labyrinth of sharp bends without any horizontals. The serfs will be able to attack only other serfs, and the nobles throw down the gauntlet only to other nobles, but we must not confuse the brawls of the mob with the elegant fencing of princes. On the strength of his three million readers, and an impregnable advertising budget to protect him from destructive reprisals, a Revel can challenge his peers to single combat (*La Nouvelle Censure*) but only because he, like them, is a power in the market and even within the state. Such sudden impulses serve to sound out the enemy and to test one's own defensive capacity; the passing whims of the great nobility are both manoeuvres and displays of strength that stabilize the balance without serious repercussions. To turn to polemic, and to talk modern, the yokel (with no media support) has only a suicidal first-strike capacity; their lordships, who have second-strike capacity, can hold one another at bay without fear of annihilation.

For what it may be worth, let us point out to those at the bottom the advantages they can gain from the existing asymmetry. Good-neighbour treaties may strengthen the hand of the Great in their internal rivalries, but they are real life-rafts for the lesser cosignatories. The mediatized feast on the crumbs left by the mediocrats—for three reasons.

1. Because what the journalist gives away means nothing to him and a great deal to the author. One man's theoretical concession is the next man's strategic gain. A top leader writer writes an article a week, a 'minor' author a book every two years. A single mention by the leader writer, and a *fortiori* a panegyric, can help launch a book (it has been known to happen) or a name (through the chain reaction it triggers), but it obviously does not damage the personal position of the leader writer or even the interests of his article. The top journalist will not be judged on that detail, but *I* will be. The choice of my photo to illustrate the article rather than X's will not lower the paper's circulation, but it will increase the sales of my book or my name (because on Monday morning, all the other editors will be scratching their heads in perplexity, worried at the idea that they might have missed the boat). After all, the editor-in-chief of a daily, say, has fifty pages to fill every day. What difference does it make to him if he uses me or someone else to fill them? And so, the higher the position of my friend in the hierarchy of decision-makers, the more the asymmetry works to my

advantage, and if I have the heart to phone him three times a day for a month, he will end up adopting the old adage, 'It costs me so little and makes them so happy'. To my knowledge, there is not a single example of a journalist not giving in in the end. If you are willing to pay the price, the gamble pays off at a hundred to one. Just look at this week's papers.

2. Most journalists, particularly the best, do not know their own power. They think of themselves as people, whereas they in fact personify a social and technical relation of which they are, so to speak, the bearers (like the individual capitalist in capitalism and the bureaucrat in a bureaucratic country). The asymmetry also works within the mediatic machine and fools those who make it run: here it is between the analysis of causes, which they are in a position to know, and the synthesis of effects, which they are not in a position to see. 'If only you knew', says the assistant editor-in-chief to the novice, 'my power is non-existent. I'm just the icing on the cake.' Yes, and he says it in all good faith: it is true that he is scarcely listened to inside the company, or not as much as he deserves to be. But that doesn't matter to me, or not a lot, since on the outside, in the sphere of effects, he *is* the cake, complete with candles. The journalist's minimal influence is the cumulative influence of his paper's name, of the hundred or so journalists who work on it, and of the thousands of journalists who have worked to make that name and that paper since its founding. The individual, the 'weight' of his name or the precise extent of his influence are much less important than his position and the licence under which he works. As heraldry has replaced the study of genealogical records, the lowliest member of the family allowed to print under the blazon will do if you want to benefit from the prestige of *Libération*, *Le Monde* or *Le Nouvel Observateur*.

3. It follows from this asymmetry that a single reliable and decided element can neutralize a majority on the editorial board and carry the decision. Strongholds are taken from within and one friendly element inside the most important citadel is enough for us to able to occupy it, even if it does mean entering in single file. A service door is all it takes. There is no chain without its weak link: seek and ye shall find. (Look back over the last ten years and you will see how ten clear-headed men can, without too much difficulty, circumvent and infiltrate the five decisive media in a strategically located country with a population of fifty million.) It goes without saying that you can only conquer thus inside the perimeter of the ruling class, within the framework of its overall interests and on condition that you never get the wrong target.

7

The Scale of Incomes

What the historian of the present computes, the taxman calculates, without undue fuss. Whereas one hesitates over the shifting scale of prestige, one can always consult the income scale—its rungs never lie. Each step up the ladder represents a social distance. That is the advantage of the parallelism between relegation and depreciation in societies where money is the indicator.

The proverbially low salaries in education have kept their relative value for a hundred years. In that sense, they are still equivalent to those in the army or the magistrature (despite a certain logical rise in army pay). A primary teacher begins his career on the same salary level as a leading sergeant and ends up on the level below a lieutenant.[11] An *agrégé* entering the profession is paid as much (or as little) as a captain, and a *professeur* nearing the end of his career earns as much as a colonel. The homogamy typical of teachers still ensures their families a fairly enviable *aurea mediocritas*, and even if the annual bonuses are not quite as tidy as in other sectors (Customs, Taxes, Post Office, Highways and Bridges), the overtime (authorized up to half the salary) is not badly paid. The salaries of the lower intelligentsia are uniform and normed on an indexed scale, with a maximum differential of 1:4.[12]

[11] A primary schoolteacher with the Certificat d'aptitude pédagogique starts his career at 2,635.79 francs, plus housing and family allowances. At the end of his career he is earning 4,455 francs (1978).

[12] It will be noted, however, that there is a historical anomoly at the higher levels of the academic institution. The top people in education are not on the 'figure' scale, which covers most civil servants, but on the 'letter' scale, which is divided into 'groups' and 'grades' and which covers some 12,000 top civil servants in the major state bodies. A rector of an academy is in group D, far above a prefect (group C) or a brigadier (group B). The rector of the University of Paris is one of twenty or so highest-paid civil servants in France, along with the First President of the Court of Cassation, the secretary general of the government and the prefect of police. This anomoly is an inheritance from the past: the original civil service scale was drawn up by university academics after the Liberation. It is a typical and localized

The world of publishing has the relatively higher salaries typical of the private sector, but there are no great disparities. Only the profits made by series editors are non-proportional, depending upon the number of books in the series that the editor can sell. For an intellectual, the benefits of working for a publisher are benefits in kind and time, apart from the annual bonus and sometimes a share in the company's annual profits: secretaries, review copies, photocopying and telephone facilities and above all an *expense account*, which means that his personal social capital can be increased virtually day by day and at no cost to him. That is why a position in publishing cannot be valued in terms of salary alone; it is not so much that it is lucrative in itself as that the perks are priceless.

The real break comes at the level above—that of mass information; the only thing above it is the cachet of show-biz, which it resembles more closely every day. Salaries in the mass media are out of all proportion with those in the university or publishing, and the difference that has always existed is now assuming American proportions. The lower intelligentsia, stuck in old Europe, has undergone a relative pauperization compared with the high intelligentsia. The ratio between the salary of a recent *agrégé* starting work and a channel director or chairman of an editorial board may be as great as 1:50. French society pays its ideological managing directors three or four times as much as managing directors in nationalized industries and twice as much as managing directors in the private sector.[13] The figures for those at the top of the apparatus are lost in a mist of confidentiality (which the works council can sometimes break through) but obviously bear no relation to the ceiling of the union scale for journalists. High as they may be (with the truly remarkable exception of *Le Monde* and, at the bottom of the scale, *Libération*, whose journalists all receive a standard salary of 2,700F), the fringe benefits (flat, chauffeur, car, travel, hotels, plane fares) outweigh them, as do the indemnities for

---

example of the retinal persistence that gave the Fifth Republic a hierarchy of prestige adapted from the Third Republic.

[13] In 1977, the director of *Europe I* was earning 110,000 francs a month and the editor of *L'Express* 70,000 francs (this has since been slightly reduced). A top reporter on *Le Point* earns 15,000 francs a month. The lowliest *animateur* in the audio-visual media earns no less than 30,000 francs a month (which, as Maurice Maschino points out, is what a woman factory worker makes in a year—and what a peasant in Mali makes in sixty years). TV stars can multiply that figure by three or four, because they also make appearances in the press, on radio and in publishing (Bouvard, Pivot, Chancel, Gicquel, Drucker, Martin and the rest). See Maurice Maschino's investigation: 'La machine à abêtir', *Le Monde Diplomatique*, February 1979, especially the section 'le salaire de la médiocrité'.

resignation. Madness? Waste? Modern society has method in its madness. It would not consent to such sacrifices if they were not 'somehow' profitable. As for the beneficiaries, one might well ask if their classic argument—job insecurity—still has any political validity, given the stability of the times, were it not that the technical concentration and the lay-offs are also, in their own way, the result of a certain political logic.

Civil Service Salaries in 1977
(*Le Nouvel Économiste*, October 9, 1978)

'Figure Scale'

	Minimum Salary	Maximum Salary
Categories C and D (515,000)		
Unqualified personnel (D), or with school-leaving cert. (C). Office staff, typist, usher, postman.	2,096 F (index 187)	3,645 F (index 340)
Category B (490,000)		
Supervisory personnel primary teacher, sub-editor, nurse, administrative secretary, air traffic controller. qualifications: baccalauréat.	2,688 F (index 248)	5,292 F (index 478)
Category A (410,000)		
Civil administrator, secondary teacher, engineer, post office inspector. qualifications: university, ENA, polytechnique	3,473.46 F (index 324)	8,789 F (index 810)

'Letter Scale'

10,733 civil servants	Group	Grades	Index	Monthly* Salary
Magistrate (second class) in the Cour des comptes, civil administrator (special appointment), magistrate, master of requests to the state council, colonel, inspector general in ministry, sub-director of ministry, chief engineer, Highways and Bridges, Chief engineer, Mines, TPG.	A	1 2 3	874 913 950	9,480 9,907 10,455
Brigadier, regional director of taxes, sub-director of ministry, TPG.	B	1 2 3	950 1,007 1,064	10,455 10,949 11,573
President of administrative department, ministerial section head, magistrate (first class) in the Cour des comptes, master of requests to the state council, inspector of finance (first class).	BB	1 2 3	1,064 1,094 1,125	11,573 11,710 11,933

(cont.)

			*	
Prefect, director of ministry, senior magistrate in the cours des comptes, full professor (agrégé)	C	1 2 3	1,125 1,151 1,178	11,933 11,933 12,823
Inspector of taxes, treasury paymaster, director of ministry, engineer (class 1), Rector of Academy, inspector of taxes, state councillor, senior magistrate to Cours des comptes, inspector-general, highways and bridges.	D	1 2 3	1,178 1,235 1,292	12,823 13,447 14,073
Director of ministry, president of the tribunal of Paris, state councillor, tax inspector general, magistrate to the Cour des comptes	E	 2	1,292 1,349	14,073 14,696
President of department or chamber, state council, prefect (special appointment).	F		1,406	15,322
21 individuals including: Rector of the University of Paris, General Secretary to the government, First President of the Court of Cassation, Vice-President of the State Council, First President of the Cour des comptes, Prefect of Paris, Ambassador of France (with ambassadorial rank).	G		1,558	16,988

* Net salaries for unmarried persons + Paris weighting allowance.

There are 1,520,000 tenured civil servants in France, plus 108,000 labourers (mainly working in Defence), 420,000 non-tenured police officers, 5,000 magistrates and 305,000 soldiers. All are paid with reference to the Civil Service Scale.

Six

High Clergy
and Low

I

A Contrast and
Two Causes

Even on the most generous official figures, the disproportion between the
tiny numbers involved and the size of the audience is striking in the
extreme. Never in any society have so few men made so much noise as the
members of the high intelligentsia of France. In terms of column inches in
the whole of the press or time on the radio and TV news, primary teachers
as a group (318,379 people in 1978) certainly took up less room than any
one member of the high intelligentsia. We need not mention such
obviously disqualified socio-professional categories as domestics (234,355
people in 1975), commercial employees (736,595) or labourers (1,612,725).
Noise is not to be taken here only in the sense of sound effects or a volume
of messages in the means of communication: it is only natural that the
media should be preoccupied with the mediamen who occupy them rather
than with fishermen or office workers. The background noise provides the
political and social columns not only with their form but with their very
substance. This 'marginal group' informs and produces an increasing
proportion of the facts and events from which the life of a nation of some
fifty million people is woven each week by the TV, the radio, the papers
and rumours, and which political organizations, unions and professional
organs quite foreign to the intellectual milieu have to take into account.

We may explain this amazing disparity between the effect and the cause
in terms of two features, the second deriving from the first: physical
concentration and mediological profitability.

Concentration.

The field in which the symbolic is exercised is isomorphic with the
administrative field in politics. That has always been the case in France. It

is no accident that the most centralized state in the Western world gives most room to the intelligentsia. 'Opinion is made in Paris. It is manufactured with paper and ink. It makes revolutions: the provinces accept ready-made revolutions. Opinion is the intelligence sold by thirty newspaper proprietors. It is all the writers capable of writing a book or a pamphlet: there are 500 of them in the whole of France and not fifty of them are talented enough to be dangerous'—Balzac 1840.[1] The geography of the intelligentsia is modelled on the nervous system of the State, and the organization of the land of influence on that of power, but without anything to balance out the metropolis. An intelligentsia with a normally small head has become swollen-headed, and it suits a macrocephalous society. The relation between the high and the lower intelligentsia is the same as that between the cerebellum and the nerve endings, the capital and the provinces. The high intelligentsia 'informs' its lower slopes, just as Paris informs the provincial desert. By reduplicating this traditional centralism, the monopolistic and technical concentration of the organs of opinion has greatly exaggerated its effect, placing the majority of decisions in the minimum of hands. The network of intellectual power reflects the structures of authority, and is spun like a spider's web, as are the means of communication (roads and railways) and telecommunication (from the Chappe brothers' optical telegraph to the telephone and telematic circuits). It is as difficult to get from Nantes to Besançon or from Grenoble to Bayonne by train as it is for an assistant teacher to communicate with the head of a laboratory or, in the opposite direction, a composer with a smallholder is to go on TV in the rue Cognacq-Jay; the assistant has to Everything works vertically and centrifugally. The only way to break down the barriers is through revolution (two months every hundred years). In between revolutions, we have the media system controlled from the centre. The only way the composer can get a message to the smallholder is to go on TV in the Rue Cognacq-Jay; the assistant has to force the doors of *Le Monde*. It is a vicious circle. *Le Monde* is open only to the head of the laboratory, and the farmer cannot send a message back to the composer because he has no access to the small screen. Communication works downwards. The local studios of FR 3 cannot introduce a poet from Marseilles to his fellows in the region without previous permission from the channel controllers in Paris, and every day the Hersant network reproduces the editorial brilliance of the big names of the capital in the four corners of the country by lumitype.

[1] 'Lettres russes', in *La Revue Parisienne*, Balzac, *Oeuvres diverses*, III, p. 344.

France is therefore the land of the *strategic optimum*: the smallest possible number of actors can obtain maximum output from minimum input, provided that it is made at the nerve centre. The same economy applies to hegemony. Intellectual 'seizures of power' benefit from the same process of increasing stakes as the riots, armed risings and coups d'état of our history, all of which spread out from a single centre (July 14, 18th Brumaire, February 1848, December 2, the Popular Front, the 1944 insurrection, May '68). The greater the technical complexity, the easier it is to buy shares. The higher the fixed costs of producing opinions, the lower the cost of annexation. There are only two or three 'vital' papers, not fifty. There are only fifty opinion leaders, of whom half at most are 'talented enough to be dangerous', not five hundred. Anyone who takes control of one Maison de la Radio, one TV studio, two or three editorial boards and, for good measure, three or four publishing houses (optional) within a perimeter of three or four hectares, takes control of the means of distribution and circulation of basic social ideas throughout the country (plus the overseas Departments and Territories, the independent neo-colonies in Africa and the whole of the French-speaking zone). Despite appearances (for evanescence is its being and its dispersal is the source of its strength), the high intelligentsia has more social power than ever before: it can now broadcast in all directions at once. The concentration of symbolic resources is monarchical; the flow is distributed by concentric waves. And the pivot of the system is a pinhead.

No matter what consensus or favourable conjuncture is invoked to justify them, such hegemonic bids for power, which paralyse a body politic by striking at its head, would be materially impossible in a federal state like Germany, the United States or Switzerland, or in a state with strong regional elements, like Italy or Britain. Just as 'taking and holding' power in Washington or Rome has nothing like the impact of taking or holding power in Paris, because Wisconsin or Emilia Romagna will go on ruling themselves as they see fit, so the multiplicity of university centres, radio and TV channels, papers and periodicals, associations and clubs spread across the whole country in the USA or Italy spreads the risks and the basis of symbolic authority in a much more equitable manner than in France. Is this mere folklore, or theatricals? Those very serious-minded people who deal in militancy, or even science, should not laugh. If it is a comedy, what is at stake in it is nothing less than the 'production of society' by a few men who *select* the ideas that will become ideologies and the facts which will become events. The mediocrats no longer occupy only the centre of the world of the stage; they will soon be taking over the stage of a world in which the intellectual frivolity of the politicians is already exonerating and excusing the political frivolity of the intellectuals. Mockery of the vapours and crazes of Paris is permissible only if one forgets or ignores the historically determined material configuration of their ideological supports. Messieurs Havas, Belin, Bell, Marconi, Hertz and a few others carried the gossip of Paris to the four corner of the country some time ago and Paris still has the best acoustics on the whole planet, perhaps even better than New York's. The great men of Timbuktu, Bangkok or Bogota call the tune in Timbuktu, Bangkok or Bogota. But anyone who sets the left bank of the Seine talking always stands some chance of hearing a faint echo of his voice coming back to him from every corner of the Western world—including the Third World. What Baudelot and Establet have established for the petty bourgeoisie in France, that 'the position it occupies in society is out of all proportion with its numerical strength', is a fortiori valid for its finest flower. Those whose heads are in the clouds are inside everyone's head. A hundred and fifty years ago, the vagrant proletariat of the suburbs was, in the eyes of the bourgeoisie, the 'dangerous class'. Of all the fractions of the bourgeoisie, the intelligentsia is now the class that is most dangerous to the people. This narcissistic circle, a real public 'thought company' without which the public could no longer think, now has the means to show a whole nation the world turned upside down and inside out, with left and right reversed, since the outside world can no longer be seen directly, but only through the Great Central Mirror. Classified ad for tomorrow: 'Will exchange phrygian bonnet for funnel—Marianne'.*

Profitability.

The strength of a system of political domination lies in its not showing its strength, and one is more ready to obey a state that one can love without realizing it is a state. In our part of the world, active consent to the domination of one class is organized by what have been called, since Althusser, the State Ideological Apparatuses, which allow existing social relations to be reproduced as painlessly as possible. Those who run our state are constantly moving between the private and the public sectors (just like the top civil servants who come and go between the business

* Symbol of the Republic.

world and the world of politics) and are professionally trained by the business schools, management, MIT, and their practice, to minimize costs. They are right to prefer special editions from the information apparatus to special intervention brigades and the sensational to strong sensations. The school apparatus needs almost a million civil servants (850,000) to integrate/train/distribute fewer than fifteen million pupils into the various branches of production. The information apparatus does not of course take specialization and supervision quite so far. But it is not a bad operation when fifty opinion leaders—with five hundred sub-mentors to take over further downstream—are enough to make this world acceptable or even desirable to thirty million adults—especially since the state takes the profits but socializes the cost by allowing private capital to participate (press and production companies), even if it does subsidize it. To work through information means to work economically, in every sense. One good organic intellectual in the control room is still profitable at 70,000F a month, plus bonuses and perks. The higher the output, the better the impression. A radio mike on a 'peripheral' station (which is really central) put to good use from 6 till 9 every morning is worth a hundred pulpits and a thousand gadgets. Country priests had their flocks, police officers have those they administer, and audio-visual stars have fans. The top symbolic police are the only force in the world to add public adoration to their functions.

What seems to be an amazing waste of resources (radios, TV, posters, leaflets, spots, films, magazines) can also be seen as a precious saving for the system as a whole. Is there not a connection between the surplus of surveillance and the shortage of imaginary and information apparatuses in socialist countries—and between the gigantic symbolic panoply and the discrete nature of the coercive apparatuses in capitalist countries? Omnipresent Party, omnipresent media: our vendors of pretty pictures have the same control function as the officials of the correct line—and the same executive status. But because of their higher productivity, they are more profitable. The maintain a permanent preventive counter-revolution as visible and painless as the normal workings of the system of which they are a part. In other words, because the TV news, *L'Express*, *Marie-Claire* and *France-Soir* each has the fire-power of an armoured regiment, the Ministries of the Interior and of Defence can cut their spending accordingly. If by some mishap all the media were put out of action tomorrow, the state power might be forced, for a time, to bring up its second line of defence 'to defend Republican order'. As we saw in '68, a long break on TV soon leads to overworked CRS.

Fortunately, the system of domination is very different in the economic hunting-grounds outside the metropolis. There, the profitability of the technology of inculcation is at its lowest and naked force has to be used openly. That is why, just as the system slips and slides internally in wartime, it can only be frontally attacked outside its own perimeter. The graveyards of the centre are on the periphery—an old lesson of history.

Two Classes,
One Struggle

The feelings that the lower intelligentsia inspires in the high intelligentsia are rather like those the second order of the clergy inspired in the first, two hundred years ago: a mixture of scorn and fear. The high intelligentsia despises the lower as a *backward* class and fears it as a *dangerous* one. Backward because it is still duped by dated 'vulgates' (Marxism, progressivism) and outdated 'mythologies' (laicity, the working class, public service, nationalization);[2] dangerous because, being made up mainly of civil servants with socialist leanings, it may identify its own emergence as a ruling class with the domination of civil society by a bureaucratic state. In one recent polemical opuscule, this vague sensibility crystallized into a thematic. I propose, writes its author, to consider this fraction of the intelligentsia as a 'statist' class because of its origins and its destiny. 'Statist' means 'dangerous', the state being the bad object, as opposed to civil society, the bringer of redemption. 'Whereas the high intelligentsia is, as we have seen, turning away from the Marxist vulgate and professional politics and is beginning, late in the day but with some acuteness, to look at the problem of totalitarianism in modern societies, the lower and middle intelligentsia, which is much stronger numerically and more influential in electoral terms, is looking at the problem of power and

[2] The place and function of the term 'vulgate' in the high intelligentsia's scale of values as an instrument for polemical inferiorization and as an emblem of nobility would require a study in itself. 'Vulgate' is insulting because the root of the word is 'vulgus', the common man (and therefore the opposite of what we, the intellectual elite, are). The trouble is that the word is also close to *vulgare*, 'to spread', and that the expansion/diffusion of an idea, theory or image is the most central of all the black boxes of cultural cybernetics. What is diffused and why? And what would have happened to the word of Christ in the West without Saint Jerome's translation of the Bible into Latin, the so-called Vulgate? Thus, the social position of the ideologues conceals the most strategic of historical problems from them: *how a thought comes into being in the world*.

how to take it. It is trying by all possible means to ensure that if the left wins it will sanction its emergence.' Thus Jacques Julliard, in *Contre la politique professionnelle*. He claims that since it dreams of nothing but nationalizations and authoritarian planning and hides its 'appetite for power' behind socialist phraseology, this fraction reveals both its lack of moral virtue and its failure to understand modern society. These pages deserve to be read carefully, for they exemplify the ideology of the ruling ideologues and the great traditionalism of today's audacities.[3] For such *topoi* do have a pedigree. In 1898, when the enemy was not the Marxist vulgate but 'naturalist and positivist vulgarities', Barrès used the same reductionism in *Les Déracinés*, in Boutellier who, as a scholarship man and a poor *professeur*, identified his ambitions with the Republic. (In the same way, the partisans of Legitimism discredited the idea of a constitutional monarchy by making jokes about social-climbing commoners.)

The feelings inspired by the high intelligentsia in the lower would appear to be a mixture of fascination and distrust. *Fascination* at the sight of a pleiad of stars embodying its dreams of personal and social success (public promotion as a measure of self-realization); an alternatively mocking or fierce *distrust* of facile ambition and of the unseemly pomp surrounding spectacular success. A researcher in the social sciences, for example, who knows his trade but is forced to consider it a *job*, usually finds something to smile or sneer at in the way his tenured superiors can gain public prestige from something they do very badly in private. There is no symmetry or reciprocity between these feelings of resentment, if only

---

[3] *Carefully*: the skim-reading we are obliged to carry out to get through a mass of papers and magazines encourages superficial thinking. More and more productions work on two levels. On a first reading you tend to agree, because you are carried away by the self-confident style and surprised at the pieces of information you pick up, but as soon as you begin to *take your time* their vacuity becomes obvious. Jacques Julliard's somewhat rushed book exemplifies the phenomenon. This latest collection of theoretical, semantic and statistical inaccuracies about the intelligentsia provides the reader with one of the most accurate pictures of the reigning code of intellectual *doxas*, which make probabilities look like the obvious. If the things a period fails to notice are the focus for its stereotypes (a focus that will subsequently make it possible to recognize it as this period and no other), there may be a necessary connection between the rarefaction of time for reading and the proliferation of stereotypes. As we gain time, invisible begins to materialize for us. The faster we go, the more hollow the stereotypes become. A speed limit in all areas and all activities is now an absolute necessity if we want to retain a certain mastery over our relations with meaning, nature and History. It is no accident that 'in praise of speed' is a favourite theme of the bourgeois avant-garde (the French '*Hussards*' took the race car over from fascist Futurism). (The Hussards were a loose group of novelists centred around Roger Nimier, 1925–1962, whose *Le Hussard bleu* gave them their name. Nimier himself died in a car crash. *Translator*)

because the feelings of the high intelligentsia can find systematic and coherent public expression while those of the lower intelligentsia can usually only be expressed in asides, solitary whispers and private comments. The inequality is statutory, since the high intelligentsia has the means to exercise its right to private ownership of intelligence and culture, its monopoly over access to the central means of mass distribution. Compartmentalized into disciplines, fragmented into categories, dispersed throughout the provinces with no means of communicating with its members, all the lower intelligentsia can do is mutter away in its corner and receive whatever is sent by the centres of legitimation: the big publishers, the Parisian magazines, the pilot broadcasts and the fashion journals.

This, then, is a battle in which the fronts are reversed and in which the endless toing and froing fools the actors themselves. Mastery of the networks of maximum distribution optimizes the power of the new intellectual leaders by allowing them to rule in the name of the plebs and because they are in contact with it. It simultaneously selects the elite and renders it anti-elitist. The appeal to the base against and over the heads of the intermediary apparatuses is both a political *line* and a *programme* common to all the heads of the high intelligentsia, for it is there that they find the greatest profit: this is the ideological expression of the mediological position of the high intelligentsia, which overhangs and straddles that of the 'intermediary apparatuses' in such a way as to phantasmagorize reality. The variations on the theme are endless and come in all keys. Thus we have a call to 'God's little people against the ecclesiastical apparatus' (Clavel), to 'the plebs against all the pigs' (Glucksmann) to 'flesh-and-blood proletarians' against the Sganarelles of the proletariat (Jacques Julliard), to 'simple, lucid men against the master censors of the institution' (Bernard-Henri Lévy). Every prosperous thinker is hanging out a sign with letters of gold saying 'I am just an elementary popular thinker'. 'Down with the notables!' has become the rallying cry of all the notabilities. There is an intellectual bonapartism, just as there can be a different bonapartism in religion and politics—often the same one.[4] The

---

[4] It is only to be expected that Maurice Clavel, the most logical and therefore the most traditional (new equals old) of the ideologues of modernity, should profess all three at once. His constant slogan is: directly from summit to base: from General de Gaulle to the people of France; from the Pope to the faithful; from the Holy Ghost to its creatures. As a sample of this plebiscitary Second Coming: 'I admit that I wish with all my heart for a sort of cultural revolution from below in the Catholic Church, a cultural revolution that would lead to a cultural revolution in the world. Yes, I know, this notion of the "little men" is exasperating.'

material procedures of fame have combined with the new balance between social disgust and social craving to permute the signs in the old equations without altering their solutions. An establishment of pariahs or a curia of iconoclasts, mingling the cult of impiety with the eroticism of execration, has thus been built up on the basis of a set of coherent discourses and practices. It has always been a feature of aristocracies that, within them, one feels closer to the people than to the average bourgeois. In the present case, the new high intelligentsia—a plebiscitary oligarchy, invested and ratified by a public opinion which it is its prerogative to control and inform—can and often does allow itself the luxury of short-circuiting the lower clergy's contacts with the 'poor and disinherited' because *it* is the contact level between specialist research and the general public (the average man). The connection with the base goes via the summit, just as the provinces are connected via the capital. The specialist does not translate his discoveries into the language of the average man himself; they are translated by the general practitioners of the high intelligentsia who take all the credit and often exclusive rights as well. In that and many other ways, the universalization of the media will be to this century what the extension of universal suffrage was to the end of the last century—the last hope of the ruling classes and the direct opposite of what it was expected to be. The real function has caught the ideological discourse on the wrong foot, and it did so all the more easily because the discourse hid the function from the eyes of its victims, who were supposed to benefit from a mode of allocation of powers that seemed to be all to their advantage. We will see later how this feint works in the political arena, where parties rush to the media that kill them in a perfect imitation of the bull charging the muleta. It has the same piquant effect in the symbolic arena. Just like the bourgeoisie which, from 1848 to 1968 (or 1978) constantly crushed the masses in the name of their own democratic discourse and majority rule, the ruling high intelligentsia is objectively justified, by virtue of the new mediatic regime, in censuring the ruled in the name of the ruled themselves: after all, it is the only voice they will listen to en masse. Here as elsewhere, those who monopolize public speaking and those who speak in the name of the public are one and the same.

In order to explain why the relations of force between the high and the lower intelligentsia are in inverse proportion to their numerical strength, we must first identify the real determinants of each and see where they differ. The pertinent differences are not, we know, differences in trade or profession: the divide cuts through all disciplines and intellectual professions. They do not lie in qualifications or professional competence, which is why the classification of workers as skilled and unskilled cannot be applied metaphorically (as Julliard tries to do) to skilled/unskilled intellectuals, general practitioners/technicians. Here, the distinction works the other way around. Officially, skilled workers (category 61 in INSEE's Code) are defined as those 'who carry out a trade requiring an apprenticeship' and unskilled workers (category 63) as being employed in 'a position which requires some training, but no real apprenticeship'. If words still have a meaning, it has to be admitted that the high intelligentsia consists of unskilled workers and the lower intelligentsia of skilled workers. Anyone can see this in his own discipline. Many intellectuals rise from the lower to the high intelligentsia in only a few years. Usually, their hierarchical promotion means that they lose their professional qualifications and in becoming general practitioners (entitled to talk about everything), give up research and fall behind developments in their own field. They live off the scientific credit of their early work until the moment comes when they have to think on an overdraft and cover the deficit with public loans. What they gain in productivity they lose in creativity and their social visibility rises at the same rate as their professional credibility falls. The increasingly frequent 'interventions'—articles, forums, interviews—the personal diversification, the increased pace of work and the botching required by the demands of publicity have the effect of replacing a 'real apprenticeship' with 'some training': the skilled worker regresses and becomes unskilled. The difference must then lie elsewhere, in status and function. The high and the lower intelligentsia represent two modes of existence, two social positions, two insertions into the economy which, although sometimes complementary, are essentially distinct.

Two modes of existence: in the lower intelligentsia, a shared situation creates a community of interests; in the high, identical conditions do not generate internal solidarity, but increase the desire for demarcation. The multiplicity of interests, statuses and indices typical of the lower intelligentsia, which basically includes the higher and middle executives in the public service, does not prevent it from having a certain awareness of itself as a professional collectivity, any more than its dispersal across the whole country weakens its cohesion. Hence the high level of unionization, which falls as one goes up the ladder: primary teachers have the highest rate of unionization of all branches of national activity. *Esprit de corps* is widespread at the lower levels, in mutual benefit societies, leagues, federations, friendly associations and so on. Further up the hierarchy, there are fewer people at the meetings (in factories too, workers are more regular attenders than supervisors). Although the members of the high intelligentsia are imbricated with one another, much more concentrated in terms of geographical, social and institutional space and have eminently integrated equipment, they seem much less cohesive from the outside. A molecule of loosely-knit atoms, the first order is distinguished from the second by this paradox: high organic density combined with a low level of organization. At this level, solitude is juxtaposed to solitude, but they are not federated. The very practice of the trade tends, towards the top, to personalize roles and erect barriers. The higher one climbs, the easier it is physically to ignore friends who have become colleagues and who are therefore indifferent. It is impossible to teach in a *lycée* without rubbing shoulders with one's colleagues. A professor in the university can come in, give his lecture and go away again without meeting anyone. A series editor works at home and a top leader writer dictates his articles over the phone without even going out. Power creates voids. Let us weep for them in their loneliness.

Human relations in the two orders are therefore very different. Whereas the lower intelligentsia exhibits solidarity, the high intelligentsia displays complicity; the former makes collective demands, the latter devises individual strategies. In the public service, the interests of the individual merge with those of his colleagues, the salary scale being the same for all. In general, the interests of the individual are those of the institution. Relations with superiors are not like those between client and patron, courtier and monarch or follower and clan leader, since the superior can do nothing to hurt his subordinate. He can delay promotion or block a transfer by sending a bad report to the administration, but he himself may get a bad report from his own superior: there is a virtual reciprocity of constraints. Even the 'individual file' has been abolished in the universities. What distinguishes a teacher's career from that of someone in publishing or a journalist is not simply the immovability of the civil servant, but the way the latter is promoted. A career depends on qualifications, and these are regularly tested in competitive exams. Moreover, it depends less upon an employer or a chapel than on a collective commission which, in the universities at least, is union-controlled. The lower intelligentsia is not subject to the humiliating obligation to please, distinguish itself or give 'favours'. Its subjection to the state is collegial, anonymous and programmed, without effect on the health, the coronary or the stomach. The scale goes by the individual teacher (and not by the institution as it did until 1887), but the individual is not tied to the scale. Rises and salary cuts apply to all, and the individual does not need to put down his neighbour or suck up to his boss to speed up his promotion. Vertical promotion is slow, but renumerations at any given level are equal. Standardization of the scales after the war did away with the big differentials in salary that once gave the Parisian *agrégé* such an advantage over provincial colleagues. The Paris provinces opposition, a social value-added typical of the high intelligentsia, does not affect the lower intelligentsia. To sum up, the divide between the personnel of the lower intelligentsia, who are all on different levels of the 'letter' scale, with varying status and rates, is not incompatible with an egalitarian frame of reference, both mental and professional, when it comes to defending the gains made by specific categories. The members of the high intelligentsia, who are all more or less at the top (income, titles, functions), work full-time at manufacturing inequality in their own heads and around them— silence about incomes, protection of sources. All the civil servants of the lower intelligentsia get their annual bonus (which, in the public sector, is bigger the further up the scale one goes): it counts as salary and is declared as such. Salary scales are official (and based on a points system) and everyone knows what his neighbour is earning, from the usher (index 200) to the tenured *agrégé* with a chair (Group C in the Letter scale—index 1125). It is not usually a lot and is a subject for jokes. Royalties, fees and salaries are no laughing matter in the high intelligentsia, where a seemly discretion reigns over such minor details.

There is a 'but': job insecurity. As a general rule, the high intelligentsia lives in a permanent state of anxiety and the lower intelligentsia in security. Protected by its civil service status, the lower intelligentsia gets along, sheltered by the salary. But the high intelligentsia is subject to the caprices of the market, social relations and the fluctuations of fame. An author's success is (relatively) unpredictable and the success of a career may depend upon a reversal of alliances, a press company going bankrupt, or the outcome of the elections. By its very nature, the high intelligentsia lives on credit—personal credit—and is permanently exposed to the judgment of others. Will my article be accepted? When will it come out? Where, in what form? Will my book sell? Has the postman been yet?

Nothing in the paper this morning? There might be a review tomorrow . . . A tragic watch. Every press attaché knows the whispers that greet the author who 'was just passing by' and prowls the corridors, worried about the silence that greeted his masterpiece (and there are thousands of them): X's article hasn't come out, Y told X it wasn't bad; what about next week's programme? Yes, yes, just wait. Feverish agitation and doubts; the glorious uncertainties of fate. The lower intelligentsia has holidays, but not the high. Life at the top is more intense and therefore more dangerous, like life in America. The lower intelligentsia is petty bourgeois, openly and shamelessly so. It tempers the material mediocrity of its income with the tranquil confidence typical of a petty bourgeoisie compromised with the state.[5] In terms of ideology and mentality, the high intelligentsia is closer to the senior executives of the economy: it rejects the past and political 'archaisms' (no collective memory), and sometimes has terrifying visions of the future. Amnesia and fear often go together. In any case, the old national antinomies (France/Europe, right/left, capitalism/socialism) are laughed at more often in the high than in the lower intelligentsia, which is still reluctant to bring itself up to date and adjust to technological modernity, international competition and market imperatives.

[5] See Baudelot and Establet, *La Petite bourgeoisie en France*, Paris 1976.

Seven

A Competitive Society

I

Principles

Competition between top and middling intellectuals is inevitable. Although we have to resign ourselves to that fact, there is no reason why we should not try to understand it. Removed from material production, the intellectual is predisposed to satisfaction with entities that are usually only the hypostases or tautologies of a social position made still more opaque to him by his own philosophical metaphors. To my mind, the intellectual's condition implies an authentically metaphysical dimension, which is not an illusion but an existence, a ghost imprinted in a body. If materialism means purely and simply ignoring that dimension, then I am not a materialist. If it means thinking it is intelligible, then of course I am. To locate the economic base of a *fatum* is not the same thing as to study the economy of fatality. It means founding it in reality, in reason.

Unlike the lower intelligentsia, which is peopled mainly by teachers, researchers, scientists and coaches, the high intelligentsia is made up of creators of original works; novels, articles, essays, poems, but also films, paintings and records. No two intellectual works are alike: their singularity is part of their definition. But in one respect all intellectual works are as alike as two peas in a pod: they are *objects*. And these objects are exchanged in a market: they are *products*. There are so many misadventures in these metamorphoses. I am alone when I write a book; only I can write it; it is between me and myself. But I do not print, reproduce or sell it. Something makes me sit up. I'm delighted or infuriated. Only I can talk about it; I must do so: I write an article and send it to my favourite newspaper. But I do not decide whether or not to publish it, I do not proof-read it, work out how much space it will take up, add the sub-headings or do the lay-out. The arrogant solitude of the creator: the strange dependency of the producer. There are so many practical antinomies in these misfortunes:

the work, which was the opposite of a product, just as the original is the opposite of the series, and the creator of the producer, is transformed into its opposite before my very eyes. This transformation is the equivalent of an alienation, in the strict sense. It is heart-breaking for an author, because his innermost being—his mind, talent, memory—comes back to him as something alien, an external thing in which he has to recognize himself. This thing is his *mind*. But the heartbreak is also a form of satisfaction: every author wants to see his manuscript printed and bound, and non-publication makes him even more unhappy than bad sales. The joy of the appearance and the sadness of disappearance. The grace of doing and the disgrace of being. Let us curtail this list of antimonies. They merely point the way. Every writer is a malaise made flesh, but there is logic of discomfort.

What sort of producer is a writer? Anyone who produces an original text that is distributed (by whatever means). That text has been produced by a certain *labour*, but the writer continues to own the fruits of his labour. He is therefore quite definitely an *artisan-owner*. He has had this status since and thanks to the French Revolution, which, by recognizing private ownership in land and commodities in general, also legalized literary and artistic property. The law of March 11, 1957, brought a more precise definition (jurists are necessarily required to think clearly and distinctly): 'The author of an intellectual work enjoys an incorporeal and exclusive right in it, effective against all persons, by the mere fact of having created it.' There was indeed an attempt in 1936 (the Jean Zay bill) to put author's right under the sign of labour and not property; but the weight of acquired privilege carried the day. Being a historical product of bourgeois law, the modern writer is a property-owner and not a proletarian. To be more accurate, he is a *rentier*, as author's right can be likened to a rent (in the broad sense of a premium derived from a monopoly position). Our author is therefore also a man with property to leave. It is because author's right is legally considered to be property that it can be inherited by those entitled to do so. Property, rent, inheritance: it is not surprising that almost all French writers in the nineteenth century, major and minor, sided with the bourgeoisie against the workers every time the latter threatened to erect themselves into a party or movement. The facts are there—and they remain, self-evident and repetitive (look at the paper or the small screen).

This incorporeal property would be sterile if the intellectual work itself remained incorporeal. Since intellectual producers, like all others, have been separated from their means of production (in the eighteenth and nineteenth centuries), the incarnation of this product requires, as we have seen, the intervention of a third party, the *publisher*, through whom converge industrial capital (the print shop) and commercial capital (distribution and advertising)—one to materialize the unique original in the form of a commodity that can be reproduced and exchanged, the other to transform the commodity into coin of the realm. The writer therefore leases his property to the publisher, without whose aid his property could never take on commodity form. This specific intermediary, who has concessionary rights in the exploitation of the work, bears the cost of transforming the use value that has been produced into an exchange value. Today, not even the proudest of novelists or the haughtiest of meta-physicians can escape this mediation: the enjoyment of a work of art or the diffusion of a concept is no longer possible without a market operation. And it will become even less possible, given the decline of the university and the political parties, the disappearance of patrons and the stagnation of the research institutes. It will be noted that, despite the prevailing injustices, the author's juridical position privileges him in comparison with the *salaried* journalist, who is usually required by statute to surrender all (literary and artistic) rights over his articles to his employer (only a few freelances can retain copyright). The writer is to the salaried journalist what the cinema director is to the TV director. The latter is not considered to be a true author: unlike the former, he does not fully own his works, which belong to the TV company and can be sold by it. This anomaly exemplifies the time-gap between fact and law. Given the new supremacy of journalists and TV authors, their juridicial inferiority is somewhat scandalous. Here, the jobs came before the rights; the statute will now have to follow.

The conditions under which texts are currently leased to and exploited by publishers call for rectification in a number of ways, and it is only right that a handful of authors, including some of the bravest (see below) should be carrying on the fight of Balzac and Mallarmé and campaigning for an improvement in our status. There is the uniquely French anachronism of the *droit de passe* (the 10% cut taken by the publisher on the total royalties), an inheritance from the nineteenth century, when authors were paid on the basis of print runs and not sales; the absurd nuisance of the old 'preferential clauses'; an excessive percentage on subsidiary rights (book clubs, paperbacks, audio-visual adaptations). The vast majority of authors are reluctant to become involved with such details, since it would be degrading to think of their novels, poems or philosophical works as what they are: commodities. And publishers reject the term 'employers' in favour of 'distributors' because they are reluctant to destroy the charm of their *tête-à-tête* with those grown-up children who come into their offices one by one, baring their souls in the form of manuscripts. The author as genius, ashamed at having to turn grace into cash; the publisher as apostle, always ready to make one last sacrifice; what, without flattering ourselves too much, can we put in the place of these clichés?

Certainly not the image of the employee, and still less that of the worker: writing is work, but the writer is not like any other worker. The paradox is that he or she is a gentleman or a lady exhausted by his or her leisure. The writer is a sensualist who is productive—in the strict sense of creating surplus value. The proof is that 'they' buy the painful product of his pleasure from him (or that he can rediscount the pleasure that the fruit of his labours will give others). Who are 'they'? Le Seuil, Polydor, Maeght or Artmedia. In that respect, there is no difference between a novelist, a painter, a singer or an actor. Let us be serious, look things in the eye and have a good laugh. The writer gets a great kick out of writing. If he is a worker, in the sense of a 'labourer', he is the only one living under communism as described by St Marx or St Fourier. For him, work is not slavery, but a need and a passion. Our literary slave cries out for more, hurls himself into it and if he works himself to death, he does so in the same way that others die of hope. He has all the work and all the sleep he wants, but he doesn't have to take the tube. No timetable, no stoppages, no rules. If he does clock in, he does so in secret, for himself and mainly out of an excess of masochism. He really is the most privileged of men. No one is forcing him to do what he does. He works away at his lace at home, with no neighbours spying on him, no foreman to suck up to and no boss to take in. Sometimes he even makes money. He takes his pleasure first, on the blank page, before giving pleasure to his clients; his pleasure may not be the same as theirs but it is certainly more intense. Not many people make a living from their vices, but how many people are paid by society to devote themselves to their favourite pleasures? Writers who have hallucinations about being factory workers should have the decency to moderate their proletarian enthusiasms. True, the same people often convince themselves that they are hastening the revolution by leaving out the semi-colons. Those who shit ink sometimes make very light of human blood.

The government no longer considers us members of the liberal professions and we owe it to the devotion of a few of our number that we are, collectively, considered wage earners and can therefore claim social security benefits. Our gratitude should not, however, blind us to our semi-luxurious salaried status, the specificity of which is not readily reducible to the classic schemas of economic activity. Although the writer does not produce the commodity in its entirety at home—as does the classic artisan—he is not forced into fragmented labour, like the worker. The latter is paid by the hour, but the writer is on piece-rate (in the USA, publishers pay the authors of best-sellers by the page, without even reading them). The peculiarity of the relation of production uniting author and publisher lies in its ambiguity: it is an archaic relation (artisanal: wages are the exception), but the product obeys the laws of the capitalist mode of production (the average rate of profit, and so on) and the ultra-modern laws of commodity circulation. The other peculiarity of the branch is that the 'employee' is paid in arrears (hence the expression 'advance') in accordance with the volume of profit he has produced for his distributor. Payment in arrears minimizes the risks for the publisher and increases the solidarity between him and the author: it is in the interests of both to improve the other's position in the market. Branches of production where the producer collaborates directly with his employer in marketing the product are few and far between.

What sort of product is a book? The atypical nature of the product explains the strange way it is marketed. A book is not a commodity like other commodities: if I want to savour.*Charmes,** *The Caine Mutiny* will leave me cold. Every book is unique in two ways. First, it is the irreplaceable product of an irreplaceable worker; and second, it gives rise to a single act of consumption (even if it is mass consumption). Its singularity defies planning, limits industrialization and means that both author and publisher can hope for the moon. Every book is a throw of the dice: 'Anything can happen'. No market research and no recipe can guarantee a best seller. It may be advisable to take a certain slot, maintain a certain profile and put the emphasis on a certain category of works. It may be advisable to drop a certain unfashionable style or an 'outdated' ideological content, but no matter how you try to ensure success, the unexpected will always slip through the net. Hence the need for the publisher to spread his net as widely as possible and balance possible losses

* Collection of poems by Paul Valéry (1922).

against potential successes. Book production may be standardized, but there is by definition no such thing as a standard book. The individuality of the object is the individulity of the author. And it is precisely this singularity that the publisher buys from the author when he buys his product. On the one hand, this is to the advantage of the author: if his labour power were interchangeable, like that of the worker (given an equal level of qualifications), he really would be a proletarian. As it is, he enjoys a certain relative autonomy *vis-à-vis* the publisher or the exploiter. On the other hand, the contract he signs with the publisher ties one individual to another rather than a seller of labour power to an owner of means of production. The relation is valorized personally because the law of value cannot work impersonally here. How can the value of a manuscript, a picture, a song or a show be established. No 'socially necessary abstract labour', no 'average conditions of production' can be invoked in this case. What is bought is therefore less the product than the person of the producer. The producer is the productive capital: is the publisher buying the producer in order to sell his work? No. He is buying the work in order to sell its author. That is the secret of marketing in this sector.

What is being sold in a book that sells? In publishing, the displacement of the centre of gravity towards marketing, which is typical of all the spheres of a commodity economy, is expressed by the new importance of sales representatives, the first jury to confront the future author—who is called upon to 'defend' his project before men who will themselves have to defend it before the commercial buyers. Representatives, acting as spokesmen for the potential audience, sometimes persuade an author to change his title, introduction or conclusion. The shift can be seen mainly in the growth of the advertising budget. Why don't we see ads for bread in the streets, or posters, stickers and advertisements for this or that dairy? Because the demand for bread and milk exists before the supply. But since the need for novels and essays is, to say the least, diffuse, it must constantly be reinvented—hence the stress on all the processes of 'making known' and the necessity for an intense 'promotion drive' around the book-product and the film-product. The need is created, stimulated and reproduced by lecture-debates, 'meet the author' sessions, signings in department stores, interviews, cocktail parties, demos. When the use value of a product is uncertain, you have to clutch at anything that can help transform it into an exchange value. In that respect, a philosophical essay or a novel poses the same problem as a fitted automatic oven or a sports-car. When it comes to cultural commodities, marketing is a necessity, not a luxury. The prophets who sneer at the very idea that they too might be mere commodity producers are never the last to invest in marketing. Madame de Cambremer again: those who minimize the importance of marketing are never the least reluctant to maximize their net margins.

'What is selling? One person talking to another,' says Bleustein-Blanchet.[6] Selling a thought means selling a thinker who interpellates the purchaser eye to eye. The credibility of the product is indexed to the familiarity of the producer, his personal appeal, his silhouette, his glamour. In transforming all that is human into a source of profit, the logic of profit has not forgotten the bodies of those who serve the intellect. Capitalist barbarism with a human face makes capital of the human face, which is why TV appearances and illustrated articles are so important to the writer, not only in terms of their immediate effect on sales, but as a vital jumping-off point for a prolonged campaign by multiple means. A lay-out artist in advertising who is told to promote a book tears his hair out if he cannot get the writer's face into his inset, if, that is, the writer has not been on TV often enough for his effigy to function as 'information' in its own right. 'Information' is neither true nor false, but a signal.

The fact that the eternal desire to be seen has become a functional necessity of the market creates a new ground on which author and publisher can meet. The publisher escorts him to Pivot or Paugam, dolls him up and makes him look pretty before he goes into the ring and then sits at the ringside, half coach and half supporter, rolling his eyes until the end of the fight. The price of this understanding with the publisher is additional conflict with every other author, since the image-making apparatus and the conduits of fame are limited in time and space. We have already mentioned this unpleasant scarcity. We can now add that competition on the cultural market is not between brand images, but between personal images, between producers who confront each other directly, and not between products. It is well known that products of equal value do not come on to the market on equal terms. What is new here is the imperiously and naively extra-cultural nature of the criteria that direct the demand for cultural goods. It is the pleasure provided by the author's image and speech that determines the market value of a text rather than the pleasure provided by the text itself. The visible valorizes the readable. It would be considered a remarkable innovation in the shoe trade if demand

[6] *La rage de convaincre.*

for moccasins and bootees came to be governed by the personal appeal of the manufacturer rather than by the quality and price of the footwear itself. Presumably it is because a text is believed to bear the imprint of a soul, lodged in a body and complete with halo and tics, that it seems so normal to hear people say 'Did you see so and so last night? What a fantastic writer!'—'Have you read the book?'—'No, but he's a scream the way he tells stories.' Or, 'That my idea of a philosopher.'—'You were convinced by his arguments?'—'No, by his looks . . .'

Such anecdotes express much more than a mere change of direction in the cultural market at a given moment in its evolution ('fashion'): *a culture is changing under the impact of its market.* To be more accurate: the very content of a culture is being shaped by the new forms in which cultural values are realized on the market. A new type of production is being induced by a new mode of consumption. There is no point in telling tele-consumers that a writer feels a need to *write* stories precisely because he cannot tell them orally and that if he could, he would not be a writer but a singer, a clown, a lawyer and a wonderful dinner companion. Or that a philosopher can only be judged by his philosophy and not by his diction or the colour of his eyes, for in this case the market, which is ruled by the TV, has switched the shelves and the products, not the labels. They are now selling images of the bookstand (and, if need be, very bad books on the image-stand). The display ads that publishers buy in the printed media are now built around the author's photo, as seen on TV, as reproduced in your usual magazine last week because, when the literary accounts are drawn up, the presence of the images, the timbre of the voice and the grain of the skin now count for more than the quality of the texts or the density of the writing. This cultural fascism is all smiles and no barbed wire. But the movement from the religion of the smile to face-hunting pays off, the latter being merely a negative version of the first. Culture with a human face and fascism both make use of the naturalist reduction, which reduces the intellectual to the physical, a person to his contingency and consciousness to the body. It is a reversal of the spiritual and angelic reduction which meant that for more than two hundred years the adjective 'intellectual' was synonymous with 'disembodied'. 'That which is purely spiritual, which has no body. The Angels and the Blessed are intellectual substances. The rational soul is said to be an intellectual force': Furetière's *Dictionary*, article *Intellectuel, -lle* (adj.), 1690. Half the work for the 1990 reprint has already been done: 'That which is purely visible, which has no interiority.

Stars and presenters are intellectual substances. Intellectual power descends upon bodies that are displayed'. New academicism for old?

What is this living creature who cannot live without selling himself? He is rarely a voluntary prostitute and although soliciting may be his forte, it is not his ideal. Our study of the producer of books in himself has turned our modern street-walker into an economic abstraction, but in his material life he is also a member of an editorial team, a tenured lecturer and an executive in a publishing house. The writer would not walk the streets so feverishly if he had not become more or less all these things at the same time: subject and object of fame, a reviewer of novels and a novelist under review, a real interviewer and a potential interviewee. For he could neither reach nor retain his position as a star interviewer if he did not from time to time succeed in becoming a star interviewed by another. Nor could the series editor keep his position very long or improve it if he did not become a successful author. A leader writer's authority comes from the books he publishes, and the success of his books from the prestige of his articles. In a word, every member of the high intelligentsia is playing piggy-in-the-middle all by himself in his individual echo-chamber, and if he stands still for even a moment, all the walls will fall in. This existential maelstrom soon has our man spinning like a top, until he reaches his own 'level of incompetence', the level that makes him a success. It is a dizzying spiral. In order to consolidate his position, he has to prepare the ground for the success of his next book: lunching, going to cocktail parties and colloquizing without a break. He increases the value of his stock by plunging into the pool of producers and exploiters, so he has less and less time for writing, for his work proper. The more botched the book, the harder the author has to work at his lunches, cocktail parties and colloquia. The writer (or the theoretician, or the essayist) becomes slightly poorer each time around, but the public man gets richer and his fame increases. In other words, 'he gets by'. He has to make a living. The writers of the past had private incomes. If Gide or Mauriac published books that did not sell, their estates at Malagar and Cuverville ensured that they would still survive. Public life and creative work were in different compartments. Yesterday's authors, usually teachers by profession, had two jobs. Julien Gracq can survive the silence that surrounds his person.* The salary and career of a *lycée* teacher who produces books are not indexed to his sales or

---

*Pseudonym of Louis Poirier, a novelist with some surrealist overtones, perhaps best known for *Le rivage des Syrtes*, (1951).

the thickness of a file of press clippings. Today, that stoical provincial middle class is no longer competitive. It has to submit to the imperatives of publicity or resign without protest. The place or, to be more accurate, the cultural market (which, if it was ever open, has now been closed by the media) is jumping with these one-man networks, Jacks of three or four trades, who are condemned eternally to undo this stitch for the sake of a holding job on that, to wear themselves out running backwards and forwards and finally to tangle themselves up in their own nets. 'Is that how men live?' No, that is how these men are forced to live and tear themselves apart in order to survive.

2

Applications

The new economy of literary production presumably means that one day we will be able to dispense with the product; doing away with the 'thing itself' and replacing the embarrassing uncertainties of creation with simulated models of cultural *animation* would be perfectly in keeping with the substitition of the descriptive, which inspires all spheres of social activity, for practice.[7] The old principle stipulated that nature plus labour equals wealth. In the present case, a human being transforms *potential wealth* (personal aptitudes) into *value* (a text) by expending a certain amount of labour power (the *work of writing*). He thus produces a commodity (a book) whose specific use value serves as a basis for its subsequent transformation into an exchange value. Experience reverses these classical theorems. Exchange value is not constructed less by the use value produced than by the person of the producer or, more accurately, by his 'social surface'. When an author sends a manuscript to a publisher now, the transaction has less to do with his text than with his address book, that being to mediatic technology what the patent is to industrial technology. The patent holder is assumed to be able to make it work. In paying the author an advance, the publisher is not paying for the product, but mainly for the means to sell it. When he acquires the book under contract, he also acquires those means, the author's *social capital*. And just as capital is accumulated labour, so the social capital incorporated in the advance represents the accumulated cost of the author's lunches and dinners, the services rendered and the alliances forged within the high intelligentsia. The address book is the crystallized form of this productive

[7] X publishes a book, Y replies with an article, Z intervenes in the debate. If you know the product lines of the moment, the state of the ideological market and the profiles of X, Y and Z, you can write the script and stage the show yourself.

industrial capital (as are the marketing firms' files on papers, parties and associations), a material token of the non-material network of contacts that ensures its owner a differential position in the general competition between himself and all other authors. The monopoly situation of which copyright was once the index is changing: it now applies to a social network rather than to literary productivity. This rent from contacts will increasingly become the discriminating element within the collectivity of cultural producers and will determine the volume of their respective renumerations. As can be seen from the scale of advances on manuscripts, which now ranges from 1 to 500,[8] for the same quantity of labour and with equal potential wealth, an eminent member of the high intelligentsia can produce ten, a hundred or five hundred times more value than a humble member of the lower.

It is his fame, whose means of production and reproduction are the mass media, that the author sells to the publisher, for that is what he must sell to the public. This is why publishers try to get a book out of anyone who is famous nowadays. For the market, the essential thing is that there is a star involved and it doesn't much matter whether he is a star of crime, football, the church, war, screen, porn, politics or music. If the star is well known to be illiterate, someone will 'record his impressions'. One-third of his fame will go into his pocket, one-third into that of the rewrite man and one-third to the publisher. Far from having caused a fall in the market value of textual production (or publishers' turnover)—it is constantly rising—the devaluation of the work of writing has the surface effect of transferring the value on to the person of the writer. It goes hand in hand with the (ideological) decline of the values of truth ('Down with ideology!') and the rise of the (eminently ideological) values of the lived experience, the eye-witness account and the live broadcast. Far from detracting from it, the tape-recorder adds to the market and ideological value of the product, both guaranteeing its authenticity and, thanks to its rapid obsolescence, speeding up the realization of other products on the market. This turnover of capital repays the publisher ten times over for what he loses on the heavy cost of stockage. Fast foods have valorized the catering industry in the eyes of investors as much as modern 'fast writing' has valorized the publishing industry in the eyes of the banks. Not only the stars profit from stardom: it has become the only way to make an investment profitable in the shortest possible space of time. If non-stars did not pay so dearly (in loss of

[8] From 1,000 to 500,000 new francs (1978).

earnings) for their obscurity, the race for the spot, the air and the mike would not be what it is: the *raison d'être* of those who serve the intellect.

Hence the new conception of labour amongst advanced intellectuals: the practice came before the concept. The productive labour of the intellectual is no longer 'intellectual labour'—a naive concept of olden days—but the extended reproduction of his social relations (priority being given to relations with the popular press). The size of his sphere of relations will determine the volume of his income. Nothing is lost and everything is created, day after day. This sheds some light from an exotic source on a mystery whose esoteric nature has discouraged more than one neophyte: how the first violins spend their time. It is the privilege of talent to practise less and play better, or the prerogative of a position to be able to work ten times less than the vulgus and sell ten times as much. What strikes the observer most about the thinkers of the culture show is how little time they have left to think once you subtract their working breakfasts, radio breakfast shows, lunches, dinners, interviews, statements, travel, phonecalls, press conferences, TV debates, and the rest. You don't need to be Rilke or even to have read his *Letters to a Young Poet* to know what the smallest gap in the surrounding background noise costs in terms of loneliness and rumination, or even social and affective poverty. Every day, the humblest intellectual experiences a rule to which the only known exception is the top intellectual in contemporary France. Their diaries can be compared only with those of big business or the leaders of political parties. Like them, they work in teams, with a secretariat and a public relations specialist, with modern equipment (reprography, video, files) and have a difficult home life. Arranging to have lunch with one of these personalities takes at least a month, unless you represent a nationally or internationally important newspaper—and that's for friends; the ordinary supplicant gets an amused smile from the secretary, 'Sorry. We're snowed under with appointments. Call back at the end of the month'. Being snowed under can be constructive—constructive of a social capital that will be completely renewed when the next book comes out (and that can be written in a month, after eleven months of 'contacts' and 'interventions'). What seems to be a systematic waste of time from the point of view of the traditional *otium* is in fact a systematic use of time too precious to be wasted in isolation. Victor Hugo, before he went to sleep, used to put a sign on his door saying 'Poet at work'. Today's creators work over the telephone, for—who knows?—a chance call may produce a contact, a project for an interview or an idea for a plan of campaign. It is also productive labour to invite a big mediocrat to wander around the estate and enjoy the blue water in the swimming pool. As soon as he takes office, the President of the Republic, or even a mere *député*, begins to prepare for re-election seven or eight years later; re-election will merely sanction the programmed day-to-day work of public relations. The modern electoral intellectual, be he eligible or not, has to think of himself as being in the middle of a promotion campaign every day, especially during the holidays, as though his book were going to come out tomorrow morning, for when it does come out in two years time, the author will only be collecting the dividends on his weekly (news items, paragraphs, articles, reviews) and monthly (polemics, events, TV appearances) investments. From that point of view, every gesture counts and the most furtive call to a friend is a long-term investment. Ultimately, writing and publishing a book will surreptitiously be classified as the incidental expenses of existence or, to be more accurate, the work will be seen as a *means* to redeem, at fixed intervals, a social capital whose accumulation has become the *end* of the individual. They say that just after the war, René Char told Camus, or vice versa, that 'an author owes the public his work, not himself'—not the most lucrative of mottoes. The ethics of writing may have clean hands, but the new economy has cut them off.

The fact that decisions to buy are not amenable to planning, least of all in a market economy, does not mean that one should not *prepare* the ground on which they are made. The preventive race for fame is an eliminator; the final decision is made on the field of personal images. But not all competitors can win at the same time: if I want to be in a position of strength in the market, my advantage lies in the weakness of others. Personal strategies—it is up to everyone to maximize his fame by making the most effective interventions possible in the media—cancel each other out completely. No one says it, but everyone knows; the silence is part of a game that will in all probability end in a draw. In the last but one analysis—the last being of a metaphysical order—all writers compete with each other because, although every book has an irreplaceable use value, there is always a limit to the demand for a given type of use value at any given moment. The inescapable consequence of commodity logic is that, in a given productive sector, he who does not sell creates value for his competitor. If we assume that ten producers have to share a market in which the volume purchased is limited to the equivalent of 1,000 hours of labour, and that two of them sell the monetary equivalent of 800 hours of labour, the other eight will have to share the equivalent of 200 hours. They will therefore have produced value for the first two, quite unintentionally. If they share the same distributor, he will have no cause for complaints: the squares contribute to the profitability of the stars. Someone will object that the literary market is not homogeneous, that it is compartmentalized into specific clienteles that are unequal, but faithful. A novel does not compete with a collection of poetry, and an essay on social anthropology is no threat to a play. 'The' audience is an amalgam of potential audiences, none of which can be superimposed on a given genre (Françoise Dorin does not stray into Beckett's territory, or Henri Troyat into that of Alain Jouffroy). But as the mass media make the cultural market more uniform, and as the supports become increasingly unified, those barriers begin to come down; protectionism is eliminated from the sub-markets, in much the same way as small and medium-sized firms in the provinces were wiped out when the Common Market undercut their prices and standardized the product lines. Someone will argue that there is no pre-given limit to the demand for cultural goods; it is not, however, completely elastic. The cultural market's absorptive capacity may well be rising—in varying degrees, depending on the product—but it cannot go beyond a certain ceiling imposed on it from the outside by social conditions and the income of the potential consumers. The statistics show a strong rise, under the heading *culture and leisure*, in cultural consumption; only *health and hygiene* is rising faster.[9] This is yet another reason for increased rivalries and inequality between the producers.

The absolute individualism of the creators does not predispose them to see the play of interconnections that governs their careers; the logic of their individual destinies can be apprehended only at the level of the category as a whole. But for his majesty the subject, a totality is as ludicrous as sociological or historical objectification is repulsive. Let us take the novel as an example. Every novelist tends to have an image of his 'career' and his 'colleagues' that includes the reality of the novel market; but it is an *inverted* image, rather like the image of the reality of the world on the small screen. Everyone knows that the commercial success of a novel, or any

[9] Up by 264% in France between 1959 and 1974. The overall figure conceals a lot of disparities. The growth in spending on entertainment and papers is much lower than the average; that on radio, TV photographic equipment, records and audio-visual equipment, above. Spending on books, prints and reproductions is simply *average*.

book come to that, pivots around Pivot and a few others. The annual demand for works of fiction may be assumed to be relatively stable. Which books will be in demand in 1979?—those whose authors attain maximum social visibility that year. Of the two thousand authors who publish novels for a market that can absorb an estimated one hundred units, five will win prizes and twenty will be invited to appear on *Apostrophes*. The first five will come out on top, since a literary prize is also a formal guarantee that the author will appear several times on TV and ensures that the peripheral media will be interested in his fame, his house, his daughter and his collection of mustard pots. As instruments to channel demand, literary prizes used to be homogeneous with the products they promoted (a literary jury is supposed to make its decision on the basis of a reading, not a spectacle, on the basis of literary quality and not the *hexis* of a sub-editor), but they have been subordinated to the new mode—the realization of the value of literary commodities—a mode which is heterogeneous to the nature of the project and whose unbounded savagery brooks no resistance. Logically enough, this subordination of the literary to the audio-visual has given a new lease of life to the procedures of the autumn prizes, and their commercial effectiveness has increased considerably over the last twenty years, the problem being that the effectiveness in question no longer belongs to them: it is lent them by the 'media regime'.

Television is not in itself creative of value. It intervenes in the market (for novels, household appliances or perfume) only to decide which value is or is not to be transformed into a price and realized in an exchange. Nor does it create the social need to which any value created must necessarily correspond. Without it, the social demand would still be shared out, but in a very different way. It is an excellent—and now the very best—instrument for equalizing the rate of profit, but its economic function is basically not very different from that of the hawkers on the quays of Piraeus, the criers in a medieval market or a newspaper advertisement in 1860. Television, which is eminently unromantic, has still created a romantic misunderstanding amongst novelists. It is quite obvious to Jacques-Alphonse Dubout that the value of his novel has risen because he sat next to Pivot last Friday night. Hasn't he seen his sales go up from 1,500 to 15,000 and his name climb to No. 7 in *L'Express*'s best-sellers list in the week following a performance in which he was so witty, seductive, insolent, pathetic, startling and, in a word, heroic. What the individual producer takes to be the most concrete of facts is, when seen at the level of production as a whole, an illusion. For this value added has been subtracted from Alphonse-Jacques Boudu's novel. Dubout is not wrong to be so pleased about the TV, 'that marvellous instrument of democratiz-ation' (sic). He is simply forgetting the limits on the elasticity of demand and that Boudu, the author of an unusual masterpiece (published by Editeurs Français Réunis on top of everything else*) and a teacher in a secondary school in Carpentras who has no top journalists amongst his contacts and suffers the double handicap of a stammer and a squint, was, without knowing it and without leaving home, getting a very bad deal. Boudu knows that he isn't photogenic and sometimes glimpses the connection between the telegenic and the eugenic; he willingly forgoes the audio-visual. He therefore felt no jealousy towards Doubout, no connection—his is a different world. But they do live in the same world: a world of negotiable paper, where every best seller stands on the inanimate corpses of a multitude of non-sellers or worst sellers. Boudu will applaud Doubout's success without a second thought, without ever thinking that the triumph of that book is one of the things that stopped his book from being a success. And Doubout, who is not interested in politics, much less economics, will think to himself, without ever giving a thought to Boudu, 'That's the way it goes. All it takes to be asked to appear on Pivot's show is talent and a bit of luck'. Wrong, like all 'natural' thought. But the completely 'natural' presence of Jacques-Alphonse Dubout on the screen conceals the socially determined absence from the literary competition of Boudu, Alphonse-Jacques, from the eyes of those concerned, the viewers and Pivot himself.

---

* Left-wing publishing house, close to the French Communist Party.

3
Corollary

To sum up; the division in behaviour and in positions within intellectual society marks an opposition between two universes. The lower intelligentsia lives and thinks as it does because the problem of realizing value on the market does not exist for it. It does not produce a commodity, but a use value, a service which, since education is (basically) a state monopoly, is not subject to competition. That difference does not explain everything, but nothing can be explained without it. A perfunctory materialist will therefore not flinch from the blasphemy of pointing out that the lower intelligentsia wants the state because it lives by the state and that the high intelligentsia wants freedom because it makes its living from the free market. One's income does not necessarily determine what one thinks, but in the long run experience proves that a mental attitude becomes untenable when it no longer fits in with the way one produces one's means of subsistence. It is never easy to think one way and live another. An intellectual who lives on the right and thinks on the left is in a precarious position and is constantly torn in two. It is not surprising that there are fewer and fewer of them, or that there are more and more men and women who are sincerely convinced that the words 'left' and 'right' are meaningless: it is cheaper to change a way of thought than to repudiate a way of life.

In 1927, Thibaudet agreed that both literary and economic inclinations were leaning to the right, but made the distinction that writers, unlike economic experts and advisers, could follow their inclinations and still get back on their feet again. Talent was therefore quite evenly distributed. In 1947, Sartre accepted that the writer was fed by the privileged, but saw him as a traitor, functionally in contradiction with those off whom he lived: 'The writer is therefore a parasite on the ruling elite. But functionally, he goes against the interests of those on whom he lives. That is the primary conflict which defines his situation'.[10] The Sartrean conception of literature as negativity in action, as the call of one liberty to another through the unveiling-transcendence of facticities common to reader and writer seems to shed more light on the Sartrean philosophy of the founding cogito than on the literary activity itself. But that does not alter the fact that talent was, by the force of post-war circumstances and climate, 'on the left': the 'collaborators' did not yet have the right to speak. Curiously enough, Sartre suggested in a note that the extension of his readership would help the writer escape from the grip of the wealthy. One cannot help but think of the socialist theoreticians of the nineteenth century, who were confident that the extension of universal suffrage would wrest the state and its legislative organs from the grasp of the ruling bourgeoisie. In reality, the extension of the virtual readership has been accompanied by a tremendous concentration of the means of reaching that readership into the hands and under the hegemony of the ruling elite. The narrowing of the channels is less important than the nature of the processes of valorization, which are intrinsically 'bourgeois', being founded on the tryptich of instantaneity/individuality/visibility, the tripod of the Great Oppressive Lure. Fifty years after Thibaudet and thirty years after Sartre, one cannot but wonder if the new literary economy is not going to make the attempt to find one's feet more uncertain and perilous. When, without realizing it, the buyers become sleeping partners in the books they buy, what becomes of Sartre's conflict between essence and existence, between the function and the position of the writer? In the cultural field as in any other, the act of putting the economic instance in command is not politically neutral: it expresses political domination and a class position. Is it a coincidence that in 1978, *vox populi* is saying over and over again that talent has moved from left to right or, in other words, that there is no longer a left and a right? Those whom we no longer dare call collaborators—the defeated of 1947—are back in force, under different names and different banners. France has probably entered one of the most reactionary periods in its history and its barometric high intelligentsia, more avant-garde than ever, marches ahead of it with a boldness that deserves real admiration. It is perhaps time to ask whether the term 'bourgeois intellectual' has not ceased to be a stereotype and become a tautology. By what miracle can the individual intellectual now escape the

[10] *Qu'est-ce que la littérature*, Paris 1948, p. 129.

historically determined nature of his society, the geographical position of his country, the place of its economy in the international division of labour—and his own material system of production, distribution and promotion? Only by accident, will-power or a moral philosophy. Adventurers, fighters and apostles will never represent anyone but themselves, at least in the here and now. And they will have enough to cope with in trying to escape the public ridicule that has banned them. In any case, if it is true that only an analysis of the global intercommunications directing the transfers and confiscation of the flow of value for the benefit of the industrial West can account for developments in European affairs, then the evolution of those in France whose vocation it is to turn events into delirium would appear to be in line with the refashioning of their base.

The answer to the question, 'But who are you talking about?', must be 'Those who get themselves talked about', those who make their mark on our times. So what—someone will say—given that those whose discourse will be important tomorrow are still *elsewhere*, in the wings or in third place, as they always have been? Let us be quite clear about what we are doing. Work on the history of the present necessarily lays us open to mistakes that will look like injustices tomorrow. So much is obvious. In order to try to understand the 'errors' of the present, the idea it has of itself, the images it takes from its stocks and the figures it issues, one has to adopt them. All one need do to understand once and for all that 'making a mark' is not a synonym for 'remarkable' but the strongest antonym of 'memorable', is browse through the family albums and prize-lists of each period's imaginary pantheon of France. The names that 'made their mark' one period are a joke in the next; the marks of respect shown to their elders provoke the disrespect of the sons—but there is no guarantee that the grandsons will not find their laughter comical in fifty years time. Anyone who wants to look his time in the eyes should not gaze too long into the eyes of statues. Convinced that any human society must erect statues, that nothing is more easily moved, and he will use those around him to discover what they reveal about the society in which he lives. It is difficult for a period to watch itself living 'live'—that is the whole point. If its best mediators are the intellectuals, the best way to reach it is to go through them, turning the mediation back on itself, so to speak.

Historical reality has rarely disgusted the national 'ideal type' so much as today: in that sense, he remains faithful to French intellectual history, that succession of years zero and absolute beginnings. He has decided to eradicate historical materialism, but today's anti-Marxism conforms so closely to a Marxist lesson on the nature of things that his behaviour could serve as an illustration in a class on dialectics for primary schoolchildren. He chooses to call the least symptom of intellectual rigour 'dogmatism' and that is the perfect way to perpetuate dogmatisms, which one can escape only through theoretical rigour. It is the same old play between being and nothingness, the eternal vicious circle of bad faith that forces masters and dandies alike to be what they are not so as to avoid being what they are. The 'intellectual of 1979' expresses his hatred of the people by declaring his love of the plebs, his distrust of reason by rejecting the state in the name of reason of state, and his desire for order in an appetite for disorder. The harder he tries to escape himself, the sooner he finds himself back where he started. His discourse must be read in reverse, because his consciousness inverts reality. In a word, his political and social consciousness comes down to a punctilious denial of his social being. But it is his social being that determines the denial.

To tell the truth, the game is fixed: our champions are not particularly distinguished. For this social being cannot be himself without denying his sociality. The collective fate of the Order is a frantic search for an individuality ratified and reinforced by an economic order that indexes the market value of the product to the marginality of the producer and confuses the race to dissidence with the race for profits. Maximum individualization guarantees maximum socialization. Estrangement from others is the condition for group membership. The lack of cohesion among individuals—which distinguishes the intelligentsia from other social categories—is a collective mode of existence. This negative cohesion appears at every level and marks our profession, our psyche, our electoral and elective affinities and, more simply, our daily misery.

The high intelligentsia rejects organization, not only by remaining outside parties and unions, but also by resisting autonomous attempts to form any professional grouping. Not that it is wrong to do so, from its own point of view: It is certainly not in its interests to defend basically antagonistic interests as though they were shared. *Escritor escritori lupus.* Wolves do not form unions unless they come up against tigers, and though publishers may not be lambs, their claws are not big enough for that role. Even if they were honest, frank carnivores, the problem of uniting the wolves would remain. Where competition is the highest common factor, attempts to organize and negotiate collectively with other groups cannot succeed. How else are we to explain the recurrent failure of the associations, unions and syndicates of French writers? An association can survive only if it is based on determinate social interests that allow its members to unite around a common objective. An organization of writers is therefore abnormal as such, and most of those that have appeared in France have been like Aphrodite appearing out of the foam. They rise from the wave-crests of enthusiasms or hopes external to the profession (1936, 1944, 1968, 1978) and disappear with them. When the profession returns to its own inertia, it returns to its initial state of disaggregation. The lucidity, devotion and obstinacy of the best break against its weight (every association lives on the subscriptions paid, and therefore lives in poverty and by its wits). The Union des écrivains (founded on 21 May 1968 by Bernard Pingaud, Roger Bordier, Guy de Bosschère and Guillevic) had an elected *working committee*, with two professional and ideological commissions, a bulletin, a delaration and goal ('the goal of the Union is to define itself by defining the writer'), but the writers themselves did not follow its lead after the first few years. The Syndicat des écrivains de langue française (SELF), founded by Marie Cardinal, Yves Navarre, Pierre-Jean Rémy and others on December 20, 1976, has an executive committee, statutes and a bulletin; but how can the future be anything but uncertain when French writers already have the greatest difficulty in presenting their case to the administrative authorities. The Société des gens de lettres, which enjoys a de facto monopoly over official representation of the corporation at home and abroad, has fewer than 2,000 share-holder members and works mainly as a fund for collecting and handling royalties, pensions and mutual aid.[11] As for the Centre national des lettres, it is a registered organization answerable to the Ministry of Culture; most professionals keep their distance from it and use it as a tool. It owes its utility and its continued survival to the fact that it is so removed from the profession. All authors benefit from what the Union des écrivains finally obtained—social security, a single definition of function, and so on—and from what SELF produced—a modification of the *passe*, a new model contract—but at best they forget their work and at worst they despise it.

Our species prefers workers' control over individual fame to collective workers' organizations. The preference is rarely made explicit; the

---

[11] To be more accurate: 1,501 shareholder members, 2,187 members and 1,817 trainee members as of 1 January 1977. (Jean Rousselot's administrative report for 1976.)

majority usually express it by their polite indifference, but a minority
sublimate it into a metaphysics of inequality. Completely in keeping with
his own position of strength in the internal relation of forces (and his
position as a salaried employee in a publishing house), Philippe Sollers, for
example, has criticized SELF for 'presenting French publishing exclus-
ively in terms of relations of forces' and has made his views quite clear
'Nothing lends itself less readily to an arithmetical set governed by an
"equals" sign than the activity of writing. It may be possible for there to be
equality in the distribution of material wealth, but certainly not in
sexuality, for example, or in language. I am therefore convinced that a
union of writers can only generate a normative and repressive ideology.
And as such a union would have to be on the left, it would add that
repressive and normative weight to its ideology.'[12] The very word 'union'
thus stimulates a medullary reflex, the liberal professions' typical scorn for
the 'regimented' little functionary, coupled in the present case and in
honour of the perils of the moment with the phantasy of petty state
officialdom—not 'Better Hitler than the Popular Front' but 'Better
marketing than officialdom!'. An intellectual who joined a coalition would
be betraying his true public function, which is to be hunted, beaten and
gagged, because if he isn't he will never be invited to dine with princes or
sit on high in official places. If he is not excluded from the pack, what claim
has he to be heard by it? His dignity lies in his indignity, and asking a
writer to join an association he does not control is like asking the most
cosseted of exceptions to return to a dreary norm. The mediocre resemble
one another and the down-to-earth assemble together. When the French
high intelligentsia meets as a committee, it clears its name by calling it
CIEL (Comité des Intellectuels pour l'Europe des Libertes[13]). Separat-
ists by allegiance and troublemakers out of a sense of duty, the spoilsports
are neither associative nor cumulative and take the front of the stage only
because they are convinced that 'they' will not rest until 'they' drive them
off it. Over the last ten years, the indices of legitimacy of the dominant
discourse have been inverted, and the President who does not begin his
speech with 'I speak to you as a seditious individual . . .', the Academician
who does not start with 'Pariah that I am', or the general who does not sing

[12] Reply to Pierre-Jean Rémy in *Magazine Littéraire* (March 1976) under the heading
'L'Ecrivain est-il comparable au chirurgien-dentiste?'.

[13] A map of CIEL and its constellations will be drawn up elsewhere (see *Traité*). (The
acronym CIEL also means 'sky'. *Translator.*)

the praises of absence without leave can be sure of losing their audience from the start.[14] The main explanation for the existence of strong, active and united writers' unions in other countries, notably the Nordic countries, is the lack of political gravitation in the intelligentsia of those countries. A German intellectual joins a union and agrees to be added and subtracted after the 'equals' sign because he has no hope of counting for much or of causing any serious trouble. If France cannot follow suit, it is because of a surplus of political gravitation rather than a deficiency. A voice that carries weight does not count. A voice that is meant to carry will ring out much better from a panoptic luminous ghetto than from the hubbub of an anonymously professional meeting.

This is the ultimate explanation of the refrain we started with: it is not true that there is no such thing as the intelligentsia, but what is true is that this group of antis is the anti-group par excellence. The only certainty in this 'We do not exist' is the first word: the intelligentsia exists not as a *we* but merely as a collection of *I*s. Not that the *I*s are wrong: they are the first to be convinced of their glorious abnormality, of their indomitable luck. In the eyes of each individual, the element of chance in his rise to the high intelligentsia conceals the institutional element. A *title* is acquired via nomination, but a social *position* is taken under enemy fire, and a *function* is exercised from day to day. The individual battle for promotion obscures the picture of the strategic organization imposed on all those promoted. Waterloo: Fabrice is still looking for the village in the mist, and Napoleon died uncertain that he had found it.

This class of outclassed beings who dream of being declassed, has made a virtue of necessity and an ideology of its atomism. There is nothing new in that: Hegel had already taken the intellectual animal as the emblem of absolute individualism. This specific latency—the most probable ideology of our species—will vary with time and place. The configuration we have termed liberal/libertarian—which is not a coherent set of positions, but a contradictory sum of negations—constitutes the form in which it is naturally, so to speak, manifested in France in the seventies.[15]

[14] It is debateable if it really is good tactics to keep telling the 'great intellectuals' one wishes to mobilize that they are outlaws from society. (Roger Bordier, 'L'Ecrivain français au ban de la société', *Le Monde*, 2 February 1970). Such flattery can only fill them with joy, as the longed-for pinnacle soars up from the very lowest depths.

[15] For a brief description of this figure, see *Contribution aux discours et cérémonies du dixième anniversaire*, Paris 1978. (Partial translation in *New Left Review* 115, May–June 1979', 'A Modest Contribution to the Rites and Ceremonies of the Tenth Anniversary').

The very least one can expect of a class responsible for the production of ideas is that it should start by helping itself. The high intelligentsia, which sometimes sells off-the-peg garments, now dresses itself in made-to-measure suits, for there was something about this ideological tweed, the shade of the colours and the softness of the cloth, that seduced a negative group with the internal unity of an archipelago. Stretchy, stain-resistant and as soft as anyone could wish, this cloth reconciles the necessities of material life (the liberal warp) with virtue's *point d'honneur* (the libertarian woof), the reality of the commodity economy with the politics of brand images, and at the same time ensures the best possible circulation of individuals within the amorphous and multivocal space of the media. What is woven is less important than the movement of the shuttle. For the most distinctive feature of the present liberal-libertarian syntagm is the hyphen: it ensures that the journey can be made in both directions by maintaining homogeneity within heterogeneity. It makes it possible to come and go between *L'Idiot International* and *Le Figaro-Magazine*, between *L'Express* and *Libération*. Between *L'Observateur* and *La Nouvelle Action Française*. It is up to the individual to find his own route from Aron to July; it is a fantasia of somersaults and dizzying reversals of fortune. No blow is irremediable and no retreat is irreversible. Vote-switching and results mean that every player gets a winning number.

The community of those who have only their differences in common constantly finds itself confronted with a problem to which there is no stable solution: how can I get my peers to recognize me as peerless? How can I establish myself as someone exceptional in a world where the exception is the general rule? It is not easy to be collectively unique. The members of the family solve the thankless aporia—how to show each other consideration and at the same time devour each other—on a day-to-day basis, showing consideration because they all depend on one another for recognition, devouring because that very recognition presupposes that the other anihilates himself before my being and bows before my superiority. The 'community of animals' has therefore invented its own peculiar form of civilization, which might be termed the politeness of malice. All societies based on scarcity are reservoirs of cruelty, since poverty generates mutual dependence: everyone needs everyone else to satisfy his basic needs. This latent humiliation spontaneously creates its own compensation: malevolence. The man of culture lives this 'culture of poverty' every day. As he wanders through Paris in an anxiety state and with withdrawal symptoms, he bears with him this resentment, this ill-vented bitterness: watchful, on the defensive, risking a furtive smile at the first colleague he meets, always torn between a desire to scratch and a desire to stroke, pouncing and dodging. But always putting a good face on it. Hasn't his press agent just told him he must 'defend his book'? A beautiful expression that takes it for granted that no sooner has a book appeared than it is surrounded, threatened by hatred and attacked by envy simply because it exists. Our man is therefore quite right to counter-attack. Even those who have all they could wish for sometimes let slip irrational frustrations, as though they were never sufficiently praised, admired or understood, as though they suspected every passer-by and even their best friends of being slightly dishonest debtors who will clear off when it is time to pay up. Hence the cathartic outbursts of bile, the viperine spasms and the preventive attacks that make up their personal identity. It is impossible to appreciate oneself without depreciating one's neighbour. Any intellectual worthy of the name stands out by always speaking ill of his colleagues and especially of his closest friends. These symbolic little killings are like life-insurance payments. In France, one becomes a noble by putting others down. La Bruyère would be out of his element here, but not Gurvitch or Mauss; we are in effect dealing with a 'total social phenomenon', not a moral failing.

Let's not be over-dramatic. Where individualism rules, the cure is in the illness. Self-preservation ensures that the killing is never for real. They scratch indirectly in notes and allusions. No one likes to make frontal attacks or to use the whip, properly. The evil one speaks is not meant to hurt and no one expects us really to think as much of a book as we said we did in our last tribute. Such kindnesses and obligations are inconsequential. No one can outwit an antagonism, but you can play on differences. The federation of solitudes would be impossible if intellectual society took its quarrels and bickering too seriously. The over-dramatization of differences, the emphasis and hyperbole surrounding personal relations, and the hysteria of gesture and word should be seen as a means of avoiding *doing* by *saying*, as circumscribing a play area that guarantees everyone's immunity and preserves the secret connivance of the players. The business world does not require displays of friendship; the world of politics goes in for matiness, and sometimes has room for camaraderie. The great intellectual world works on friendship alone, but what it calls friendship is a speculative investment. The more friends there are, the bigger the take, and vice versa. Just as a politician sees his circle of close friends grow and shrink in proportion to his party's share of the vote or his position in the state apparatus, the personal contacts of the intellectual rise and fall with his 'importance' (which has its visible and audible scales), and therefore with his social utility. Maurice Clavel's telephone never stops ringing; Louis Althusser's is much more discreet. The former can introduce me into a number of sanctums, but the latter is still a mediatic cul-de-sac: no contacts in TV, no page in a weekly, no radio slot, just a collection of theoretical works whose clandestinity is preserved by the press, from whom he has received not a single interview in thirty years of activity. What good is Althusser to me? Clavel is my friend. Men at the summit of power, which is merely the place where the contacts are thickest on the ground, have nothing but friends—friends of power. Provided they call their 'contacts' 'friends', they can consider themselves happy. The quarrels of the milieu are therefore legendary: the newspapers are full of its schisms, quarrels and break-ups. Most are equivalent to demands for the renegotiation of existing compromises and derive from diplomatic pressure or a gradual escalation by a partner who wants to strengthen his hand. But *where only individuals and not values are involved, everything is negotiable* and there is never any end to the game. Non-correspondence between principles and behaviour, between saying and doing, is a useful rule of conduct, and one that is rich in nice surprises: you pick up the phone and hear the almost affectionate voice of a 'friend' asking you to dinner after having dragged you through the mud in the press yesterday— *of course* it was 'just a joke'. Or you see two colleagues arm in arm, when one of them told you only this morning that the other wasn't fit for hanging. Or you find an article by so-and-so in a paper he told you was quite despicable only last week, even though only an innocent would have taken that to mean he would never write for it. A milieu full of noise and commotion, where the firemen are hand in glove with the arsonists and where adversaries calmly prepare their polemics together in the summer (a bad polemic is worth ten times more than a good advertisement). This is a milieu where no one owes anything to anyone, because they all owe everything to everyone; where saying you are on the left doesn't stop you mixing with the right and combining honour with utility, or wheeling and dealing over the corpses of yesterday's mugs, who still believed in it; where all it takes to be something is saying you are something or getting someone else to say it. The ethnographer would pinch himself—were it not that he had, without realizing it, become a full member of this strange ethnic group whose structures and constraints keep us all busy.

Conclusions

Conclusions

The Cycles of Misery

Is it really a new *ethos*, or the structure of a specific consciousness? 'The above substantial individuality, to begin with, is again single and determinate. Absolute reality, which it knows itself to be, is thus, in the way it becomes consciously aware of that reality, absolutely universal, without filling and content, merely the empty thought of this category.'[1] Thus Hegel, with the first position of the archetype of the animal, gives us the key. The individual posits himself as absolute, denying any constitutent relation other than that which unites him to himself: 'the relation to what is other than itself, which its limitation would involve, is *now* overcome', in this figure of consciousness, which, like all the others described in the *Phenomenology*, is not 'a history within history, but a history which makes History intelligible'. Or perhaps here in France, in the late twentieth century, in the consciousness of the intellectual figures of the moment, the great collective brain in which we all think and live? All that has been said about today's intelligentsia comes to no more than a marginal and wordy exegesis of the twenty pages in which Hegel 'recounts' not a failure, but a 'deception'. We therefore have no more at the end than we had at the beginning, but to discover this we had to reach the end. Myths are made to be repeated, and it is not our fault if the Hegelian myth of the intellectual animal is a myth of origins which, as we all know, are never discovered until the end of history, when the irremediable has been accomplished.

The odyssey of the intellectual, this endless spiral, is ultimately a

[1] 'Self-contained individuals associated as a community of animals and the deception thence arising: the real fact', is the sub-title of the passage in question (Hegel, p. 417). I cannot begin to express my debt to Roger Establet, whose commentary is, to my knowledge, the most illuminating that exists on *The Phenomenology of Mind* as a whole.

dialectic that does never completes itself; it is full of reversals, but it always revolves around itself. Its motor contradictions are in themselves enough to prevent the intellectual both from finding himself as he wishes, as an essence, and from losing himself once and for all, in order to find himself elsewhere. 'Individuality which takes itself to be real in and for itself' initially had its concept to hand. But that singularity is still no more than a hollow generality, since there is nothing objective to attest to it. If it is ineffable, originality can only be formal. Singularity has to be expressed as difference and opposition, through a determinate work. That is why the intellectual cannot simply put Montaigne's motto ('It is an absolute and almost divine perfection to be able to enjoy one's being and remain true to it') into practice, because he expects recognition, which means reciprocity, not reconciliation. A cell closed in on itself, his consciousness wants its work to give its definition a meaning, but the work is meaningful only in terms of the definitions others give of it. Autarky then disappears and the cell opens. The intellectual writes both for and against his peers. On the one hand, he finds his source within himself. His consciousness refuses external conditions (which make a mockery of his independence and chain his spirit), principles (for, for himself, the individual is his own origin and end, and the universal is mere appearance and mystification), and systems (which dissolve his singularity into the impersonal abstract). On the other hand, his roots are in alterity; cut off from others, he languishes and dies where he stands, for he exists only by and for his audience. In a word, he might be defined as both 'being-for-others' and 'being-against-others'—which means that others will alternate between being his Heaven and his Hell and that his social life will be a Purgatory, a perpetual coming and going between the two. One day, he shuts himself up, plunges into himself, or goes out incognito; the next day, the same man rushes to be interviewed and takes off his dark glasses. One day, he blithely ignores a specialist review that pans his latest book: that he has been misunderstood seems to him the most obvious sign of his genius. A week later, a casual remark from a stranger cuts him to the quick. This rift suggests a twofold and impossible postulation.

Artistic production (and intellectual production in general) cannot be *normalized*, but one might well wonder whether any creative project isn't necessarily but unwittingly *normative*. Its singularity may conceal a universal proposition which it simultaneously actualizes and hides; a proposed set of references and values implicitly valid for every man *qua* man, and which are submitted to every reader, spectator or listener for immediate and unhesitating adoption; a proposition that is polite, or comic, but which is secretly imperious, perhaps more so than the author may think or want it to be. The written work contains within it a vision of the world, and the plastic work an idea of the world; spontaneously and by definition positing itself as a totality, every vision or idea of the 'world' bears within it a tacit demand for exclusivity. If there is only one world and not two, there should in theory be only one correct, 'real' vision of the world 'as it really is', that is, as it appears to me. If that is the case, the egocentricity of intellectual creators would be an unwitting imperialism that has sufficient self-awareness to reduce the risk of confrontations with others or of abdication of sovereignty; and that would form the almost transcendental basis for economic competition. Being that which cannot be spoken, thought or represented, but that without which no diction, thought or representation is possible, this a priori form of intellectual perception would make the creator a scandal for the creator, any symbolic producer an intolerable challenge to his fellow. We all know how many people in our milieu resent alterity as a personal affront. Such is the mark of failure, carved on the heart of a heartless society, which expresses the spirit (*esprit*) of a social corps with no *esprit de corps*.

This society cannot in fact generate a real community, because, for the intellectual, this would be no more than a means to realize himself and attain his concept. When it discovers its inessentiality, the essential ego refers to a 'we' which, being inessential in its turn, refers it back to itself. As in a batch of culture in which every microbe feeds by destroying the next, there is no organic totality, merely an endless process in which everything is detotalized by the individual, who is then retotalized by the other and so on. Every book refers to other books which destroy it and are in their turn destroyed by others. An individualism without works or values generates an organism without organicity—a trading company that can look like a charming family circle. But this family of people with no family resembles a copy of bourgeois society itself. 'In the community of animals, "work" has the same meaning as "commodity" in liberal economics. In the one, the commodity is the product of concrete labour dissolved into its monetary equivalent. In the other, individual works are both commodities and money.'[2] They have value not so much because of what they are (works of art, a corpus of theses or textual substance) as

[2] Establet, p. 112.

because of what they can give their author in social equivalents (visibility, fame, credit); they are means of payment within the general circulation of individual values; in the last instance, that is, they are instruments of mutual devaluation. The works themselves are annihilated in their intrinsic necessity to the advantage of their relative position. A mediatized society devalues words and over-values the indices of the market-place and the moment—the inflation of the descriptive being equivalent to a deflation of the semantic. What is said is less important than who says it, and where and when he says it. In a word, the only work common to the intellectual animals is the dissolution of all works, each work being dissolved by all the others.

Is it possible to break out of these circles of misery from within? The supreme irony is perhaps that they cannot be described without being reproduced, since anyone who mentions their tricks will immediately be suspected of playing a different trick—or of disguising grievances as good intentions. The prodigious annoyance these pages have inspired in the reader, if indeed there is a reader, will probably cause them to be dismissed as a discourse of disguise. Close friends make the best enemies, and why paint a self-portrait in the form of a caricature?

'When an intellectual talks about the intellectuals,' writes Maurice Duverger, 'he is talking about himself. Thoughts that should be written in the first-person singular are put into the third-person plural.' But how can they be in the first person when a succession of 'Is' seems intolerable? It would in fact be more modest, for there is a great deal of pride and a certain amount of cowardice in making a general, abstract 'other' responsible for one's own ideas. We have already had an opportunity to take stock of the mingled pride and cowardice that persuaded us not to use the first-person singular (for we initially drew a distinction between the impersonal 'I' of rational exposition and the confessional 'me' of original writing). In the order of discourse, reference to 'me' offends Reason as well as modesty. We have therefore chosen to take any risk to avoid that—and primarily the obvious risk of being accused of having too many scores to settle with the intellectuals (with ourselves) not to make bad mistakes in our sums. If in the eyes of the reader, settlement and drawing up of accounts are one and the same, we quite readily endorse that suspicion. To unite consciousnesses without restricting their independence is not an easy task, and profane history scarcely seems predisposed to honour of its own free will the old social contract drawn up by the philosophers. In spite of everything, the wide world harbours enough fervour and energy for those who placed in intellectual society their hopes of finding an 'I' which would be a 'we', or a 'we' which would be an 'I' to pack their bags with a light heart.

'One day, we are assaulted by what others think of us and realize that this is the strongest thing of all', said Nietzsche. But what can the assailants do against an empty fort?

2

Nine Gates to Hell

> Until now, progress has always been thought of as a promise of something better. We now know that it also announces the end.
> MILAN KUNDERA

1. Technology and ideology stand not in inverse but in direct proportion to one another: the more complex the former, the simpler and therefore the more powerful the latter.[3] The new technology of information greatly reduces the practical power of ideologies. The rise of the mass media has the direct effect of making the mediaman a mass man for the first time in history. The displacement of production by communication gives the functionaries of distribution the advantage over those who operate on things. The controllers are beginning to take control of the workers. The age of the intelligentsia is beginning.

2. The age of the intelligentsia will be the age of the greatest unintelligence. There is in effect an inverse ratio between the informational value of a message and its communicability. The more demonstrative the thought, the more costly the transmission and unpredictable the reception. The economy of reason makes reason anti-economic. The selection from below effected in intellectual society by the mass media is rigorous and final because it obeys a rigorous law against which there is no appeal. The mass media ensure the maximum socialization of private stupidity. That social stupidity may be open to a mathematical assault. Otherwise, it is unassailable.

---

[3] These theses put the local analysis presented here into the theoretical context of mediology. They will be made more explicit on another occasion.

2. Information is expensive. Information theory terms the expenditure of energy inherent in an transmission or reception of information 'neguentropy'. It has been established that 'information increases as the logarithm of the number of equally probable states'. One might well ask if this law, which has allowed the physical notion of information to be translated into mathematical form, does not have as its corollary *a law of diminishing returns* governing technological developments in social information. If so, entropy or loss of energy would rise in geometric proportion to the extension of the circuits and the increased volume of the transmissions. In other words, the accuracy of information becomes more and more improbable as the sphere informed is extended. Bad information drives out good information because *truth is becoming more and more expensive.*

4. The fall in the number of news pages in the written press, the regular increase in the length of weather and sports flashes on radio and TV news, the growing inaccuracy of agency reports, the contraction of literary criticism into printed pastilles, the disappearance of theoretical polemic in favour of ideological signalling: according to the professionals, all these phenomena of involution are due to lack of space, time, money and interest (on the part of the consumers). That lack appears in fact to be the mark of an underlying tendency which is making the cost of truth prohibitive. Truth is a luxury that rich societies are less and less able to afford.

5. The methodical promotion of idiots would be merely an entertaining exercise in sociology were it not that it expressed a more serious total ideological phenomenon: the irresistible rise of the irrational in a civilization based upon the practical applications of the results of rational labour. Each stage in the evolution of mankind attests a constant ratio, of relative value, between the means of production of delirium and technical capacities, between the volume of illusions and the volume of power. The rise of the irrational (of which sects, mages, gurus and prophets are a sign) does not invalidate this law. The rise of the irrational parallels the rise of the threshold of applied scientificity; it is its compensatory effect. The more the 'objective' world is 'rationalized', the more the irrational takes hold of the subjective. Science cannot impose its own performance without ipso facto perfecting that of non- and anti-science, just as the more tightly individuals are enmeshed by increasingly constraining social controls, the more their individualistic desire to escape them increases.

'Ideological' does not mean the opposite of 'scientific'; it designates something that follows science like a shadow.

6. If, in that respect, there is nothing new about the present period, are we giving in to the facile arguments of millenarianism when we ask whether scientific and technical progress is not approaching a qualitative threshold that will dictate a leap backwards on the road of civilization? The demand for the irrational is reaching critical mass under the pressure of an accelerated rationalization of the social and material environment, at the very moment when intellectual activity finds itself subject to the law of supply and demand. Although there has never been a social demand for logical abstractions, Western societies have until now kept their maniacs of the Word in reserved spaces. The destruction of the pockets of knowledge on the one hand and the developments in information and telematics on the other will continue to provide spiritualism and idealism with a mass clientele, and with the added bonus of a fine clergy of traitors. The more the world is mastered and modelled, the more its objective reality becomes blurred and estranged from its users. At the end of modernity, we find God and the Devil again—and the priests.

7. The advance of the sciences makes the process of establishing the truth more protracted and complex: the development of the media shortens the process of administering the truth and makes it primary. A major part of today's disenchantment is born of this contrast. But so are tomorrow's panics and suicides.

8. If mankind commits suicide one day—or day after day—all at once or in small groups, it will do so to music, nuclear war or not. 'Minimal encoding, maximum reception' (Michel Serres). Music is a universal form of communication because it has nothing to communicate. It is more profitable to transport a sonic signal than a sign because it costs the neural apparatus less to receive a signal than to decode a sign. Our most likely future is one of multi-directional, non-stop pop music, and the very movement that packs the discos is emptying the lecture theatres. This neurologically controlled shift, which has its origins in the physics of the universe, underlines the urgent need to call a halt. Michel Serres, who likes music can in fact explain why Johnny Hallyday dominates the scene of social ideas. Johnny Hallyday, who cannot explain it to himself, can only stop his fans from going to listen to Michel Serres. The asymmetry is

classic, but it is full of danger once we go beyond a certain point.

9. Since the best information, from the media's point of view, is that which communicates least, what is meaningless becomes what is most easily understood. The increasingly noticeable insignificance of our official programmes illustrates the economic law that optimal information (in the media sense) equals minimal communication (in the mathematical sense). The apogee of the reign of the media recreates pure noise. The curse of information is turning back on itself and swallowing its own tail: the final truth of the media is the sea serpent. The end is in the beginning.

There appear, a priori, to be two practical ways to escape barbarism.

If we believe that the progress of mankind requires us to come full circle as soon as possible and start 'somewhere else', we will choose to go one better, accelerate the circulation of false rumours until they become dizzying and eliminate every last hint of the old criteria of truth and reality. We will actively join in the delirium, demand to be more and more astonished, applaud the mages, each evening trump the morning's novelty with another.. Such would be the road of what might be called *revolutionary decadence*, a peacetime equivalent to the revolutionary defeatism of the First World War. If we are to escape the middle ages to which the mediatic gallop is bearing us, let the jukebox rave on, let the eardrums and the brain pound until they burst and take us back to their own inner time, up against the wall and silence. Back to the age of the real again. But what if it is like the stone age?

The alternative to decadence is a more positive policy of exchanging the criticism of weapons for the weapons of criticism with regard to the mediocracy around us—a respectable moral reflex, but one that is both private and punctual. Direct action is no doubt justified by the aporia in which any discursive critique of the media finds itself: the object of criticism (and a boycott is part of the very wording) has the material ability to reduce the subject to nothing by withdrawing it from circulation. But any solution to a historical and collective question has to be historical and collective. Moralism is the last resort of the desperate.

In the present case, it would be unreasonable to despair, as one of two things will happen: if the last resort is indeed approaching, the other, earlier resorts will eventually appear. If they cannot be found, we will know soon enough. In any case, the stranglers will not have the last word.

Index